ALL I REALLY
NEED TO KNOW
I LEARNED
FROM WATCHING
STAR
TREK

ALL I REALLY
NEED TO KNOW
I LEARNED
FROM WATCHING
STAR
TREK

DAVE MARINACCIO

Published by Crown Publishers, Inc., 201 East 50th Street, New York, New York 10022. Member of the Crown Publishing Group.

Random House, Inc. New York, Toronto, London, Sydney, Auckland

CROWN is a trademark of Crown Publishers, Inc.

Manufactured in the United States of America

Design by Lauren Dong

Library of Congress Cataloging-in-Publication Data
Marinaccio, Dave.
    All I really need to know I learned from watching Star Trek /
Dave Marinaccio. — 1st ed.
      p.   cm.
    1. Conduct of life. 2. Star Trek (Television program)—
Miscellanea. 3. Marinaccio, Dave. I. Title.
BJ1581.2.M35 1994   93-44654
158'.1—dc20   CIP

ISBN 0-517-59798-5

10 9 8 7 6 5 4 3 2 1

First Edition

For
G.A.B.

INTRODUCTION

I **work in one of the noblest enterprises ever conceived by man, advertising. My work environment is
a stress-filled one. About the only thing taken for
granted is that today's problems will be completely different from yesterday's. At its best, it can be said that the job
offers variety. Unfortunately, it's the same old variety day
after day.**

In situations of change, it is natural for human beings to
look for touchstones. As a human being, I had always sought
a center to my life, an example to follow. What I hadn't realized was that I was already following a path into the future. It
was pointed out to me at a business meeting.

I was comparing a current problem to something I had
watched on television the previous night. I can't recall the
particular problem, but I do recall saying, "Well, we could be
diplomatic, but as Scotty said on Star Trek last night, 'The
best diplomat I know is a fully charged phaser bank.'"

"You turn everything into Star Trek," a coworker responded.

She was right. For years I've related everything in life to
Star Trek. But why not? Captain James Tiberius Kirk is the
most successful person I've ever observed. He's a great
leader, a good manager of people, dedicated, moral, adapt-

able, at the top of his profession, gets the girls, is well known and respected. There are worse role models.

Most importantly, I was practically a Phi Beta Kappa in Star Trek. As a kid it was my favorite TV show. As an adult, virtually every night after work I would walk in the door, collapse on the couch and hit the remote control. Like most men, the remote control is part of my arm. Unlike most men, I can actually watch an entire program. Just so long as the program is Star Trek.

Anyway, that comment at work helped me discover something I already knew. I realized then that I already know what's necessary to live a meaningful life—that it isn't all that complicated.

ALL I REALLY NEEDED TO KNOW about how to live and what to do and how to be I learned watching Star Trek. These are the things I learned:

• Each person or each species, no matter how alien, has the right to live their lives as they wish. (As long as they're not trying to take over the galaxy or eat you or something.)

• Everyone has a role in life. Sulu is the navigator. Uhura is the communications specialist. Do your own job and the ship will function more smoothly.

• Whatever you are doing, answer a distress call. The most important time to help someone is when they need it.

• If you mess something up, it's your responsibility to make things right again. (Say you disrupt history and cause the Nazis to win World War II. To correct matters, you have to let Joan Collins walk in front of a car even though you're in love with her.)

• The more complex the mind, the greater the need for the simplicity of play.

• If you can keep your head in a crisis you've got a fighting chance.

- The unknown is not to be feared. It is to be examined, understood and accepted.
- Close friends become family and family is the true center of the universe.
- End every episode with a smile.
- And lastly, with time and patience you can even learn something from *The Next Generation*.

Everything you need to know is in there somewhere. It may be dressed in some real lame costume. But it's there. Every situation you will face in life has already been faced by the crew of the Starship Enterprise NCC 1701. How to respond to challenge. How to treat your friends. How to pick up girls. How to get ahead on the job. How to run a business. How to bandage a wounded silicon-based life-form. Everything you need to know.

Many of the things that Star Trek teaches us are unintended. That doesn't make them any less important.

James T. Kirk is the model ship's captain. He's always in fighting shape. He has to be to handle the 2.5 fights per episode. Yet, there it is right in front of us. And right in front of him. A potbelly. Not your five nights a week at Dunkin' Donuts New York City Police Department potbelly. But a very comfortable, let's not push back from the table just yet potbelly.

O.K., on Kirk it looks good. Of course on Kirk everything looks good. From the pointy sideburns to the uniform to the pointy-toed boots. But the potbelly is special. No question about it, it belongs there. Apparently, in the twenty-third century people will be at ease with their bodies.

I'm forty. I work out three or four times a week. Each workout includes 180 sit ups and 40 leg lifts. However, I share every single workout with a potbelly the captain would be proud of.

Spot reduction, the concept of losing weight in a specific area of your body, is impossible. Aerobic activity will burn the fat off a human, just not off the parts a human desires the fat to be burned off of. At least that's what the health and nutrition specialist at the Old Town Athletic Club told me.

Problem is, I'm not fat anywhere else. Just in the stomach.

I figure any reduction would have to take place in that particular spot. Don't ask me why it doesn't.

Incidently, this potbelly thing is really a male problem. Women tend to gain weight in their thighs. A moment on the lips, a lifetime on the hips, as my mother used to say. Without a doubt the greatest inequity between men and women is the simple fact that a man can suck in his gut but a woman can't suck in her thighs.

At any rate, when I see James T. Kirk standing there on the transporter pad, phaser hanging neatly on the side of his slightly bulging waistband, I feel good. And so should you.

Working for an advertising agency means working for many different clients. I've created ads for literally hundreds of products, from Adorn hair spray to McDonald's hamburgers to Weyerhaeuser particleboard. Some companies are dominated by one personality, others develop a corporate culture. From what I have seen, both types of businesses can be successful. The key is that there be clearly identified corporate goals and a decision-making process.

When I worked on Sunkist Orange Soda, they had the most bizarre decision-making process imaginable. After the agency presented the new ideas for television or radio commercials, everyone in the room voted.

Junior writers got one vote. So did the president of the soda company. Obviously, we would stuff as many of our folks into the meetings as possible. Guess what? When the agency had the most people in the room, the agency recommendation stood a solid chance of getting approved. As strange as that process was, at least a decision got made. A lot of client meetings end in analysis paralysis. Nothing ever happens.

While decision-making processes are important, clearly identified corporate goals are more important. In my experience, the best-run companies have a basic philosophy that the people in the company know and understand. Sometimes this philosophy is formalized in a mission statement. Here is the best mission statement I have ever heard.

These are the voyages of the Starship Enterprise. Her five-year mission: to explore strange new worlds, to seek out new life and new civilizations, to boldly go where no man has gone before.

Crew members of the Starship Enterprise know exactly what they are supposed to do. Suppose you are the dumbest person on the ship. How long do you think the mission will last? Five years? Very good. And suppose you encountered a strange new world? What should you do? Explore it, perhaps. There is even an emotion telling you how you should go about exploring it. Boldly.

Now try a simple test. Ask a number of colleagues at your place of work, "What is the single most important thing our company is trying to accomplish?" I've done this myself. Chances are you will receive many different answers. If you run a company, this exercise can be extremely enlightening.

Now ask yourself, if your business encounters a strange new world, what would your dumbest employee do? What if your company encounters a strange new opportunity? Without a basic philosophy, even a business's smartest employees have to improvise when they meet a new or challenging situation.

We could do worse than rewriting the Star Trek mission statement for whatever venture we are on. A simple statement. One that spells out who were are, what we are doing, and how we would like to go about doing it. Maybe even deal with the question of why we are doing it. Make the language exact, the goal specific, and even your worst employee will make you proud.

The Klingons are a rotten lot, immoral, aggressive, ruthless, coarse and generally evil. They are responsible for most of the troubles in this galaxy. They are not like us.

They are a lot like the Russians were in the dreary years of the cold war. They are a lot like the Iraqis were in the dusty days of the war in the Gulf. They are the enemy. All enemies.

Over time, the appearance of the Klingons changed. In the beginning, on the original series, they kind of looked like Mr. Spock—darker skinned than Mr. Spock, but similar.

In *Star Trek: The Motion Picture*, the Klingons looked different. Bony protuberances ran from their noses to their scalps. A fierce enemy had become more fierce for the big screen. What didn't change was the concept of Klingon as enemy. This new face was more faceless. Less individual. Less human. More alien. Easier to hate.

By the time William Shatner kicked Christopher Lloyd (costumed as a Klingon) off the cliff and into the lava flow on the Genesis planet in *Star Trek III*, we had no problem hating the new Klingons as much as the old.

Now there is a Klingon on the bridge of the Enterprise. Enterprise NCC 1701D is the designation of this ship, *Star Trek: The Next Generation* Starship, commanded by Jean-Luc Picard.

Worf is the name of the Klingon, and he is not the hated enemy—he is a beloved member of the crew. Security officer is his job in the twenty-fourth century version of Star Trek. By the twenty-fourth century, Klingons will be our friends.

Nature abhors a vacuum. Drama demands conflict. Ergo, Klingons as enemy have been replaced by the Cardassians. The Cardassians are a rotten lot, immoral, aggressive, ruthless, coarse and generally evil. They are responsible for most of the troubles in this galaxy. They are not like us.

Bottom line. There has to be evil to define good. If a Cardassian shows up as a beloved crew member on *Star Trek: The Generation After the Next Generation*, then a new enemy would appear. (The Romulans have been enemies in both the original series and *The Next Generation*, so they become the odds-on favorite.)

How about no enemies? Only friends. It is possible. If we can solve our differences with the Russians, maybe we don't have to replace them with a new enemy. Maybe we can replace them with a new idea. Think positive. No enemy.

Except, of course, the French.

Of all the things that Star Trek teaches us, the simplest and the most obvious is that mankind's future is in space. Time after time, Captain Kirk gives this little speech about how restless man is. That he is an explorer. That man must have challenge. That he must struggle to survive.

Perhaps this explains why the Enterprise, traveling the universe, exploring countless planets large and small, near and far, never encounters paradise. Utopia doesn't exist in space.

I live in Washington, D.C. We have all your money. Almost every day on the way to work I can watch federal workers digging up flower beds and other federal workers planting new flowers, perhaps pansies. Soon after, other federal workers rip up the recently planted pansies and plant tulips. It's gorgeous.

I sometimes wonder if there are specific government workers who only rip up the flower beds and others who specialize in planting. Or even if there are pansy, tulip and daisy specialists. It's possible.

Meanwhile, other federal workers are mowing the lawns, pruning the trees and washing the sidewalks.

Driving to work in the morning, I often look at the beautiful view I'm afforded just by living in the nation's capital and think about the people in Boise, Idaho, and Hartford, Connecticut, who are paying for my lovely drive. These pretty beds of tulips are your tax dollars at work. And two weeks later, with the tulips still in full bloom, they are ripped out by the ripping crew and the planting crew puts in begonias.

Specialization in this city is close to a disease. We have at least five different police forces that I am aware of. My personal favorite of all the law enforcement divisions is the Secret Service Uniformed Division. Doesn't that strike you as just a little bit funny? If they're the Secret Service, wouldn't the uniform give them away?

On the side of the white cars they drive around America's capital is a shield. The official shield of the Secret Service Uniformed Division. Who is this supposed to be a secret from? Even illiterate criminals can figure out that a car with a shield on the side is a police car.

Even with all your money, all these cops and all these flowers, Washington, D.C., isn't Utopia. Not even close. Truth is, it's a mess. Our murder rate leads the country. You know the story.

Just think of the tremendous amount of money we spend on this place, including money we don't even have. Still no Utopia. And there never ever will be one.

But when I talk to people who don't believe in the space program, they usually feel that we should spend the money here on earth. Let's fix the planet. Take care of the people here. It's a nice thought, but there isn't enough money in the world. Even if there were enough money, watching Congress should teach us there's no way we would ever be able to agree on how to spend it.

How about this. Remember Spain, the place where they had the Olympics? Suppose when Ferdinand and Isabella ran the place they decided not to explore the Atlantic. Instead, they decided to spend the wealth of Spain to fix up Barcelona. To take care of the people there. The Golden Age of Spain would never have happened. Someone other than Columbus would have discovered the New World. Some other country would have reaped the rewards and enjoyed a golden age. And I guarantee you Barcelona would not have become Utopia.

Luckily for you and me, they invested their money in ships of exploration. And their ships of exploration discovered America. I mean, why do you think people speak Spanish in Los Angeles, San Antonio, and Miami? Isabella and Columbus, that's why. We should do the same thing and invest our money in ships of exploration. Spaceships.

Okay. Maybe this is a little preachy. But it is just so damn obvious to me. The same people who think the space program is a waste of money won't leave their houses in the morning until they check the satellite weather channel.

Mankind will go out into space or our species will die

prematurely. I'm too old to be a part of it. I will never stand on Mars. But humans will. As surely as James T. Kirk stands on the bridge of the Enterprise, as surely as Jean-Luc Picard stands on the bridge of the Enterprise D, humans will stand on Mars. We will struggle. We will fight. We will explore.

Face it, even if we created heaven on earth, after a while it would bore us out of our skulls, and we would seek out a new challenge. Space is the ultimate challenge, and that's one thing we cannot resist.

We already have found Utopia. For man, Utopia is endless challenge. And by answering that challenge, maybe we'll find ourselves.

It's absolutely undeniable. True on Star Trek. True in real life. The reason that Captain Kirk gets the girls is that—drumroll, please—he's the captain.

I hate that. Give the fairer sex every chance to look into your soul and see you for the prince you are, and you'll come home from the dance alone. Wear an Armani suit. Make the big bucks. Be the boss. These are the ways to a woman's heart.

As Tony Montana so aptly observed, "First you get the money. Then you get the power. Then you get the women." Yeah, I know that the money part wasn't actually in any episode of Star Trek, but Kirk does drive around in a pretty flashy spaceship.

To be fair, the masculine gender is just as shallow as the distaff side. Men, James T. Kirk included, are suckers for a pretty face. Given the choice of the woman who will make him happy and the woman who will look good on his arm, a man will go for the arm ornament every time.

Once Captain Kirk actually fell in love with a great-looking robot. Hey, she may have been a robot, but what gams. Romancing a robot seems extreme until you take a look at William T. Riker on *The Next Generation*. This guy is after the female of every species in the galaxy. Weird thing is, he isn't interested in human women.

Of the thousand people on the Enterprise D, who has Riker had affairs with? Counselor Deanna Troi, a Betazoid empath, and Ensign Ro Laren, a Bajoran. Also, this guy Riker always takes his vacations on a planet called Risa, which is the Club Med of the twenty-fourth century. So who does he have an affair with on Risa? An alien, of course, who almost takes over the ship and enslaves the Federation.

Listen, Riker, you are very seriously flirting with Space AIDS or something close. Let's show a little restraint. And let's give our earth women a little respect.

But I digress.

So here we are. Women like powerful men. Men like beautiful women. The only real positive thing I can say about this situation is that there are exceptions to every rule.

In the episode where Kirk and Spock went back in time and ended up working in a soup kitchen, Kirk still got the girl. Even as a soup kitchen worker, Kirk carried himself very well. Plus, he was head and heel above the rest of the guys slurping up their dinners. Compared to them, he was a well-dressed, fairly powerful bum with all his teeth.

The lesson here is, be the captain. Or if you're not the captain, groom yourself, dress the best you can, don't slouch and never speak with your mouth full. This is probably good advice for women as well.

Phone just rang. On the other end was a friend with some happy news, a baby boy named Max. The news reinforced something I actually learned before Star Trek.

If you want to have a family, you have to settle down. Fathers and mothers do not trek around the galaxy. They put down roots and face the most demanding challenge of all, the three o'clock feeding.

Skiing is a wonderful sport. Thirty-five is a wonderful age. West Virginia is a wild and wonderful state. The first time I visited West Virginia was when I learned to ski at the age of thirty-five.

Most pro athletes retire by the time they are thirty-five, unless you include golfers as professional athletes. Among other things, thirty-five-year-old humans have lost reflexes and flexibility during their excursion through life. That fact is painfully apparent to athletes who continually use their reflexes and flexibility. The more sedentary masses, however, don't truly realize that these abilities are no longer available to be called on when needed. Skiing, I was soon to find, is an activity that tests both the reflexes and flexibility of its participants.

One might reasonably ask why a thirty-five-year-old man would take up skiing. Two reasons. The obvious, a twenty-five-year-old girlfriend. And second, a philosophy gleaned from my favorite television program, that the unknown is not to be feared, it is to be examined, understood and accepted.

Undoubtedly, this philosophy can lead to strained ligaments, but it's a heck of a lot of fun. Besides, when did Captain Kirk ever back down from a challenge, especially when a woman was involved?

So it came to be that I was standing with two boards strapped to my feet, slippery snow beneath and a friend shouting instructions at my side.

Most ski slopes have a bunny hill. This is an extremely gentle slope where fledgling skiers cannot build up enough momentum to seriously hurt themselves or others. I believe the name *bunny hill* comes from the Latin *snow bunny*, which is a young woman who cannot ski but enjoys wearing very colorful and attention-getting ski clothes.

Allison, my friend, had given me the instructions for the snowplow. This is a method of skiing slowly and under control. Pointing your skis toward each other (but not crossing the tips), you head downhill. The sides of your skis, which are angled slightly forward, will pile up snow, like a plow, and keep you from gaining speed.

Allison had not given me the instructions for stopping. And there was a compelling reason for stopping a few feet ahead: Japanese ski school. Ten short, dark-haired Japanese men standing side by side on skis. I was approaching from the side.

It wasn't a question of *if* I would hit the line, it was a question of how many Japanese ski students I would knock over. Strictly a matter of physics.

Any Physics 101 student will tell you that speed times mass equals momentum. Let's calculate. Including the ski equipment, long johns, sweaters, etc., I weighed about 195 pounds. My speed was probably 1.5 miles per hour. Therefore, I figured I was going to knock over two Japanese ski students.

As the last few feet between myself and the inevitable disappeared, I screamed, "Look out! Look out! LOOK OUT!" The noise caught the attention of the man nearest me. He turned toward me with a puzzled look on his face.

Like in a nightmare where the action takes place in slow motion, I languidly hit the gentleman with the puzzled expression on his face. He fell in equally slow motion into the gentleman next to him. In the sixties, we didn't believe in the domino theory. Now I had vivid proof. Skier number two fell into skier number three.

As the skiers in line were novices, none of them knew how to get out of the way. One little, two little, three little skiers. Skier number three gave me hope as he momentarily regained his balance before he toppled into skier number four.

I now realized the name *bunny hill* comes from the English *Benny Hill*, meaning thirty minutes of nonstop slapstick action.

The event continued to unfold, and I was still moving. So this is the snowplow. Bodies were piling in front of my skis. If only I had the reflexes and flexibility of your average professional golfer.

Mercifully, the fifth skier in line was stopped from falling by the sixth. A hush filled the nearby surroundings. No one spoke. Eyes did all the talking needed. They said, "You are a total idiot."

We managed to untangle ourselves. I put my tail between my legs and my skis under my arms and walked away.

Allison, my friend, wanted to tell me what I had done wrong. Listening was not a strong point of mine at this particular moment. Leaning the skis against the lodge, I retired to the bar.

Skiing is a wonderful sport. Forty is a wonderful age. Over the past five years, skiing has become a favorite pastime. Colorado and Vermont have been added to my skiing itinerary since that first trek to West Virginia. An unknown experience has been examined, understood and accepted. Skiing has become a wonderful part of my life.

I hope someday to ski in Europe. I plan on avoiding Japan.

Kirk is a military man. His method of dealing with conflict is to meet it straight-on. The problem with this approach is evident on almost every episode.

By the third commercial, the ship is in danger, the crew is in danger and there is no easy or apparent way out. Then it gets worse. Before you know it, Mr. Scott is screaming over the communicator that the ship is going to blow up.

Good drama, but a hardly the way to go about your day-to-day business. A more rational approach, and one occasionally used on the show, is the tactic Kirk tried in the episode called "Space Seed." Ricardo Montalban, portraying Khan, has just been thawed out from a frozen state and Kirk wants to find out more about him. Cleverly, Kirk invites Khan to dinner and lets Spock put Khan on the hot seat with some very pointed questions.

This is exactly the format used by many Italian parents to teach their children how to deal with conflict. The Italian parent in this scenario is my father, Alexander Teresio

Marinaccio. My father would sit us down around a large wooden table. Over the course of the next hour, every family member would confront every other family member. Your actions, your personality, even your clothes were called into question.

Volume was extremely important. The louder, the better. Alliances were formed and broken in minutes. The experience was intense. We called this exercise dinner.

Those dinner-table discussions served me well in future years. They taught me to stand on my own two feet, to make my case and hold my ground. They also taught me that there are times for repose during an argument—I mean discussion—times to just sit back and watch.

Letting someone else carry the action for a while allows you to rest, observe and analyze. As Yogi Berra, the great Yankee catcher, once said, "You can observe a lot, just by watching." Which is the tactic Kirk employed with Khan.

The larger lesson is not to run away from conflict. In my home, running away from conflict would have led to missing dinner every night, which in turn would have led to starvation. Besides, conflict can't be avoided in life and shouldn't be. In conflict there is information and growth. In conflict there is, or can be, profit. Whatever doesn't kill you makes you stronger. It doesn't matter whether you use Kirk's straightforward approach or my father's very loud approach. Stand your ground.

Captain Kirk isn't married. Neither am I. Both of us enjoy the company of women. We both chase them and occasionally catch them. But neither of us have found that one girl.

The captain is married to his ship, the Enterprise NCC 1701. He truly loves the ship. He is obsessed with it. There is no room in his life for another love.

I've remained single for a different reason. Sure, I spend a lot of time at work. But I've never been accused of being married to my job. No, work isn't the reason for my long bachelorhood.

The real reason I've never taken a bride is my brothers and sisters. This isn't blame, it's an explanation. Imagine if you will a family with three boys and three girls.

The oldest, Alan, met Betty and married her.

Amber was the next oldest. She met and wed Harry.

Alice Jean met Arthur and they tied the knot.

I was next oldest. Let's skip me.

Barbara was second youngest, still is. She met David and they got hitched.

Mark, the baby, walked down the aisle with Karen.

A small number of sons, daughters, nieces, nephews, cats, dogs and parrots followed. And they all lived happily ever after.

I'm not kidding. All my brothers and sisters fell in love, got married and stayed married. Stayed in love, too.

In a country where one out of two marriages end in divorce, all my siblings have beaten the odds. I'm not saying they have perfect marriages or they haven't experienced tough times. They just picked the right person and made a lifetime commitment.

Needless to say, this is a pretty high standard to live up to. And it puts me under tremendous pressure. If I don't make a lifetime match, I spoil the whole set. Divorce isn't an option for me. Imagine yourself in a similar circumstance.

Since none of the major Star Trek characters ever got married, there are no other role models for me to look to. Well, that isn't exactly true. Mr. Spock got married in one episode. But Vulcans are like salmon. They have to go back to the place of their family origins to marry. Also, they get engaged at the age of eleven or so, then marry at a predetermined time in the future. When Vulcan blood begins to boil and causes a very high fever, it's time to find a justice of the peace. On closer examination, maybe Vulcans aren't really very much like salmon. But they aren't very much like humans, either. And that's my point.

When Spock did get married, the whole thing turned out to be pretty much of a mess. The marriage wasn't even consummated, so it really doesn't count. So where does that leave us?

It leaves Kirk with the ship, Alan with Betty, Amber with Harry, Alice Jean with Art, Barbara with Dave, and Mark with Karen.

And it leaves me right where I started. Maybe someday?

We haven't talked about Mr. Spock very much to this point. The enormous popularity of the Spock character was one of the major reasons for the success of Star Trek. Half logical Vulcan, half emotional human. I don't want to say Mr. Spock is smart, so I'll just describe him as the thinking man's Albert Einstein.

For all his intelligence, Spock is troubled. Completely torn in two between his conflicting halves. Mr. Spock pretends to be perfectly adjusted. He is, in fact, perfectly schizophrenic.

Regular viewers of the show know that Mr. Spock is putting up a front, a facade that denies his basic nature. He elevates his Vulcan heritage while hiding from his human side. As likable as the character is, Spock is basically dishonest. He just isn't being himself.

This can be a tremendous problem unless you happen to be in advertising. In advertising the last person you need to be is yourself. In fact, being a schizophrenic is a definite advantage.

One day you're writing a perfume ad that is supposed to appeal to young women. The next day you have to convince an elderly investor to move his individual retirement account from a mutual fund to certificates of deposit. You have to put yourself in so many different pairs of shoes it's like working at Florsheim.

Once I tried to impress a new boss by walking into his office and identifying myself by saying, "Hi, I'm Dave Marinaccio and I'm a schizophrenic."

The new creative director looked up from his desk and replied, "That makes four of us."

While this type of behavior is a positive boon in my professional life, even admen go home at night—most nights. And at home, denying your basic nature is not a very good idea. Just look at the tormented Spock.

Ask any fan of Star Trek to recall their favorite moments of the series and inevitably one of those moments will be when Spock smiled. Or the time Spock fell in love, or the time Spock cried. Or when Spock crossed the line and acted human. I think we enjoy this so much because these are the times when Spock lets his guard down and is just being himself. This is the real Spock.

My favorite scene of this type occurs in "Amok Time" when Spock enters sick bay and discovers Captain Kirk isn't dead. Spock is ecstatic. He thought he had killed the captain earlier in the episode. After catching himself in a huge smile, the Vulcan first officer regains his emotionless mask.

Doctor McCoy, however, has witnessed Spock's lapse and begins to needle him. Kirk comes to the rescue. "C'mon, Mr. Spock," Kirk says. "Let's go mind the store." Kirk and Spock turn away from McCoy and walk out of sick bay together.

There are two great lessons in one scene. The obvious lesson, taught but not learned by Mr. Spock, is just to be yourself. It feels good. Or to put it more poetically, to thine own self be true. True for me, true for you, true for the Vulcan first officer.

The second, more subtle lesson is delivered by the captain. Kirk knows Spock lives in a world of self-deception, but he lets him ride. Kirk could have ganged up with McCoy to confront Spock. Instead he supports Spock. Gives him a way out when he needs one.

There are plenty of times when Kirk implores Spock to let his human side out, but not now. Not when it will hurt him. Not when he's vulnerable. For Captain Kirk, part of being himself is being a good friend.

No one on the Enterprise has very much stuff. You know, stuff. The things we all accumulate over the course of our lives. Sure, there isn't that much room on the ship to accumulate stuff. Even the captain's quarters are about half the size of a room at a Motel 6. We're talking small.

But I think there's something a little bigger going on here. Mainly that possessions are not the way to judge if a life is full. People don't need to fill their lives with things. What the humans on the Enterprise have are full lives, interesting lives.

During the 1980s, possessions were king. A favorite bumper sticker of mine that became very popular in the recently passed decade said "Whoever dies with the most toys wins." The eighties were the "me" decade. While addressing the stockholders of a fictitious company in the movie *Wall Street*, Michael Douglas pronounced the eighties credo: Greed is good, greed works. Let us all bow our heads in remembrance of the values of the 1980s. And say a little prayer that they never return.

Excessiveness marked the eighties, but the idea of collecting and having a lot of stuff has been around for a long time. Keeping up with the Joneses was a favorite pastime in the

1950s. Long before that, Herbert Hoover won the White House by promising a chicken in every pot.

Let me tell you a strange little story. When I was growing up, I had a friend who had a dream. No, not that dream, a head-on-the-pillow type of dream. His dream was this. He went to a furniture store to pick out furniture for his apartment.

Paul, my friend, is a nice guy. Even-tempered. Good musician. Kind of boring. Paul dreamt he was buying furniture. Some folks don't even think about buying furniture when they're in a furniture store. Paul had this dream when we were in high school. High school!

High school is anguish. Everything is magnified. Information is pouring in from infinite angles. Bad advice and good advice are indistinguishable. Idealism abounds. Life is exploding. And Paul is dreaming about buying furniture. You know, stuff. Ohhh, that's a very nice Chippendale chair, but will it fit with my Bauhaus-influenced Barcelonas?

I bet his living room looks very nice today.

On the Enterprise, the choices are much more limited. Because there is less room, the things that people have say much more about them. Kind of like your dorm room in college. Everyone had the same bed, the same desk, the same closet. Individuality was expressed in your choice of wastepaper basket and posters. If you walked in a room and saw a large picture of Barry Manilow in concert, WATCH OUT!

Captain Kirk's quarters made the most appearances on the show. Very Spartan were Kirk's quarters. But predictable for a military man.

Of greater interest is the way Mr. Spock's room was decorated. Any third-rate fortune-teller would have felt right at home in his digs. The light was always very low, and there were screens and muted colors throughout. In the back was a Vulcan meditation vault. For all the logic and rationality of

Spock's day-to-day existence, in his room mysticism and spirituality were the fashion.

Spock also kept a musical instrument called a lyrette. A true renaissance man (or renaissance alien, as the case may be). During one episode he played the lyrette and sang a song about "bitter dregs." This was the low point of the entire Star Trek series.

In Spock's defense, many of us save the musical instruments of our youth and occasionally have the courage to play them. Fortunately, you and I don't have to perform in front of a national television audience. I no longer own the bass guitar I took lessons for in high school. What remains from that experience is the love of rock and roll that bass guitar helped me develop.

Which brings us back to stuff versus experience. What the voyages of the Enterprise are about is *knowledge*. What the voyage of life is about is the same. Back when the Russians and Americans were racing to the moon, Neil Armstrong and Buzz Aldrin got there first. They returned with a bunch of moon rocks for scientists to examine.

Compared with the experience of going to the moon, those moon rocks are just rocks. Somewhere in a laboratory those rocks are being examined, while all around the world imaginations are fired with the knowledge that the moon is a place we can actually go.

Given the choice, I would rather have an adventure than stuff. My adventures are scuba diving in the Cayman Islands and hang gliding in North Carolina. Cashing in those vacations could probably have gotten me a nicer car or Barcelona chairs. For me, it's no contest. Although I may not get to go where no man has gone before, I'll happily settle for going someplace where I've never gone before. And living a fuller and more interesting life.

Traveling around the galaxy at warp five, which I understand to be two hundred and fifty-six times the speed of light, you pick up a thing or two. One is that humans are imperfect. It doesn't take a degree in quantum physics to leap to this conclusion. Still, bounding around the galaxy and discovering other species provides a mirror for looking at ourselves. Aliens have strengths and weaknesses, just like us. And each time the Enterprise encounters a new life-form, we have a new measuring stick.

Many of these alien species have much to be admired. Some have no trace of war. Others are rational. Still others have immune systems that prevent them from ever being infected by disease. Some are simple gatherers, taking no more than they need from their planet, living lives of complete contentment. Much like Elsie, the Borden cow.

Strikingly, none of these species are perfect, either. In each society there is a flaw. The Gideons, who are immune to death and disease, suffer a terrible overpopulation problem. The simple worshippers of Vaal have the IQs of eggplants.

And what does this measuring stick show us? What is our greatest imperfection? I think it is this. We are attracted to the very things that harm us the most.

An example. Human beings, *Homo sapiens*, folks, us, get

addicted to heroin. We don't get addicted to health food. We don't get addicted to school. We don't get addicted to building a better life and loving each other. We get addicted to a drug that turns us into drooling idiots. A drug that eventually turns normal healthy human beings into criminals. Because the only way one can afford the wonderful feeling this insidious drug provides is by stealing.

A second example. Chocolate. I love it. Chances are, so do you. It is a multimillion-dollar industry. Perhaps more. Give a child the option of eating chocolate or broccoli and the child will pick chocolate every time. So would former president George Herbert Walker Bush.

I strongly expect broccoli, which is good for a human being, would finish far behind on a list that included cotton candy, M&M's, ice cream and hot fudge. All of which are not especially good for you.

Take the potato. The potato is good for you, but it can be made into something that has almost no nutritional value and is loaded with grease—potato chips. Which do you prefer, the potato or the chip?

To continue. Imagine the worst possible thing you can do for your skin. You got it, tanning. It causes skin cancer—CANCER!

Now, plan a vacation. Florida, anyone? How about Cancun? What should we do when we get there? How about spreading a towel on the beach and letting the strongest rays of the sun reaching the face of the planet turn us a deep brown? Ahhh, now that's living.

Is it any wonder that our most enduring method of solving problems is warfare? If you have cable TV, you can watch war all night. It's captivating. We love it. In fact, the greatest sacrifice a human male can make—coming soon to human females everywhere—is to give his life for his country.

Don't misread this. There are many brave people who have fought to make us free, who have honored principles with the last full measure of devotion. But in most cases, warfare could be avoided. It is a failing of the species to which we belong. It is usually the last refuge of wounded pride or some equally meaningless posturing.

The amazing part of all this is that humans have progressed so far, that such a destructive species flourishes. And we do. We keep on keeping on. Humans are drawn like moths to the flame that will burn and kill us. And we draw strength from the experience. We survive.

At its core the question becomes, is man basically good or evil? That is a question for the ages. From what I've seen we must be good. With all these horrible tendencies—our affection for drugs, chocolate, war, Barry Manilow music—we still reach for the stars. If we can prevail against these, then maybe life is a test we can pass. And maybe, just as Star Trek predicts, a better day is coming.

Beam me up, Scotty. If there's a single phrase that has moved from Star Trek to general usage, it's "Beam me up, Scotty." That's because this phrase works in almost any situation.

For example: You've forgotten your spouse's anniversary. At the moment your spouse discovers your blunder, you simply say, "Beam me up, Scotty." In an instant Mr. Scott will beam you directly to the bridge and out of trouble.

Maybe not. If you've seen Scotty lately, you know there's a good chance he's in the mess hall and not the transporter room.

To me, "Beam me up, Scotty" is just a way of saying the world is beyond my control. Humans are used to this condition. Relatively speaking, few things are really in our control.

In the house where I grew up there was a small plaque near the coat closet. It read, "God grant me the serenity to accept the things I cannot change, courage to change the things I can, and wisdom to know the difference." That's the eloquent way to say we are rarely masters of our own fate.

There is a popular and stupider way to say the same thing: "Sh*t Happens."

I couldn't imagine putting a "Sh*t Happens" bumper sticker on my car. When I see a car with that bumper sticker, I think the driver of the vehicle should be fined. Or have his or her mouth washed out with soap. Car bumpers are a public forum, and vulgarity doesn't belong on public display. Not as long as there are children riding around in other cars.

Besides, "Sh*t Happens" is an excuse. It's whining. Crying, "It's not my fault," like some big baby.

You don't get to pick the situations you are dealt in life. But you get to decide how you react. Individuals decide for themselves how they respond to situations. Star Trek usually shows us a positive path to take. The basic philosophy of the show is that man is improving, getting better. Even though there will always be circumstances beyond our control, we control ourselves.

What "Beam me up, Scotty" means is that you realize an event is beyond your control but you're going to react with a sense of humor and then move on. After Scotty beams Kirk out of trouble on Star Trek, the captain regains control and comes out on top. Being beamed up is the captain's way of taking a time-out. We can't always take a time-out in life when we want, but we can always call out for Lieutenant Commander Scott. The act of calling Scotty is a mental time-out. It gives you a second of relief to regain control. Then, like the captain, you're ready to move on. And win.

I have a bachelor of science degree in home econom- ics from the University of Connecticut. It's a little unusual for a man. My major was child development and family relations. Psychology and education were my split minor.

How I came to get this degree is a study in how *not* to get a college education. My first semester in college I achieved— definitely the wrong word—a cumulative average of 0.7 on a scale of 4.0. Semester two my average zoomed up to 1.2.

College was fantastic. I truly enjoyed it. In fact, I truly enjoyed it a little too much. To prevent myself from flunk- ing out, in my remaining semesters I took all the same courses as my girlfriend. As she passed, so did I. After a couple of semesters on this system I almost—almost— made the honor roll.

Her major was child development and family relations. Her degree is from the school of home economics. Since they couldn't give her two degrees, I got one. I owe it to her.

The roots of my educational demise began in high school. Up to my sophomore year, gradewise, I was fairly average. The year was 1967, now known as the Summer of Love. I grew my hair, short by today's standards but noticeable in the mid-sixties, and I started hanging out with an intellectual crowd, wearing blue jeans and tied-dyed T-shirts and attend- ing rock concerts.

As you might imagine, this thrilled my parents no end. Dad was especially upset when I decided to paint a peace symbol on the back of my hand.

My senior year I began a precipitous drop. Not quite tune in, turn on and drop out, but I skipped a lot of school and began to hang around the streets panhandling with my friends. Our joke greeting to each other was "Peace. Love. Bell-bottoms. Got any spare change?"

Passersby would occasionally ask if we were hippies. "No!" we'd say. "Never met one." Just hated the label, I guess. We weren't sure what we were, but we didn't consider ourselves hippies.

I was accepted to college mostly because of decent SAT scores. At UConn my hair got longer. I really didn't do anything, it just grew. When you stop cutting your hair, everyone asks if you are growing your hair. The obvious answer is yes. Everyone is growing their hair. And in college in the early seventies everyone was not cutting their hair, too.

One evening, while visiting in my girlfriend's dormitory, Crandall B, I met some of the young women who lived on her floor. One of the women wore a button on her shirt. It read "Star Trek Lives."

By this time, Star Trek had been off the air for a number of years. It was not yet into wide syndication. Very few reruns were on the cableless airwaves, and the home VCR was still a distant dream. So most of us had not seen the Enterprise in a long time.

It was an exciting moment. This particular young woman had attended a Star Trek convention in New York City, and ten thousand people had joined her. We talked extensively about our favorite episodes. I asked a million questions about the convention. Through this conversation, both of us felt as if we were part of something larger. What would become the Star Trek phenomenon was just beginning, and both of us knew it would grow.

Soon I would be in Star Trek overdrive. Countless reruns filled my afternoons and nights. Shown virtually any scene from any episode, I would be able to recall the entire story of the episode and quote interesting lines of dialogue verbatim.

I became aware that any member of a landing party wearing a red shirt would not survive to the next commercial. I knew that Mark Lenard, the actor who portrayed Spock's father, had been a Romulan captain on a previous episode. I knew that Nurse Chapel had played the part of Number One in the first failed Star Trek pilot.

My abilities grew until only a few seconds of any scene would reveal the entire episode to me. Like Gary Lockwood in the episode titled "Where No Man Has Gone Before," I keep learning and learning. Still I watched. Many of my friends suffered the same affliction.

Suddenly a new word appeared. A word that was meant to describe us all. The word was *Trekkie*. "Are you a Trekkie?" I was asked. "No. Never met one," I would reply. Just hated the label, I guess.

By the end of my college career, I had a degree in home economics. And something that I would carry with me for the rest of my life. A love of the captain and crew of the Starship Enterprise. Fatefully, no longer did I have the love of that resolute young woman who got me through the University of Connecticut. But that is a different story.

Star Trek II: The Wrath of Khan opens with academy cadet Kirstie Alley taking a test. The test is called the Kobayashi Maru, the no-win scenario. Bodies fly all over the screen when Alley, portraying the Vulcan character Lieutenant Saavik, fails the test.

Failing the no-win scenario isn't so bad. As you might have suspected, you can't win.

Here's the test. The Kobayashi Maru is a transport ship that has inadvertently crossed into Klingon space. Klingons attack the ship and are well on their way to destroying it. Alley's ship receives a distress call revealing this information. Hundreds of people on the Kobayashi Maru will lose their lives if her ship takes no action. If she chooses to cross into Klingon space to attempt a rescue, then she is fair game for the Klingons, who far outnumber her.

Kinda like getting into the left lane on a city street. You may move very quickly for a couple of blocks, but just one car turning left in front of you can stop you cold. Sitting there waiting for the lane to clear, you give back all the time and distance you've gained. Cars you zoomed past are now passing you.

Stay in the right lane and you pass no one, moving glacially toward your destination while the left lane breezes by. This is the no-win scenario. The Kobayashi Maru.

Trying to save the transport turned out to be Alley's downfall. Quickly swarmed over by the Klingons, her ship was blasted out of the heavens.

Character is what the test measures. How does one react to a situation where there is no satisfying outcome? Unlike presidential elections, character counts when one must pilot a starship.

Later in the movie, we find out that one person has actually won the no-win scenario. The only cadet in Starfleet Academy history to successfully cross into Klingon space and rescue the Kobayashi Maru? James Tiberius Kirk.

Kirk managed to change the programming of the computer that ran the Kobayashi Maru simulation. Whether this was cheating or original thinking is open to debate. Unlike the rest of us, Kirk never had to face the no-win scenario.

The opposite of the no-win scenario is, obviously, the no-lose scenario. This is rare on planet earth. Unless your name is Richard Gere. Richard faces the extremely difficult choice of staying at work and doing love scenes with Debra Winger, Lauren Hutton and Jodie Foster or going home to his wife, Cindy Crawford. Oh, yeah, Richard is also a millionaire.

If you're like the remainder of the world (i.e., those of us who are not Richard Gere), you probably face the no-win scenario every day.

Fathers and mothers have to decide whether they should take their son, who wants to stay home and play baseball, to visit the aunt who really wants to see him. College students must choose between easy courses that will improve their grades or tough courses that will improve their minds. Professionals wake up sick and wonder whether to go to work at half speed and infect everyone in the office or stay home and fall behind. Television networks always put the best shows on opposite each other.

So what is the value of this concept? It tells you what is really important. Difficult choices expose how we truly feel. What we believe deep inside.

Crossing the neutral zone to rescue the ship shows a willingness to take a chance and a little recklessness. Ignoring the distress call shows an appreciation of what you have, a reluctance to risk what you already hold. Each choice a person makes reveals something about the person. The no-win choice cannot be faked. Consequences are great for any option.

Life, unlike the Kobayashi Maru, is not a simulation. You may not recognize the no-win scenario when it happens in your life. You may not want to. Sometimes when unpleasant things befall us, we simply deny them.

The lesson I've taken from the Kobayashi Maru is not to avoid the unpleasant in life. Make a decision and learn from the consequences, good or bad. After bad experiences, I try to grade my performance. Examining my behavior changes it. Hopefully makes it better.

There's also a lesson from Captain Kirk. When faced with a potential no-win scenario, try something new. Reprogram the situation. Find a way out. Don't stop trying. And maybe, with original thinking, you too can win the no-win scenario.

It's hard to infer Star Trek's opinion of pets. No one on the Enterprise has one. No one on the NCC 1701 Enterprise, that is. On the Enterprise NCC 1701D, the starship of *The Next Generation,* Commander Data has a cat. Also, in the captain's ready room there is an aquarium with . . . fish? Something that looks like fish, anyhow. Either way, whatever is in the bowl behind

Picard's desk really doesn't qualify as a pet. And when you consider that Data isn't human—he's an android—no one on the Enterprise D has a pet, either.

On the original series, tribbles were kept as pets in "The Trouble with Tribbles" episode. Tribbles were basically furry little balls that purred and had an incredible propensity to breed. Sort of like rabbits on fertility drugs. Everyone on the ship loved them. Kirk eventually kicked them off the ship because there were so many of them they were fouling up the machinery.

Let's give the crew the benefit of the doubt. Maybe the reason there are no cats or dogs on the Enterprise is the same reason I don't have a pet. It simply wouldn't be fair to the animal.

Size alone would dictate that any animal on board would have to be fairly small, like a city cat. You know, those cats who live their whole lives in six-hundred-square-foot apartments on the eighteenth floor of New York City high-rises.

What kind of life is that for a cat? I've known such cats. Watching them look longingly at birds that fly past the window, it's obvious this is not a natural state.

What's really crazy is when people living in similar conditions own one-hundred-and-fifty-pound German shepherds. I have no doubt these folks love their dogs. But it's not fair to the animal.

The other day I heard an incredible idea. Virtual reality for city pets. Fit a dog with a computerized helmet and transform your living room into the Serengeti. Of course, until the virtual reality pooper scooper is invented, a real mess could ensue.

Back on the Enterprise, the crew has an erratic schedule. What with fighting Romulans, exploring strange new worlds and examining gaseous anomalies, who has time for feeding, walking and scratching bellies?

Pets care for us because we care for them. If you can't care for a pet, you shouldn't have one.

I'd love to have a dog. I almost got a couple of parakeets. Even had them named, Sutter and Tidrow. Bottom line was, I didn't think I could care for the birds. Maybe I'll settle for fish. Or something that looks like fish.

The unknown is not to be avoided. It is to be examined, understood and accepted. Fear should be treated exactly the same way. As a young man, I had an aversion to flying in airplanes. The most apt description would be that I was a white-knuckle flyer.

My first airplane ride didn't occur until I was twenty-two years old. Eastern Airlines took me from Hartford to Chicago. I enjoyed flying, face plastered to the window, until a Cleveland flight from Chicago a couple of years later.

Before the plane could get above the weather, we flew through a thunderstorm. Someone once said flying is hours of boredom interrupted by seconds of sheer terror. This particular ascent was half an hour in a Veg-O-matic. I realized something was up when the pilot instructed the flight attendants to return to *their* seats and strap in.

After this experience, flying became less enjoyable. The ride to Cleveland had shaken more than the plane. It had shaken my faith. Clearly, something had to be done.

To me the solution seemed obvious. Embrace your fears. Make a friend of horror. Get back up on the horse. Once more into the breach. Yes, my solution to being a white-knuckle flyer was to become a skydiver.

Once you've fallen through the sky in a jumpsuit, I reasoned, being in a plane will seem very solid indeed. A young woman who was a friend of mine agreed to join me in this adventure.

So it came to be that one bright Saturday morning we headed to Roosevelt Field in Warm Springs, Georgia, and a date with destiny. Atlanta Air Sports was to indoctrinate us in the ways of parachute jumping. The day's activities had been explained to us over the phone. Arrive early and sit through two hours of classroom instruction, which would be followed by a couple of hours of ground school. Finally we would be taken aloft to make a jump.

During the classroom session I noticed a problem. Our instructor, Tim, seemed much more interested in instructing my female companion than he did me. She received a high level of personal instruction from Tim. I received little attention at all.

My concern was not jealousy. I neither dated nor was I sexually interested in my friend. No, my concern was for my life.

Still, I wanted to jump very much. But questions were forming in my mind, foremost of which was "Is this a good idea?"

About this time we learned what to do if our parachute didn't open. In fact, we learned about the multiple ways our parachutes could fail to open. A skydiver falling through the clouds at an increasing rate of acceleration must be able to identify the type of malfunction that has befallen his chute. I knew exactly what I would do if I experienced a malfunction. I would die.

As the morning turned to afternoon, our class moved outside. On the tarmac we watched jumpers climb into a Cessna 182. They were ferried to eight thousand feet and then left the plane. From eight thousand feet a jumper can stay in free fall for about twenty-five or thirty seconds. From the ground, jumpers look like dots. Slowly the dots get arms and legs. "Open the chute," your brain starts to repeat as the jumpers get closer. In an instant, the skydivers are under canopy and float to the ground.

Watching this ritual time after time built our confidence. Jumpers went up and jumpers came down. Seemed to be enjoying themselves, too.

The camaraderie was contagious. "You're gonna love it," more than one jumper said to us. Occasionally a jumper would come over and observe us practicing. "Hit the back of your thigh on your PLF," one said. (A PLF is a parachute landing fall.) It takes the shock out of hitting the ground, which you do at pretty high speed even with a fully deployed parachute.

Finally Tim thought we were ready. In front of the plane we stopped for a photograph. I managed a smile.

Perhaps you've heard the question, "Why would anyone jump out of a perfectly good airplane?" One look at this plane gave me the answer. Jumping was probably a good idea if this bucket of bolts actually got us into the air.

We were ferried up to our jump height of three thousand feet. A static line was attached to my parachute. This line would automatically pull the ripcord as I fell from the plane. Tim opened the door of the plane.

Stick your head out the window when your car is going sixty miles an hour. Imagine gas and oil are pouring out of your engine, which is also producing five times as much noise as usual. Now imagine your car is three thousand feet above the ground. Magnify all the above with fear for your life. Lastly, leap from the car. That's skydiving.

"Feet out the door. Stand on the strut. Jump! Jump! JUMP!" The third time Tim yelled, "Jump," I did.

My mind went blank as I stepped into the air. At the end of the static line was the static of my brain waves. The next few moments do not exist in my memory.

The chute opened and I came out of a coma. Silence. An amazing view and silence greeted my return to the land of the living. A tremendous sense of calm filled me. Here, at 2,980 feet, I felt at ease, I felt happy.

Slowly I came to earth. Lazily I drifted downward. Nearer to the ground things started to speed up. The ground rushed up and reminded me to get ready for a PLF. The experienced jumpers had predicted my PLF would be a disaster. Newcomers just never get them right. This newcomer did a perfect PLF. I daisy-chained my parachute and walked one hundred yards back to the takeoff point.

Wow, did I feel good.

I continued jumping until they took me off the static line and let me pull my own ripcord. That summer I made fifteen jumps. Since then I have made numerous airplane trips.

Turbulence still gets my attention when I fly, and occasionally I feel a little nervous. But I feel good about myself. I examined, understood and accepted something that had scared me. I don't skydive anymore, but I wouldn't trade the experience for anything.

To say any episode of Star Trek was the best is to take away from the others. Certain episodes did make a deeper impression than others. And some fired the imagination, giving them a life beyond the show.

One such episode was "Mirror, Mirror." Most people remember this episode as the one where Mr. Spock had a beard. What happens is the transporter, a finicky piece of machinery, is scrambled by an ion storm. When Kirk, Uhura and McCoy are rematerialized, they end up in a parallel universe. Back on the Enterprise, a Kirk, McCoy and Uhura from the parallel universe rematerialize.

Normally when people from parallel universes switch places, nobody notices. It's a common occurrence where I work. However, the particular parallel universe that the crew of the Enterprise switched with was evil.

So when Kirk returned to his quarters in the parallel universe and checked his service record, he found he had assumed command of the Enterprise by assassinating Captain Pike. Not a pleasant place, this parallel universe.

That episode was on my mind while I was shaving the other morning. It was staring me right in the face. There are tiny alternative universes right here on earth. Places where you can see yourself a little askew. Mirrors.

Mirrors have always been a source of mysticism. Vampires don't cast a reflection in a mirror. Break a mirror and you get seven years' bad luck. Alice fell through one. Kilgore Trout wrote they were leaks to other universes. Oddly, you are not the face you see in the mirror. You're seeing yourself backward, reversed; it's you but it's not.

While shaving, I noticed the mirrors in my bathroom were lined up to reflect off each other. In front of me was the face in the mirror and a mirror image of the face that looked into the mirror every morning. To really see myself as others see me, I needed a double reflection. An image even more distant than the face in the mirror.

And that's how we see ourselves. Askew. No matter how objective we are, we will never really know how we look to others because our vision is obscured by our own point of view. To really see ourselves as we are, we need to get as far as possible from our own self-perception.

In "Mirror, Mirror" the captain and crew get that far away, all the way to a separate universe. They view parts of their personalities that they strive to suppress. They are forced to see themselves as barbarians. And they can't deny that they are looking at themselves.

While going to a parallel universe isn't usually an option for most of us, stepping back and looking at ourselves is a good idea even with the distortion of self-perception. I suppose I relate to this episode because I wonder what it would be like to be a barbarian or a priest. How different would my life be in a different time and place? What would be different when I looked in the mirror?

My mind tends to wander, but being a small mind, it never wanders very far.

One of the differences between Star Trek and real life is that nobody ever daydreams on Star Trek. You know, just kind of stares off into space and thinks nothing. Kirk never has to tell Spock to wake up and smell the coffee. If I were Uhura, listening to that subspace radio chatter all the time, I'd zone out completely. She never does.

If I were Scotty down in the engine room with the drone of the warp drive going on and on, I would be daydreaming before you could say Jack Robinson. Not Scotty. Matter and antimatter, dilithium crystals, these things keep him endlessly focused.

Truth is, the truth this isn't. Long voyages make humans vegetate. Ask anyone who has ever taken a long car trip. Sing all the songs you want. Play all the car trip games in the world. After a little while, your mind will take its own little journey.

On a five-year voyage like the Enterprise's, I would probably daydream for a year and a half. I've refined these little trances into an art form. Coming out of a daydream, I can usually trace my thoughts backward until I reach the point where I drifted off. Try it if you like; I don't know if it's hard or easy to do, I just do it.

Ironically, many of my daydreams put me on the bridge of the Enterprise, the place where nobody daydreams. The fact that no one on the Enterprise daydreams probably isn't a conscious choice of the producers. My guess is it's a limitation of television drama.

While Star Trek is usually right on the big stuff, it does miss on some small points. This is one. Too bad. These little excursions are good for one's mental health.

Besides, on a show that takes place in outer space you'd think somebody would space out sometime.

Central to everything in Star Trek is the non-interference directive, the Prime Directive, as it is called. It may be the most important idea in the series. The way the directive is applied or not applied is as interesting as the concept of the directive itself. But let's not get ahead of ourselves.

The Prime Directive prohibits the captain and crew of the Enterprise from interfering in the internal affairs of any of the planets they visit. Say the Enterprise shows up at a planet where a human sacrifice is about to take place. They are prohibited from stopping the sacrifice.

Behind the Prime Directive is some pretty sound reasoning. People have the right to construct their societies in any way they wish. Valid reasons may exist why the sacrifice is taking place, reasons the crew of the Enterprise may not fully understand. Cultural bias may influence the way the crew interprets what they are seeing. Therefore it is best not to interfere in something you do not completely understand.

This rule not only protects the people of the planet, it protects the crew. Noninterference keeps the crew from getting into the middle of a private fight. Since they don't get involved, they don't have to pick sides.

Here's a different scenario. The Enterprise discovers a world that is being ravaged by a plague. Antibiotics on the ship could save the world. According to the Prime Directive, the Enterprise cannot interfere. Although they might save the inhabitants of the planet, they might also be put in the position of deciding who lives and who dies. Or, during the inoculation, advanced technology might fall into the wrong hands. Potentially, this advanced technology let loose on a backward world could produce results worse than the plague. Once again, the wisdom of the Prime Directive protects both the Enterprise and the life-forms it encounters.

If you understand the preceding, you should also understand this.

The Prime Directive is treated with as much respect as a fire hydrant at a dog show. Episode after episode after episode, Kirk ignores the Prime Directive and does what he believes is right.

Never doubt the captain would waltz right in and stop the human sacrifice. If the person to be sacrificed was an attractive young woman, never doubt the captain would fall in love. Next, he would pass out the antibiotics and end the plague. Kirk does observe the directive when it fits his purposes. Rarely otherwise.

In a way, the Prime Directive fulfills its primary mission: creating dramatic conflict.

What, then, is the lesson here? A great one. People are more important than rules. Enforce the spirit of the law above the letter of the law. The Prime Directive was instituted to protect people. When the directive gets in the way of protecting people, ignore it.

A person who understands a rule knows when to break it. A person who understands a rule understands intent. The Prime Directive was not intended to condone human sacrifice. Kirk does the right thing when he interprets the rule to fit the situation.

Wouldn't it be wonderful if our justice system could make that differentiation? We hate lawyers because they use the letter of the law to their own purposes. They pervert the spirit of the law. They make the right wrong, and the wrong right. Lawyers would let the human sacrifice take place, then sue on behalf of the relatives.

Watch virtually any episode of Star Trek and the Prime Directive will play a part. But Captain James T. Kirk will play a more important part. Judgment will be exercised. And people will be more important than rules.

Here's another reason James T. Kirk is an excellent manager. When he's around, you know he's in charge. When he's not around, he clearly designates his successor. It's simple and direct. Totally unmistakable. As he leaves the bridge, he turns to whomever he wishes to be in control and says, "Mr. Scott, you have the bridge." Mr. Scott then serves as captain while Captain Kirk is gone.

Anyone who has watched a teacher walk out of a classroom can appreciate the importance of this action. A smart teacher will appoint some skinny Goody-Two-shoes to spy on the class, someone who will tell on you in a minute. And guess what? It works.

A more absentminded teacher might mumble, "O.K. everybody work at your desk." Then leave. Guaranteed, immediate and total chaos will ensue.

But heck, why use grade school as an example? Let's talk about the average American office. While showing a little more restraint than the average grade school class—fewer spitballs will be thrown and fewer fist-fights will break out—from a productivity point of view, the profiles are similar. When the boss is away and no designate is around, less work gets done.

Like most of what Star Trek teaches us, this may seem simplistic. It is. These are lessons culled from a television show, not the library at Alexandria. But the lesson itself is right on the money.

Designate someone to take over the bridge, and the ship will continue to run smoothly. Designate someone to take responsibility for a job, and the job will get done.

In advertising, there is a job called proofreading. I'm sure you've heard of it. It's important because if you spell something incorrectly it reflects on what you are saying. "Give me liberty or give me depth" just doesn't have the same power as Patrick Henry's original quote.

Proofreading is not the occupation of choice for many people. For most, it's a way station. Proofread for a bit and get promoted to assistant copywriter. In smaller advertising agencies, there is no money for proofreaders. This is a constant trouble point.

At one small office I worked in, proofreading was everybody's job. True, our general manager believed that everyone who handled an ad should proofread it and everyone was responsible if an error got through. Needless to say, many errors got through. Why? Because when everyone is responsible, ultimately no one is responsible.

Big themes. The duality of man. Good and evil. Squeezing the toothpaste tube on the end or in the middle. Star Trek was different because it dealt with these issues head-on. To examine prejudice Frank Gorshin was painted half white and half black. Star Trek routinely tackled subjects other shows were frightened to touch.

A very early episode of Star Trek involved a transporter malfunction. Kirk was beamed back from a planet. As soon as he left the transporter room and the door shut behind him, the transporter came on again. Kirk materialized for a second time. But this Kirk was different—sinister.

Later we learn that the first Kirk is all good, the other is all bad. Somehow the transporter has scrambled the captain into two separate beings. Jekyll and Hyde, if you will.

And here's why Star Trek was a remarkable show. Instead of the usual battle between good and evil, a different point of view was drawn. Neither Captain Kirk was better than the other. Evil Kirk was a savage, practically a rapist, but he was strong-willed and determined. Good Kirk was very humane and caring but also timid, weak and lacking the ruthlessness to be a decision-maker.

Each Captain Kirk was incomplete without the other. Being completely good was just as bad as being completely evil. For the time and place, this was a tremendous breakthrough. And, as we say in advertising, it had the added advantage of being true.

Inside all of us is a killer and a priest. My mother used to say this in a beautifully simple way: "There's good and bad in everyone." What Star Trek made me understand is that everyone needs both the good and bad inside them to exist. It is finally a question of balance. For me. For you. For Kirk. For everyone.

Finnegan was an upperclassman at Starfleet Academy. An upperclassman who tormented a plebe he called "Jimmy me boy." Jimmy me boy was, of course, Cadet James T. Kirk. Long after Kirk graduated from the academy, the captain of the Enterprise remembered Finnegan.

"Remembered" isn't strong enough a word. What James Kirk wanted was to beat the tar out of Finnegan. And beat him silly he did—years later, on a planet that made dreams come true.

Virtually every member of the Enterprise lived out a fantasy on that planet, a planet constructed for the sole purpose of recreation. A planet constructed by an intelligence so far beyond our own, Spock wondered why they needed recreation at all.

The curator could have answered Spock. But it was Kirk who spoke. "The more complex the mind, the greater the need for the simplicity of play." Bingo. On the nose. Home run. Yeah, buddy. I'm gonna turn all the cards over. "The more complex the mind, the greater the need for the simplicity of play."

Other phrases may sound similar. All work and no play makes Jack a dull boy. Work hard and play hard. All those clichés are close but no cigar—they subtly miss the mark.

This is a prescription for maintaining one's mental health. An understanding that intelligence requires both purpose and diversion. That the more challenging uses a mind is put to, the more important it is to have fun. CEOs should scuba dive. CEOs must scuba dive. A vacation isn't just a good idea, it's an absolute need.

To tailor the concept a bit, the more complex the task (or job) the greater the need to build in some fun. Extrapolate this baby all over the lot. Star Trek strikes again. Everything you need to know is in this series someplace.

In this particular instance, it's also stated as eloquently as imaginable. The more complex the mind, the greater the need for the simplicity of play.

When I was a young boy in Catholic school, the nuns taught us the Golden Rule. Do unto others as you would have them do unto you. Good rule. You should treat other people as you would have them treat you.

Coming from the nuns, however, we considered this rule suspect. After all, the nuns frequently hit us. Strict interpretation of the Golden Rule would imply the nuns would like us to beat them up. We knew this to be false. Even raising your hand in self-defense when being struck by a nun could get you into big trouble. Principal's-office kind of trouble. Calling-your-parents kind of trouble. Never ever even think of hitting a nun—never. This was as clear as an unmuddied lake. Crystal clear.

While we struggled with this paradox, an offshoot of the Golden Rule puzzled us even more. The subrule was this: Treat everyone the same. Again, like the Golden Rule, not a bad sentiment. But in practice? Yikes! What a mess. Absolutely impossible to follow.

What was obvious to the students at Saint Joseph's School in Enfield, Connecticut, is not obvious to many current managers of people. You cannot treat everyone the same. Far from it. Managers with a feel for people know that you have to treat everyone differently. The rules should be fairly well spelled out, but how the people are treated inside those parameters should vary by individual.

For example, both McCoy and Spock work for Captain Kirk. Both are his friends. Both are experts beyond Kirk's abilities in their fields of specialization. Spock is a general scientist. McCoy is a medical doctor. Both are treated with respect and dignity. Mr. Spock, however, is allowed to override the captain's decisions. Kirk will in fact acknowledge Spock's abilities by turning to him for solutions and recommendations.

McCoy is usually told what to do. The captain's opinions are more important than McCoy's recommendations. Very often, Kirk will order McCoy to carry out a task against McCoy's protests.

One thing allows Kirk to treat these two so differently. He knows them. He understands their strengths and weaknesses. He wouldn't use Spock as a cheerleader or as director of human resources, and he knows that McCoy is a chronic complainer.

The creative department of an advertising agency isn't a starship, though there are some alien life-forms to be found there. But there are different fields of specialization, and many of the members of a creative department know much more about their fields of expertise than the creative director. You will also find emotionless people and chronic complainers. My guess is that this makes an advertising agency much like any other office.

To successfully manage all these different types of people, do what Captain Kirk did. Try to get to know them. All you can really manage is the strengths and weaknesses of your people. Then, when you know them and manage them in an individual way, try to do something else. Treat them as you would like to be treated.

All Star Treks end the same way. The captain is sitting in his chair on the bridge surrounded by the members of the crew. Significant others from the episode are sometimes part of the group. There on the bridge the moral of the story is told. Many times the moral comes in the form of a joke. A friend of mine calls this part of the show "the laugh on the bridge." As the laugh continues, the screen usually cuts to the outside of the ship. The epilogue music comes up and the episode ends.

Over time I came to realize that, more than a terrific way to end a television show, laughter is a great way to end almost any occasion. Nice way to end a business meeting. After a kiss, it's a great way to end a date. It would even be a great way to end the world. Imagine this, the Four Horsemen of the Apocalypse come galloping through, wreaking havoc on the world. Then, after a hard ride, they dismount, tell a joke, laugh, the music comes up, the universe goes down.

At work on some Fridays after four o'clock I like to gather the creative group together. Sometimes we sit in the computer area, other times we congregate in an office. The setting isn't as important as getting everybody together. Occasionally we send a writer out to the package store for a little beer. The purpose of these little get-togethers is part work, part social, part Star Trek. I figure if you can end the week with a laugh, it bodes well for the following week. When the sessions continue past five o'clock—quittin' time—I feel really good.

Endings are more important than beginnings. I hate that dandruff commercial that says, "You never get a second chance to make a first impression." The eventual outcome of a first meeting is far more important than initial impressions. Didn't the mother of the writer of that commercial ever tell him/her, "Don't judge a book by its cover"?

The first time Chuck Yeager flew in an airplane he got sick—sick. In World War II, Yeager made Ace in one day by shooting down five German planes during one mission. Chuck went on to become the first man to break the sound barrier. He led the first perfect deployment of a Tactical Air Command fighter unit squadron. Today General Chuck Yeager is generally considered to be the best pilot in the first one hundred years of aviation. Who cares if he threw up his first time in an airplane?

Most of the time you'll have a thousand second chances to make a good impression. First impressions can be overcome by a subsequent performance. But no one ever forgets how you go out. John Belushi, a funny man, is remembered as a drugged-out suicidal maniac. He can never live it down. Can anyone even remember their first impression of John Belushi?

And speaking of endings, there's always Lester Moore. Lester was shot to death in Tombstone, Arizona, in the wild 1870s. Not many folks know the story of Lester's life except that it ended when he met someone a little faster on the draw. He lies in Boot Hill Cemetery. At the head of his grave is a marker that reads:

HERE LIES
LESTER MOORE
FOUR SLUGS FROM A 44
NO LES
NO MORE

Now that's how to end an episode with a smile.

I think it was Benjamin Franklin who said, "Guests, like fish, begin to stink after three days." Lovely thought there, Ben. To be fair, houseguests are both a joy and a pain. To be realistic, houseguests are going to happen. People will visit. The payoff for having houseguests is that you get to visit them and become their houseguest. But let's stay on the subject of people coming to visit you.

How should one prepare for houseguests? Should one prepare for houseguests at all? Hey, they're coming to visit you. Why not show off in all your native charm? "This is our house. This is how we live. I'm sure you'll be happy just to fit in for the next few days."

It's an easy strategy for houseguests. Cuts down on a lot of the work. Just clean up the place and voilà, you're done.

I don't think so.

When guests are expected aboard the Enterprise, many modifications are made. Of course, many of the houseguests (shipguests?) aboard the Enterprise are aliens. Without some modifications in life-support systems, the visitors would die. And as any competent host will tell you, the death of your visitors is bad form.

The lesson here is straightforward. Change the environment of your home to accommodate your houseguests. Making your home more like their home will make them feel more comfortable and welcome. When your visitors are comfortable, they become better guests. How far you go is up to you. The idea is to make your visitors feel at home.

When my sister and her husband visit, I put a quilt on their bed. I normally leave the quilt in the closet, but my sister loves quilts and has one on her bed. Small changes like that can have large effects in making someone feel at ease. Besides, in my sister's case I know that soon after she arrives she will be in total control of the house. Why fight it?

O.K. Your houseguests have arrived and you've greeted them. Sit back and let everyone shake off the jet exhaust. Everybody settled? What's next?

Let's return to starship NCC 1701. Usually one of the first acts on the Enterprise after receiving guests is a formal dinner. Officers attend wearing their dress uniforms. The menu is top-drawer. Sometimes the food is from the visitors' planet, other times it is an earth favorite. Wherever the food comes from, it is made obvious, by a toast, that this feast is in honor of the visitors.

Feed the guests. Yeah, a great way to start a visit. Let's not take that part about the formal dinner too seriously. But a dinner in honor of your houseguests, with an appropriate toast, is a great place to start.

Next, ask yourself honestly, why did your guests come to visit? Did they come to see you? Did they come to see the city you live in? Is your home merely in a convenient locale? If you live in Orlando, you know the answer.

If they came to experience something other than your wonderful presence, take them out to eat. This is also good advice for bad cooks.

If your houseguests came to spend plenty of quality time with you, cook them dinner. Show them your silverware and wine collection. Do not treat your guests as guinea pigs. This is not the time to try out that oh-so-interesting recipe that you never had the opportunity to cook before. Play it safe. Serve a trusted standby that everyone loves. And don't forget the toast.

All right. You're off on the right foot. Is there anything else we can learn from Emily Post . . . ehh . . . Captain Kirk? Well, he usually assigns a crew member to give the visitors a tour of the ship, to be taken at their convenience, of course. Unless the guest is a beautiful woman, in which case he leads the tour personally. He also tries to keep everything as normal as possible during the visit.

If there is anything interesting around, at the very least give your houseguest the option of a tour. I live in Washington, D.C., about ten blocks from the White House. If a potential visitor gives enough warning, there is a VIP tour available that anyone can get just by asking. This is a big hit. You don't even have to go along.

As for the acting normal part, do what's normal for you. Be yourself. That's who they are visiting. I'm as much myself as possible (while following James T. Kirk's lead).

Great people talk about ideas. Average people talk about things. Small people talk about people. This is also the difference between television shows like Star Trek, a show about ideas, and shows like *Melrose Place,* which deal with who's zoomin' who. Star Trek episodes usually deal with themes like the dehumanization of man in a technological society. Typical prime-time fare deals with gossip.

It is truly amazing how much of our lives are filled with gossip. Titillating items about whatzisname and whatzername. If the time spent on gossip in the average office were added up, the loss of productivity noted would be in the billions.

Gossip is often confused with conversation. In fact, it often takes the place of conversation. Take gossip away from some folks and they would turn into mimes.

Bookstores and newsstands are gossip-crazy. Name your favorite type of gossip and there's a specialty magazine. Or ten. Entertainment, politics, finance, farming, pick a subject. We even create fake gossip like the *National Enquirer* because the factual gossip isn't enough for us. Give us dirty laundry. Why does anyone know who Marla Maples is? I mean really, who cares? Couldn't we live without that?

It becomes a game. Who knows what about who's doing

what to whom. The person who knows the most dirt has the most power. It doesn't even matter if the story is true, what matters is if it is juicy. And it matters if you're in. 'Cause if you're not in, you're out. Heaven forbid others might know more than you do. The game becomes self-perpetuating. Each turn of the screw deserves another. No matter who is getting screwed.

On Star Trek, the members of the crew don't gossip. There is plenty of opportunity for gossip, especially with Kirk's libido barely under control. But somehow the crew of the Enterprise figured out something that escapes a lot of folks—there are a heck of a lot more interesting things to talk about.

Ideas are one.

Kids walk into my office. Baby goats they are not. Young, aspiring advertising professionals. YAPs? They are well groomed, fresh faced, energetic. They carry books. Books in advertising are portfolios of previous work. The work of the young and fresh faced are spec ads. Spec ads are ads that have never been produced. Pretend ads. Virtually every portfolio, or book, has a spec ad for Crayola crayons and one for AIDS awareness. Usually the ads aren't very good.

I've scoured many episodes of Star Trek to see how young trainees are incorporated into the system. Can't really say I've found much help. Enterprise NCC 1701 is the flagship of the fleet. Very few cadets get the opportunity to join the crew. New members are more likely to be established professionals who require assimilation, not training.

The movies are a different matter. In *The Wrath of Khan*, the entire crew is trainees. Kirk is terrible with trainees. Maybe that's too strong. Kirk is not interested in trainees. Naturally, a situation develops in which the young trainees, under the watchful eye of the captain, must sink or swim. The training exercise is over, and now it's for real.

In one scene, Kirk turns to Spock and asks his opinion. How will this group of inexperienced trainees just out of Starfleet Academy perform? Spock answers, "Each according to his gifts."

Is this a cop-out? Sort of. It denies that you can teach someone a lesson that goes against his or her nature. Scared people will always be scared people. Brave people will react according to their gift of bravery. What is most important in life are the gifts you are given. If you are born with the gift of gab, maybe you can bore the Klingons to death.

Let us accept this premise, at least to a small degree. Kids can walk into my office day and night for years to come and what is important is the talent they are born with. The finest art schools in the nation can polish and polish them. But it won't help if they don't have the gift.

I just can't buy it. Here's why. Two things are important. For the sake of Spock, let us call the first one gifts. The second and more important factor is attitude, the willingness to overcome obstacles. To keep trying and never relenting. Persistence will overcome resistance.

By way of putting things into perspective, imagine a young fresh face walking into your office. Scrubbed clean. Eager. Feeling good about the meeting soon to unfold.

The absolute, number one, critical mistake this young person can make is this: acting like a jerk. You work hard. The folks in your office work hard. Weekdays often turn into weeknights. Weekends are often an extension of the work week. Pressure and stress are part of your daily routine. Now, ask yourself this question. Do you want to be around a jerk during a stressful sixty-hour work week? Do you want a nail driven into the bridge of your nose with a sledgehammer? Probably not.

Attitude is the top priority.

After attitude, talent or gifts are important. What Spock might have said was, "Each according to his desire and his gifts." But Star Trek got it half right.

So here it is. A young, eager, fresh-faced hopeful walks in the door. Find out what kind of a person is sitting across the desk. Is this someone you could spend long hours with? Is he or she positive?

Then find out about this person's gifts. In advertising, that means looking through their book for talent. Do they have a way of looking at products that is different from the pack? How do they think?

Kids walk into my office. Baby goats they are not. I've hired a few and they all have the same gift—a great attitude.

James T. Kirk has many attributes to be admired and emulated. He is loyal, helpful, friendly, courteous, kind, obedient, cheerful, thrifty, brave, clean and reverent. But make no mistake, Jim Kirk is no Boy Scout.

His greatest quality, one which I try to copy, is that he never gives up. He never quits.

Bones McCoy, standing on the Genesis planet, said it best. Above his head, the USS Enterprise was burning up in the sky like a streaking meteor. Next to him, James Kirk had just asked, "What have I done?" McCoy, eyes heavenward, replied, "You did what you had to do. What you always do. You took death and turned it into a chance to live."

So here's Kirk. His crew marooned, his son murdered, his ship destroyed, his reputation ruined, his career in tatters, his credit cards canceled. Not a good day for the boy from Iowa. What does the Captain do? He keeps his head. He figures out what to do next. He doesn't give up.

I've never faced the kind of adversity that Jim Kirk regularly defeats. However, I do run. Well, by many standards it's not running, but it is faster than jogging. The point is, I do go out dressed in running shorts and put one foot in front of the other.

During most runs, especially on hot days, the body wears down. Sometimes an ache will crop up to accent your tiredness. Slowing down or stopping pop into your mind.

When this happens during my runs, I think of James Kirk. It helps me keep going. Kirk wouldn't give up; he'd press himself harder, push through it and keep going.

This is not always the best advice. Once, during a 10K road race (that's 6.2 miles for the nonmetric of you), I really overheated. To gain seconds, I had skipped every water stop. The more tired I became, the harder I pushed. As I crossed the finish line, I collapsed. They threw me into the back of an ambulance and rushed me to a hospital.

As I awoke out of my delirium, the nurse asked if I could remember my name and address. This really upset me. What did she think, that I was an idiot? Then I realized I didn't know my name or address. I *was* a total idiot. Slowly it came back to me. My name was, still is, David Marinaccio. It took me a little longer to remember my address.

Neatly folded on my chest, next to the IV line, was a T-shirt. A race official noting that I had crossed the finish line gave me the T-shirt that was awarded to all the finishers.

Now, what I had done was extremely stupid. Never run a race without replenishing your fluids. It can kill you. But the part about never quitting, I'm proud of that. I was hot, tired and physically drained, and still I had summoned the strength and the willpower to run the entire distance. I didn't give up.

I still have that T-shirt. I believe it shows I have a little character. Not unlike my favorite character, a starship captain who never gives up.

To produce vodka in the United States of America, you must follow very restrictive rules. These rules require that the vodka be both odorless and tasteless. The rules work. In blind taste tests, American vodkas are indistinguishable from each other.

I learned this amazing piece of trivia in a conference room at an advertising agency in Chicago. This information was considered important because our job was to convince consumers that the vodka we were advertising was the best-tasting.

Our task was not impossible, though. You see, the very same consumers who could not distinguish a taste difference between vodkas in a blind taste test could find wide differences in taste when there were labels on the bottles. Since our bottle had a label on it, we were confident we could become the best-tasting vodka.

The researcher who told us these wondrous facts closed the meeting with a phrase that is an advertising mantra. She said, "Perception is reality." Her point was that we should treat these taste differences as if they were real.

To reinforce the perceived differences, we would create a "point of difference" from other brands of vodka. In our case, we would tell the public that our special filtering process is what produces the smooth, smooth taste you can find only in our bottles. Ironically, it is the filtering that makes all American vodkas absolutely tasteless. But hey, perception is reality.

In one episode of Star Trek, the Enterprise is grabbed by a giant hand. The ship cannot move forward or back, up or down. Engaging the ship's engines to pull free of the hand only results in the hand's squeezing harder.

The hand, of course, is an illusion. It is really an energy field made to look like a hand. By examining the hand, the Enterprise begins to unravel the mystery that is holding them motionless in space.

Unlike advertising agencies, the captain and crew of the Enterprise never accept perception as reality. If they did, they would still be in orbit trying to shake hands.

In "Spectre of the Gun," Kirk, Spock, McCoy and Chekov find themselves transported to Tombstone, Arizona, circa 1881. The entire town is an elaborate illusion. But the illusion is real enough to kill you—if you believe it can.

Once Mr. Spock realizes that the laws of physics don't operate in Tombstone, he concludes that the entire situation isn't real. He convinces the others of his discovery, and this becomes the key to resolving their predicament. What Spock does is find the reality behind the perception.

Perception is *not* reality. This is a running theme on Star Trek. Time and time again, situations that appear to be one thing are shown to be another.

It isn't necessary to watch Star Trek to learn this lesson. Think of the people you know. Some folks who appear cold and uncaring are often warm and decent when you get to know them. Smiling, friendly, outgoing folks can be downright mean when it counts. Image is shallow. What's important is the substance of a person.

Perception is perception. Reality is reality. Illusions must be examined to be exposed. But it is an effort well worth making. Because when you peel away the perception and find the reality underneath, you've also found the truth.

By the way, the vodka didn't sell and the brand went under.

Anyone with even a passing interest in Star Trek should know this rule: Never, ever, ever wear a red shirt—not under any circumstances. Don't do it.

Pick any episode. Captain Kirk, Mr. Spock, a series regular like Uhura and some guy you've never seen before are standing on the transporter pad. If the guy is wearing a red shirt, he will not live past the first commercial. Somewhere on the planet below certain death awaits.

I've watched these guys in red shirts get shot, be blown up, be disintegrated, have all their blood drained, have every cell in their body explode and otherwise meet the most painful and horrible deaths imaginable.

The endings aren't even especially heroic. First a guy beams down, then he's dead. At least it's usually quick. Nine times out of ten, the poor fellow doesn't have a clue what hit him. Within seconds, Bones examines the fallen crewman with a tricorder, turns to the captain and says, "He's dead, Jim." By the next scene it's as if the guy never existed.

There's no wake, no funeral and most of the time his name is never spoken again.

I bought red swim trunks once. Took them with me on a scuba diving trip to the Cayman Islands. While wearing those trunks ninety-five feet underwater on the north wall of the ten-thousand-foot-deep Cayman Trench, my regulator came apart. For those of you unfamiliar with scuba, the regulator is the thing you breathe with. No regulator, no air. Under ninety-five feet of water, this is more than an inconvenience. I managed my way up to the surface. Once safely back in my hotel room, I threw the red swimsuit away.

You would think I had learned my lesson. Wrong, security-detail breath. I bought a red short-sleeved shirt last summer. Next morning I unfolded the shirt and took out the pins. Ouch! A small trickle of blood. No big deal.

Work was relatively unremarkable that day, and I hopped into my car for the commute home. A car, I later realized, is a twentieth-century version of a transporter pad. On the ride home—WHAM. I ran into a van. My front end crumbled. The van sustained no damage.

Although I wasn't killed, there was several hundred dollars' damage to my car, and I did receive a $125 fine from the United States Park Police (one of Washington's many police forces). I tossed out the red shirt that night.

I do not own red socks or a red jacket or a red sweater or anything else that is completely red. It's a wonder I'm not afraid of Santa Claus. I do find red-haired women attractive but I don't recall ever dating one. That's probably for the best.

Listen, wear red if you want to, but I'll pass.

Whenever the captain and crew of the USS Enterprise visit other cultures, the customs of the host planet are observed. Alien societies are taken at face value and not judged by human standards. Even when Scotty's life hung in the balance in "Wolf in the Fold," his trial took place under the laws and penalties of Argelius II.

A friend of mine lived in a building on Peachtree Street in Atlanta. Of course, since every street in Atlanta is named Peachtree Street, that doesn't really tell you where he lived. His apartment was located in Midtown, an urban area of the city populated by numerous high-rises.

The particular building my friend called home was also the home of a large flock of pigeons. Like many of the residents of this building, my friend would occasionally feed the pigeons.

I've never really cared for pigeons—or air rats, as they are also called. Pigeons are dirty and always begging. They make a mess of any place they hang around. They even walk funny.

Let's face it, being a pigeon is no walk in the park. Worse still, they now face a fight for their ecological lives. Seagulls have swept into the cities to fight for their spot on the food chain. Even inland cities are now populated by gulls who find human trash and waste an absolute bonanza. They are bigger and faster than the pigeons, maybe smarter.

I don't have a shred of scientific proof to back up this observation, but it sure looks that way to me. Hey, I may not like pigeons, but I think they have a tough fight on their hands.

My friend recognized many of the pigeons that hung around his apartment building by their markings. One day he noticed that a bird he was familiar with had broken a wing. As the bird walked, he leaned to the side, his bent and ruffled wing dragging pathetically behind.

So heart-wrenching was the sight of this injured bird that he became an object of human pity. Passersby who saw him would break off pieces of their sandwiches for the poor little broken-winged bird. People would always make sure the aeronautically challenged pigeon got something to eat. He became a star. His weight ballooned. Surprisingly, his wing injury had become his lucky break.

Other pigeons noticed. No kidding, other pigeons noticed. Soon there was a rash of bogus broken wings. Perfectly healthy pigeons were pretending to have broken wings, hoping to gain charity from humans with food. And it worked. The faker birds got fed.

My friend had watched the whole phenomenon take place over the course of a week. He told me he didn't feed any of the others, but he continued to make sure the original broken-winged pigeon got his share. I sensed he didn't like the idea of the healthy birds pretending to be hurt. That they were fakers.

I think my friend is a smart guy. But I also think he fell prey to judging these pigeons by human standards. While feigning an injury to gain charity may be a reprehensible act for a human, the faker birds were just doing what had proven to be successful for another of their species.

We should treat pigeons like the crew treats alien species and keep our morality to ourselves. That applies to all animals and to nature in general. Fauna and flora have nothing

71

to do with our culture. Following the lead of the crew of the Enterprise suggests giving respect and not passing judgment.

Hey, the pigeons were merely attempting to stay alive and prosper. In an environment where seagulls are now competing for the same space these birds occupy, they turned misfortune into fortune. Darn clever, too.

A **starship captain is no different from a manager at K mart or IBM. One of the traits I admire most about James T. Kirk is the way he manages his people. I admire him as much for what he doesn't do as for what he does. Specifically, he doesn't use fear or threats as a management method.**

A few years ago, there was a book called *Winning Through Intimidation*. It was a very popular book, although I don't believe it was too popular with the folks who were on the receiving end of the intimidation. I don't recall ever seeing a copy on the captain's bookshelf.

Scaring people may help achieve short-terms goals, but in the long run, it causes more harm than good. Loyalty, trust, respect—these are the qualities a good manager instills. They are incompatible with fear. And they can't be cultivated by a bully.

Though Kirk never resorts to fear, he is still a tough manager. Very tough. Captain Kirk regularly demands the impossible of his crew. He can demand it of them because he expects it of himself.

Kirk never asks them to do something he wouldn't do. When danger arises, he faces it personally. The safety of the crew of the Enterprise is his number-one priority. And they know it. So when the captain asks them to perform miracles, they do it.

In almost every episode of Star Trek, Kirk comes up with an array of superhuman demands. Scotty has to change the laws of physics to keep the warp drive going. He says he can't, but he manages to do it. Bones McCoy has to treat and save a creature without knowing its anatomy, or he has to cure a disease that no one has ever been infected by before. He always finds a way to get it done. The crew constantly surpasses their own capabilities because Kirk demands it.

Thing is, it works. I mean it works in the real world. Oh, you can't cure AIDS in an afternoon or discover a new scientific principle when you need one, but you can accomplish some amazing stuff if you *try* to achieve the impossible.

In advertising, the goals are modest compared to mixing matter and antimatter. The impossible might be changing a client's mind or finding the money to use a top-notch director to shoot your commercial or selling a particularly daring concept. Most times scaling these heights is not even attempted. Trying to conquer them in an atmosphere of bullying and intimidation is inane.

Fear is a powerful emotion. So is hate. One breeds the other. And when you are reaching, trying to go where no one has gone before, you better be sure that the people you're managing want you to succeed.

Great success is built on a solid foundation, a foundation of loyalty, trust and respect that you can depend on. Without them you will fail. With them you can command a starship.

The most touching thing about Star Trek is the friendship between Kirk and Spock. To me, it *is* Star Trek.

How and why friendships are formed is one of the great mysteries of the universe. Why do two people suddenly feel comfortable around each other? How do they find common ground? What is the connection that makes a relationship special, what gives it the strength to last?

Watching kids develop friendships is fascinating. Put two kids of approximately the same age together and BAM, they become as thick as thieves. A minute later they disappear. Just as you notice they're gone, they're back, laughing at a joke no one else understands. Kids seem to be able to do this an infinite number of times with an infinite number of other kids.

A few years later, this behavior is gone. It's not so easy for grown-ups. Maybe the reason adults don't make friends is that they have friends. I'm not sure. But somehow the process is different for big people.

There seem to be two basic kinds of friends. The peas-in-a-pod, birds-of-a-feather, friends-that-are-like-twins kind. Like Patty and Cathy, they look alike, they walk alike, at times they even talk alike.

Then there are friends like Kirk and Spock. Yin and yang, the opposite sides of the same circle, perfect complements to each other. Kirk needs Spock's coolness and calculation. Spock needs Kirk's gut instincts and aggressiveness. They complete each other.

I don't know when Kirk and Spock first met. I do know I've seen every single episode of Star Trek and every Star Trek movie but can't find that moment. Although we didn't get to watch this friendship start, we get to see it grow. We watch it being forged. Each adventure is a link in the chain. Every alien menace defeated is a shared victory. The more danger they share, the deeper the friendship becomes.

Countless times this pair risked their careers for each other. Kirk's travels up and down the chain of command are a testament to his devotion to Spock. Although he has killed the captain on at least two separate occasions, Spock is equally devoted to Kirk. The simplest way to put it is, they're friends for life.

Some friends merely save each other's lives. Kirk and Spock have died for each other. Kirk to save Spock in "Amok Time." Spock to save Kirk—the ship, too—in *The Wrath of Khan.* Now that's friendship.

Perhaps you know someone like that. Met in high school and never drifted apart. Moved away maybe, lived on different parts of the continent, but never lost that closeness. See him today and you just pick up where you left off. I'm lucky I have two friends like that.

Friends are one of the gifts of life. A funny thing about friends is that all the good times don't bring you as close as one shared bad time. Friends that go through hardships with you get to know you, and you them, in a deeper, more meaningful way. You get to see their best and worst. You see them for what they really are. In turn, they have seen you in exactly the same way.

Hit a rough spot, and a lot of people will help, if it's convenient for them. True friends will help even when they have to go out of their way. When you need them, they're there.

Often they're the same people who wouldn't dream of asking you for help when they need it. You still give it, of course, but the best of friends rarely need to ask anything of each other. Experience has taught me these things are true.

I know this: Kirk and Spock understand what friendship means. When I look at these two, I can't help but wonder what kind of friends William Shatner and Leonard Nimoy are. Can it all be acting? I hope not. I hope they're the best of friends for the rest of their lives.

Once when I was out of work, my brother-in-law invited me to play in a friendly game of poker. This poker game had taken place—off and on—over a number of years with pretty much the same players. Thousands of poker games just like it happen in dens and basements all over America. I was glad for the chance to get out, engage in some macho camaraderie and forget my current troubles.

As my financial situation wasn't the best at the moment, I was concerned about the stakes. "Quarter ante with a maximum fifty cents bump," my brother-in-law told me. For the uninitiated, that means it cost each player twenty-five cents at the beginning of each hand and that a player can raise the stakes fifty cents as each subsequent card is drawn.

"How much does the big loser usually lose?" I asked.

"About twenty dollars," he replied.

"O.K. Sounds good," I said, and gathered up twenty dollars in quarters for the night's competition.

As I met the other players I realized that macho camaraderie now includes females. Five men and a woman sat down to play cards.

Seven card stud was the game of choice. Two cards face down followed by five face up. I tossed in my quarter. After the first three cards were dealt, the bidding began. It hit fifty cents immediately. Same on the next card. Same on the next card. By the time the first hand ended, I had lost two dollars and seventy-five cents.

"Hey, what's the most anybody has ever lost in this game?" I asked the table.

"Harry lost about a hundred and twenty bucks," laughed the guy in the glasses directly across from me. I wasn't hungry, but I lost my appetite immediately. If looks could kill, my brother-in-law would have been dead.

My twenty bucks were gone in about five minutes. Players looked at me the way polar bears look at seals. Exchanging ten dollars for forty more quarters, I figured this was it. Lose 'em and I'm gone.

Then it came to me, the corbomite maneuver! A little trick James T. Kirk used to save the Enterprise. When you're outgunned and everybody knows it, it's time to bluff.

Kirk was in desperate straits. (At least it wasn't his brother-in-law that got him into it.) The Enterprise was facing an alien vessel far beyond its own technology. Ten minutes were given to the captain before he was to be blown to kingdom come. So Kirk, knowing his communications were tapped, sent a message to Starfleet. He said he would commit suicide by setting off the ship's supply of corbomite. The corbomite would destroy a large part of the galaxy, so the Federation shouldn't send any ships to this area for many years.

The aliens, who were eavesdropping, fell for the trick. And they retreated, leaving the Enterprise intact. Naturally, corbomite doesn't exist, even on Star Trek. Kirk was bluffing.

Next hand was my turn for the corbomite maneuver. Dealt

my usually crummy cards, I bet to the limit. Seeing this totally defeated figure—me—running up the pot was a clue to the other players. They quickly folded. I had bluffed and won a small pot. I had won. This little victory restored my confidence and I played the night, finishing slightly ahead.

I haven't played poker since. My sister's husband and I have made up. Thanks to the example of Captain Kirk, when strength failed, I successfully used guile. And like the captain, I learned that sometimes the greatest victory is just to escape with your skin.

Walter Koenig portrays Pavel Chekov, the Russian ensign, on Star Trek. I met him once, very briefly.

One day, a friend of mine who is also a big Star Trek fan was feeling sick. Being sick is bad enough, but it was also his birthday. Simultaneously, there was a Star Trek convention being held downtown. Putting two and two together, I hatched a plan. To cheer up my friend, I'd drop by the convention and buy him a phaser gun. Who wouldn't feel better holding a weapon that could kill or stun with the flip of a dial?

When I arrived at the downtown hotel where the convention was taking place, I discovered the price of admission was twenty-five dollars, exactly the amount of cash in my wallet. Entering the convention would be useless if I couldn't buy the phaser I came for. Disappointed, I headed for home.

Walking out to the lobby, I spotted a familiar face. Chekov! Standing next to him was a beautiful young woman.

(Not only the captain gets the girls.) They were saying goodbye, and Chekov, Walter Koenig, was heading toward the convention.

A new plan formed in my brain. I followed him, slowly closing the distance between us. To reach the rooms where the convention was being held, Chekov would have to ride down a long escalator. That ride would take about forty seconds, long enough for me to pitch my idea to the Star Trek cast member.

I stepped on the escalator a single step behind Chekov. Extending my hand and gesturing a handshake I said, "Walter, I'd like to thank you for many hours of enjoyment watching Star Trek."

He turned, took my hand, shook it and said, "Thank you."

"I wonder," I continued, "if you could help me with a small problem." Relaying the story about my sick friend and the lack of funds to accomplish my mission, I finished with a plea. "If you pretend I'm with you, I'm sure the ticket takers will just let us both pass into the convention free. It would be a big help."

Walter Koenig looked at me, paused a second, smiled, then said, "O.K." And we stepped off the escalator.

As we approached the convention doors, it was like being in a mini-tornado. Every head turned to see Chekov. The crowd at the door murmured. I could hear the voices: "It's Chekov." "Hey, look. Chekov." Almost everyone who saw him broke into a smile. It was a real, honest display of what people think about Star Trek, the happiness and magic of it. And because I was with Chekov, I got to taste a tiny little morsel of what it was like to be on the inside. It was wonderful.

Unfortunately, it ended as soon as we passed through the front doors. Walter Koenig turned to me and smiled a last time. "You're inside," he said. And he was gone, taking the little tornado of happiness with him.

Heading over to the merchandising area, I searched for a phaser. They were out. Instead I purchased a schematic diagram of the Starship Enterprise that cost about twenty dollars, leaving me cab fare home. As it turned out, it cost my sick friend about ninety dollars to have the gift framed. But hey, it's the thought that counts, right?

On the way home, I replayed those moments walking through the doors and into the convention with Chekov over and over again. I had gone to do something nice for a sick friend, or I would never have gotten to cross that threshold. And there's the lesson. When you do something nice for a sick friend, nice things come back to you.

Everyone is on the bridge of the Enterprise. Everyone. Kirk the white male, Uhura the black woman, Sulu the Asian, Chekov the enemy Russian, Spock the alien and guest stars of every gender, race and creed.

Best of all, on the Enterprise they all get along. More than get along, they all help each other. They're all part of the same team.

A quick look might make you think of the United Nations, but a longer look reveals what is really at work here, the melting pot. You don't hear as much about the melting pot these days. It's a beautiful concept. Immigrants from all over the world come to America and melt together. Each loses a little of their own culture but produces a brilliant alloy in which the best of each comes out.

The bridge of the Enterprise is the America of the melting

pot. O.K., there are no pointy-eared aliens from Vulcan in America. But it is a place where all kinds of people come together and become part of a greater whole.

It reminds me of the neighborhood of my youth. Walking around the block I grew up on, you could hear five different languages: Italian, French, Polish, Spanish and English. We all got along.

While many of the parents thought of themselves as Italian or Polish, all the kids thought of themselves as Americans. We loved baseball, rock bands, watching TV, the same stuff loved by American kids all across the country.

Today is different. Does that mean that for *The Next Generation* to realistically reflect America in the 1990s each ethnic group should be off in its own corner? That there should be gangs on the holodecks, drive-by shootings in the turbolifts and a McDonald's in Ten Forward? I hope not.

The truth is, the bridge of the Enterprise has always depicted a sanitized vision of America. But sanitized is not a dirty word. I see it as a hope for the future. If our country is going to live long and prosper, then we are going to have to behave like Kirk, Uhura, Sulu, Chekov and Spock. We don't have to dress in silly little uniforms. But we will have to give up a little of our pasts to share a common future. To gain the best of each other.

When my grandfather passed through Ellis Island in 1895, he came to the melting pot. He wanted to be part of America. His future and America's future were more important to him than where he came from. In America, it didn't matter where you came from. It mattered where you were going.

It's exactly the same on the bridge of the Enterprise. What is important is what you can contribute, not whether you came from Russia or Vulcan. The crew members must give up a little of themselves, but they gain the universe.

Star Trek: The Next Generation. I remember the first time I heard the phrase. The idea that there would be a Star Trek without Kirk, Spock and Bones seemed sacrilegious. Still, when the series began, I watched.

Mostly I didn't like what I saw. Captain Picard was too cold. Commander Data was such an obvious attempt to re-create Spock it seemed absurd. Nothing seemed right. Still, I watched.

Wesley Crusher became a member of the bridge crew. A child as a navigator? These guys were totally losing it. Still, I watched.

I was reminded of the last films of the Marx Brothers. Groucho was slower and the stories were thinner. Still, slow, thin Marx Brother movies were better than no Marx Brothers movies. And so it was with *The Next Generation*. At least it was Star Trek.

Slowly, things began to change. *The Next Generation* started to grow on me about the time Lieutenant Worf's hair started to grow on him. During the first couple of seasons, Worf wore his hair in a pageboy. Imagine, a Klingon in a pageboy. A member of the most vicious, warlike species in the galaxy, and these guys had given him a haircut that belonged on Sandra Dee. It could have been worse. He could have had a beehive. To give it the real Klingon touch, they could have added real bees. Anyway, when Worf's hair began to grow, they were finally starting to get it—to understand Star Trek. They realized Worf was a Klingon and that warriors don't get their hair done by Sassoon.

Although the show was gaining steam, there were still some problems. Without a doubt, the worst was Deanna Troi's uniform. Deanna Troi, the ship's counselor, wore a special boob uniform. A deep V-cut revealed her ample cleavage. The fact that she was the only person on the ship to wear a boob uniform ran counter to the best notions of Star Trek.

Star Trek is not about cheap sex. Star Trek was out in front—perhaps the wrong expression—in understanding that women are the equals of men and in portraying them as equals. The boob uniform was thought up by, well, boobs. I haven't noticed the boob uniform in a while. I hope it's gone forever.

Somebody finally wised up and sent Wesley Crusher off to Starfleet Academy. Don't get me wrong, Wil Wheaton does a great job as Wesley. It's just that Picard was right in the first place. Children don't belong on the bridge.

Ultimately, the optimistic outlook of the original Star Trek found redemption in *The Next Generation*. It got better and better. Intriguing concepts began to take shape. Species that communicated through analogy and the dreams of an android were explored. The classics were woven into the scripts.

On the original series, Shakespeare was often a part of the show. A passing theatrical troupe performs Hamlet during "The Conscience of the King." The three witches from Macbeth make a cameo appearance in "Catspaw." The Star Trek movies are practically homages to the Bard. In *Wrath of Khan*, Ricardo Montalban's death scene is pure Shakespeare. *Star Trek VI: The Undiscovered Country* draws so heavily on Hamlet, I was expecting Mel Gibson to show up.

The Next Generation won me over completely and totally when my literary hero, Mark Twain, showed up at his acidic best, gracing the final cliff-hanging episode of one season. I wish Hal Holbrook had been playing the part, but you can't have everything. Besides, it was a very good Sam Clemens who matched wits with and then joined the crew of the Enterprise D.

In my heart I wanted *The Next Generation* to succeed. It just took me a while to warm up. Given time, *The Next Generation* was able to connect with my generation. Often we (meaning me) are a little quick to judge, quick to condemn. I'm glad I kept watching. Good things are worth waiting for.

If there's a lesson to be learned here, it is about the real next generation. With kids, a little patience is a good idea, too. Children will usually surprise you with how well they turn out, it just takes 'em a bit of time.

What will people do in the twenty-third century? What are the occupations of the future? Hmmm? The military will be intact. Hence, captains, navigators, chief engineers, communication specialists, yeomen and gunners will all be around. Doctors and colonists are a good bet. Bureaucrats are indestructible. Bartenders are indispensable. And chaplains will always be in demand.

Star Trek has a place for them all. They've all played parts in one episode or another.

But dare we dream that the future will be minus one occupation? That the future will be free of lawyers?

Alas, lawyers continue to exist into the twenty-third century. Hey, Star Trek presents an optimistic view of the future, not a perfect one. Kirk was defended by a member of the bar when he went on trial for murder in an episode called "Court Martial."

The kindly lawyer that took Kirk's case was right out of a 1930s movie. His sense of the law as an instrument of justice was refreshing by today's standards. Even the prosecutor, a former girlfriend of Captain Kirk, was that uncommon breed of lawyer that cared about justice and people. She was happy to lose the case when it was discovered that Kirk was innocent.

Amazingly, money never came up during the entire episode. Imagine two lawyers and neither interested in money. Cynics could use that as the ultimate proof that Star Trek is fantasy.

I, however, choose to believe that in the future even lawyers will join the human race. That the law as a profession will end its obsession with money and refocus on the higher meanings of the law.

I offer as proof the simple observation that no one has ever filed suit against Captain Kirk. If members of the bar were to continue their current behavior into the future, surely someone would have tried to sue the captain. Lord knows he's punched enough people to spend the rest of his natural days in litigation.

Ipso facto the future is a place where tort reform has turned lawyers into wholesome, functioning members of society. Instead of suing everyone in sight, people will actually solve their problems outside of courtrooms. Lawyers will still exist to handle the criminal proceedings of the day, but their primary concern will be finding the truth, not joining the million-dollar-settlement club.

The future according to Star Trek has puppets, paupers, pirates, poets, pawns and kings. It even has room for lawyers. But mercifully, the ambulance chaser has disappeared into history. Hooray!

James T. Kirk and all members of the crew of the Starship Enterprise are sworn to obey the orders of their senior officers. This is the military code of conduct. Survival of the chain of command rests on strict adherence to it. Disobedience cannot be tolerated. It would invite a complete breakdown of order.

For this reason, it is surprising that one of the strongest suggestions of Star Trek is to question authority. Look at virtually any authoritarian society the Enterprise visits. They're usually a disaster. Check it out.

On Gamma Trianguli VI the followers of Vaal had turned into a race of sheep until Kirk ordered phasers to knock out Vaal's power source.

Countless generations of Yonadans had lived in ignorance and servitude under the strict discipline of the Oracle until Kirk used phasers to knock out the Oracle's power source.

Near Pollux IV, the entire crew of the Enterprise was almost enslaved under the iron hand of Apollo until Kirk used phasers to knock out Apollo's power source.

. . . Wait a minute, I just had déjà vu. Sorry. Where were we? Oh yeah.

And speaking of authoritarian societies, let's not forget about Professor Gill. He reinstituted Nazism—with the best intentions, of course—on Ekos. This civics experiment failed miserably until Kirk woke the führer out of a drug-induced semicoma.

I believe I can see a pattern here. Absolute power, which is what Vaal, the Oracle, Apollo and Gill had in common, corrupts absolutely.

Authority was seen as anathema to original and independent thought. Kirk's goal was to get the residents of these societies thinking for themselves, to get people of these planets to stand on their own two (or however many) feet. Phaser fire usually got the oppressed citizenry on the road to their full potential.

When Star Trek first appeared, everyone was challenging the status quo. Cultural, sexual and civil rights revolutions were in high gear. People were marching in the streets because they believed the United States government had lost its way. "Down with the establishment" and more offensive idioms were a part of everyday speech. But I do not believe Star Trek's perspective was some ephemeral view of life dictated by the 1960s.

In fact, the most monumental confrontation with authority by Captain James T. Kirk didn't occur until the late 1980s. *Star Trek V: The Final Frontier* climaxed in a confrontation between Kirk and God.

God tells Kirk to bring the Enterprise closer to the planet that the captain, Bones and Spock have beamed down on. Kirk doesn't comply. Instead he asks, "What does God need with a spaceship?" Bones interrupts, "You don't question the Almighty." But Kirk ignores the doctor and asks again. Captain James Tiberius Kirk not only questions authority, he questions God.

As it turns out, the entity the captain was talking to was not God. Powerful, yes, but not God. For, as any good captain knows, God doesn't need a starship.

If Kirk had submitted to the apparent deity, if he hadn't

questioned, the outcome would have been terrible. Kirk's insolence saved the galaxy.

Well, it wasn't actually the captain's questioning that saved the galaxy. You might suspect that it was Kirk using phasers to destroy the entity's power source. But in this case, it was Mr. Spock using a Klingon disrupter to destroy the entity himself. Hey, that's what you get for impersonating God.

Technology changes, but people don't. No matter how powerful our computers become or how many diseases we learn to cure, we still act dopey.

Take cars. I can't say that Star Trek definitively implies there are cars in the future but whenever they show San Francisco in the Star Trek movies, there are carlike things flying around. For the sake of convenience, let's just call 'em flying, nonpolluting, technologically advanced vehicles of the future. Wanna bet that some dopey human will lock his keys inside? I'll give you odds. No matter how advanced the car, we will lock our keys inside, forget to set the parking brake or smash into the flying, nonpolluting, technologically advanced vehicle right in front of us while we are changing the radio station. Because, while the cars may change, the humans driving them remain the same. It's our lot.

Have you ever watched the fire-fighting competitions on television? Firemen from all over America compete in events like the ladder climb or the hose hookup. Obviously, these are the best, most physically fit firemen from their towns. Ever wonder who is left behind in the fire station to protect the citizenry? I'm just waiting for a town to burn down while

What is it about Star Trek that inspires the people who watch it to be so . . . inspired? My whole life I've run across people who draw parallels between their existence and the fictional characters aboard the Enterprise. I'm not talking Trekkers or fanatics. Just folks like you and me who make reference to Star Trek at work, at home and at play. What makes this short-lived television series of the 1960s so powerful?

Initially, the actors who portrayed the captain and crew had no clue. William Shatner said in an interview, "We were just actors, performing on a weekly TV series."

No, you weren't, Bill. You were touching people in a way they had never been touched before. You were transporting audiences to a place they never wanted to leave. And once you took us there, we never let you go back either.

I remember the first time I watched Star Trek. My mother and my brother Mark were there. Small bowls of Neapolitan ice cream sat in our laps. Before the episode ended, Star Trek was my favorite show. I couldn't wait for next week or to tell my friends about the show.

In high school, we often discussed episodes of Star Trek with a fervor never applied to our studies. I remember sitting in my friend Jim's Ford Fairlane talking about "Who Mourns for Adonais?" an episode that postulates that the ancient

Greek gods were really space travelers. Thousands of years later, the Enterprise stumbles upon the remnants of this group on a planet far from earth. Apollo is the lone survivor.

The discussion made us giddy. We talked and laughed and played with the idea. It was as if the Enterprise's warp drive had been put directly on our imaginations. We thought thoughts as big as the galaxy.

There were undoubtedly a thousand similar discussions taking place all across America. And with syndication, the same discussions were probably taking place all across the globe. Were two German high schoolers sitting in a Volkswagen having the same exchange? Two Swedes in a Saab? Two Italians in a Fiat? Why not? If the Greek gods were space travelers, anything was possible.

In a way, Star Trek made us all one, the people of the planet earth. We had a common vision. And in 1968, for the first time in history, NASA astronauts took photographs of the whole planet from space. So we got to see what our vision really looked like. Maybe that's it. That Star Trek and the times and science all came together at one moment. That we suddenly looked at ourselves in a whole new way. And that once we saw that perspective, we just kept it. Maybe that's why so many people still do it today.

Then again, maybe the ability of Star Trek to touch us is a mystery of the universe. If so, then just letting it inspire us is more than enough.

Lieutenant Commander Montgomery Scott is the perfect ship's engineer. His love for propulsion systems know no bounds. Given shore leave, he would rather go back to his quarters and read technical manuals. All the better to understand the most technologically advanced vessel of his time, his vessel, the Enterprise.

Scotty treats this piece of machinery as if it were a person. He coaxes it, he pushes it, at times he is more wet nurse than chief engineer.

The ultimate goal of all this loving care is speed. If the ship's maximum speed is warp seven, then he just knows he can edge it up to warp nine. And maybe just a wee bit more.

He lives in a tug-of-war. One side loves the ship, wants to treat it like a baby. The other side tortures the ship until the last ounce of speed is squeezed out of the warp drive. And then he squeezes just a wee bit more.

Scotty loves to break the rules. If he has a theory that's never been tried before, then the Enterprise is a guinea pig for his idea. Never satisfied with the status quo, he tinkers and changes and improves, making up the manual as he goes along.

The lesson I learned from Scotty is to leave all the options open. When dealing with complex problems, humans want to simplify them, idiot-proof them. We live in a society where everything is idiot-proof. By the way, you and I are the idiots things are idiot-proofed for.

There is a slight problem with living this way. Idiot-proofing is also genius-proofing. Idiot-proofing reduces the impact of judgment. On the Enterprise, all the rules can be broken if there is a good reason. Greatness is usually achieved by trying something different or putting existing things together in new and unconventional ways. It's called innovation. Idiot-proofing prevents new approaches, ensuring that the same old tried and true methods are used.

Scotty's genius could not find expression in an engine room with a governor on the warp drive. Idiot-proofing the Enterprise would mean limiting the chief engineer's creativity. Idiot-proofing would mean more rules to follow and fewer options to be exercised. With fewer options, it's safe to say, the ship would have blown up long ago.

Competent people know which rules to follow and which to ignore. When people of good judgment are allowed to exercise their insights, good results usually follow. When people's hands are tied, they are ineffective.

The crucial variable here is competence. Sure, if a bunch of trainees are running the ship, idiot-proofing is probably called for. But when you're working with the best, let 'em loose. Don't restrict them. And you, just like Captain Kirk, will be the beneficiaries of their genius.

Doctor Leonard McCoy is the perfect ship's physician. Just kidding. The character created by DeForest Kelley is cantankerous, contrary and opinionated. Underneath, of course, he has a good and caring heart. Bones McCoy's view of the world is just a bit cynical.

His cynicism usually serves him well. He sees right through Mr. Spock. He can tell off the captain if he has to. And you'll never find him backing down an inch from something he believes in.

Cynicism also gives him a gift that is useful in any age. It allows him to use technology without being subservient to it. The tools of medicine in the twenty-third century are highly sophisticated. There are the tricorder, the medical scanner, the sterile field and various computers. There are also highly complex vaccines and compounds for almost any situation.

These tools are useful to the doctor. But McCoy understands that they are only tools. When these devices fail to work or start to hinder rather than help the process, McCoy changes the way he works. He uses his years as a doctor, his judgment and his creativity to find solutions. In short, Dr. Bones McCoy knows when to shift from high-tech to low-tech.

In "The Devil in the Dark," Kirk wounds an alien creature

called a Horta. A mind-meld between Spock and the Horta confirms that the Horta is injured very badly. The mind-meld also reveals the intelligent nature of the alien. Kirk orders McCoy to heal the Horta. Unfortunately, the Horta is a silicon-based life-form. Its body structure is more mineral than animal. The creature is a living rock.

At first McCoy hesitates. "I'm a doctor, not a bricklayer," he protests. But he examines the creature. The good doctor's instruments are designed for examining human beings and prove ineffective. What follows is—in my humble opinion—McCoy's finest moment.

He puts down his tricorder and orders emergency shelter cement from the Enterprise. Emergency shelter cement is mostly silicon. So, he trowels the cement into the Horta's wound as a bandage. Sure, it means getting his hands dirty, but it works!

"I'm beginning to believe I could cure a rainy day," McCoy tells the captain. And I believe he's right.

In advertising, we use computers. In the past decade they have become the tool of choice for many art directors and designers. The computers can perform extremely quickly. Representations of print ads can swiftly be brought to near-finished quality by using any number of programs. These "comp" representations help clients see what their ads will look like in a magazine or newspaper.

This tool is a wonderful advance for our business. However, it is sometimes quicker to draw a picture or to insert an exclamation point by hand. And there are some things the computer just cannot do. Low-tech occasionally has advantages over high-tech.

When these instances occur, many art directors get stuck and forget there is a world outside the computer, a world filled with pads and X-Acto knives and magic markers. Many times these low-tech tools in the real world can do the job better and faster than a one-gigabyte hard drive. Oh, they may get your hands a little bit dirty, but you'll get the job done.

An art director who gets the job done is valuable—more valuable than one with clean hands. The same applies to anyone in an occupation that mixes new technology with more traditional implements. The best employees are the ones who use all the available resources, especially their judgment.

As Doctor Leonard "Bones" McCoy showed us, kneeling over that Horta, technology is a tool, but it's not the only tool. And there are times when it's the wrong tool. Thanks, Doc.

Advertising agencies are always bragging about what great listeners they are. They'll tell anyone who'll listen.

I think what they are really trying to tell their clients is that they can communicate with them. That they understand them. Instead, they just say they listen. Taken literally, that means they do only half the job. After all, communication isn't just listening, it's exchange.

Listening is a big industry. There are books, tapes, videos and seminars on listening. I've sat through many talks given by people who were experts on listening.

No doubt listening is an important skill. But to have a meaningful dialogue, listening isn't enough. I mean, you can't have two people sitting there listening to each other and accomplish anything. On the other ear, one person doing all the listening and another doing all the talking isn't productive either.

"Language, you depend on it for so much, but is anyone its master?" So spoke Mr. Spock in "Is There in Truth No Beauty?" Well, sort of. Mr. Spock had mind-melded with Kolos, the Medusan ambassador, when the statement was made. Judging by the wide grin on Spock's face when he spoke, the observation likely came from the ambassador, who was rattlin' around in the first officer's brain.

The short answer to the ambassador's question is "No." A solid case can be made that far from mastering language, no one even uses it adequately.

I recall learning in my child development classes to go beyond speech when interacting with children. Small children can't always find the right words to express themselves. Many times they don't even know the right words. The idea is to listen to what kids are trying to communicate instead of listening to what they are saying.

Preschool is as wild as any planet the Enterprise ever visited. Man-eating four-year-olds regularly snack on their playmates. Power plays and shifting alliances create a maze seasoned politicians would have trouble negotiating. Love buds, blooms and dies in the afternoon. And virtually all of it is nonverbal. Noisy, but nonverbal.

I mention this because in subsequent years I've become convinced that preschoolers communicate as well as adults (possibly as well as worldwide communication companies). Their exchanges are brief, to the point, and for the most part honest.

Still, economy with words isn't the answer to mastering language either.

I had an uncle who never finished a sentence. He'd kind of trail off about halfway through a thought and leave it hanging there. Then he'd start the next sentence. Drove me crazy. Even weirder was the fact that we all understood him. Somehow we all knew how the sentence would end, so he never had to conclude. Besides, in my family someone was always interrupting. So, none of us ever finished a . . .

I believe if the Medusan ambassador had shared Mr. Spock's body for a little longer he could have answered his own question. He would have understood that language is only part of communication, just as listening is only part of language. Subtle movements and actions help us interpret words. Sometimes no words are needed at all. Like a nursery school teacher, Kolos would have learned that what was being communicated is more important than what is being said. Or heard.

And understanding that, he could have had real exchange with humans. With luck, he might even have been able to decipher what a multinational advertising agency meant when it talked about listening.

You meet an unusual assortment of traveling companions on a bus. I'm not talking about going a couple of blocks in the city, although you can meet interesting people on a city bus, too. I'm talking about the kind of bus that crosses state lines.

Given the duration of that type of trip, an eight-by-forty-foot box is just too cramped to maintain any hope of personal privacy. So even though elbows, perfumes and conversations invade your personal space, it just makes good sense to go with the flow and try to be friendly. A smile or kind word can help the hours pass a little more easily. You're all in it together. Make the best of it.

Some folks hunker down in their seats and bury themselves in books. Others love to chatter away. I have a slight fault. When people talk loudly, I tend to look at them. Once eye contact is established, the talker will usually lock in on me. This makes me uneasy, so I say something. Soon, I'm in a conversation—like it or not.

So it came to be that a bantamweight boxer, an unemployed roofer with a large protuberance that ran from his nose to his forehead and I were sitting in the back of a bus headed out of New York City.

The boxer carried much of the early conversation. He also carried a bottle of cheap whiskey in his pocket. In short order he knocked off the whiskey, which in turn knocked him out.

The roofer and I had stories to exchange. I had worked my way through college as a roofer and appreciated how hard the gentleman next to me worked for his money.

As we talked, the roofer said something unbelievable. "I can drive an eightpenny nail into a two-by-four with my head."

"What?" I wittily replied.

He grinned and asked me to touch his forehead. Now, I had noticed the large bulge in his forehead, but I hadn't mentioned it. Hey, if you sit down next to a guy with a large bulge in his forehead, discretion is usually the best course to follow.

"Go ahead, touch it," he insisted. So I did. I felt as if I were touching a Klingon. Luckily, this was a very friendly Klingon.

I asked, "Can you really drive an eightpenny nail into a two-by-four with that?"

"Yeah, won a lot of money on bets doin' it." He paused. "It's hell to pay if I miss."

That cracked me up. I mean, you know that's got to be the truth. Of course if he did miss, he would lobotomize himself at the same time he lost the bet. So he probably wouldn't care much about losing the money.

We woke up the boxer when we hit Hartford. And each of

100

us went our own way. Without the bus, we would have never touched each other's lives. Like I said, on a bus you meet a strange assortment of people.

There are folks just like the boxer and roofer on Star Trek. One is Harcourt Fenton Mudd. Another is Cyrano Jones. Both travel through space in small spaceships living lives we can hardly imagine. Jones buys and sells rare and useless merchandise, while Mudd, the con man, peddles dreams.

Mudd and Jones live in the margins. The Enterprise encounters them only by coincidence, when their courses collide. They're a part of the same universe as the Enterprise, but they don't fit in the perfectly ordered world of a starship.

Jones and Mudd are a reminder of the same lesson I learned on the bus ride. Many lives have little to do with the nine-to-five world that the rest of us have made for ourselves. The variety of ways to pass through this life are endless. We think of ourselves as normal, but who's to say?

Right now, there's a guy out there driving eightpenny nails into two-by-fours with his head. I hope he doesn't miss.

Making a telephone call is a simple act. I don't mean to say it is easy. It can be one of the most difficult acts for a human to perform. I remember my sophomore year in high school. Sitting alone looking at the telephone, I would summon all the nerve in my fifteen-year-old body. This great effort would occasionally result in my being able to pick up the receiver. But I couldn't seem to dial.

If I could have dialed, the number my digits fingered would have connected me to the home of Beth K. I desperately wanted to talk to Beth. To ask her on a date. But my fear was overwhelming. What if she didn't like me? What if she rejected my advances? The closer I came to the phone, the greater my anxiety would become. I gave in to fear. I never called.

Over time I realized that if you can dial a telephone, you can do anything. That simple action is all that is necessary to launch almost any human endeavor.

You want to skydive? Call a skydiving club. Had an argument with a close friend you want to settle? Call 'im. Want to find a preschool for your kid? Call. Half the time there's an 800 number to get you started. Just pick up the phone and dial.

I am aware that people don't actually dial the phone anymore. Although button-pushing is the action required to make a telephone work today, I still think of it as dialing. Of course, I still think of time in quarters. Quarter of one, quarter past seven—those phrases seem more natural than twelve forty-five or seven-fifteen. When I look at digital clocks and push-button phones, I remember when the world was rounder. Anyhow, just grab the cordless and punch in the numbers, and the world can be yours.

It's the first step to anywhere. It turns thought into action. Dreams into reality.

Hey, Star Trek began with a call—a distress call that led the Enterprise to Talos IV. Starfleet calls are often the stimulus for an episode. Apollo took AT&T's advice literally and reached out and touched the Enterprise. That started a wonderful adventure.

But I'm sure there was an important Star Trek phone call made before any of those—the call to Gene Roddenberry from NBC telling him they had bought his TV show.

Over time, even teenage angst can be turned into wisdom. I'll never know what would have happened if I made that call to Beth K., what adventures might have been. In subsequent years I've learned to pick up the telephone and dial. The result hasn't always been what I wanted, but it sure beat sitting there looking at the darn thing. Give it a try. Pick up the phone and see what happens. It's far better to act than to wonder what might have been.

Take one second. One hundred seconds is about a minute and a half. One thousand seconds is about seventeen minutes. A million seconds? One million seconds will take twelve days to pass. Now guess how long one billion seconds is? Take a second to figure it out. Take a hundred seconds and do the math. The answer will take your breath away.

One billion seconds is over thirty-two years—years. It's a big number. It looks like this: 1,000,000,000.

As large as that number is, it is dwarfed by the number of stars in our galaxy. The Milky Way contains approximately one hundred and fifty billion stars. 150,000,000,000 looks like that.

With so many stars out there, it begs a question: Why haven't we discovered a single intelligent species in our galaxy besides ourselves? Why isn't there an artifact or radio wave or signal that positively indicates life beyond the earth? Why isn't there a single shred of proof of the existence of an alien race?

Forget intelligent races, we haven't even proved there is a space fungus or alien microorganism. For all our science and discoveries, we are the only living things in a dead universe.

I am aware of the abduction phenomenon, claims that

people have been captured and experimented on by aliens, then returned to their homes. I've seen the "In Search Of" episode on the Roswell, New Mexico, alien crash site. I've actually met people—nice, credible people—who have had UFO experiences. But these people and events have not produced a piece of absolute, undeniable scientific proof.

I, however, believe the Milky Way is teeming with life. It must be. Otherwise how could Kirk, Spock and McCoy stumble upon inhabited planet after inhabited planet? Hey, nearly every week a new alien life-form is introduced on Star Trek. Ergo, we live in a galaxy filled with an array of beings, sentient and not.

Many scientists believe right along with me. The United States government funds a project called SETI (the Search for Extra-Terrestrial Intelligence). Actually, it *used* to be called SETI. The new name for the project is the High Resolution Microwave Survey. Brave congressmen worried that the name SETI, which contains the letters ET, might prove an irresistible target for political cartoonists. By changing the name, Congress hopes to avoid this cartoon peril. I mean, who cares if the project is good science and important? What's truly important is that our elected representatives maintain their sense of self-importance.

So today a project called the High Resolution Microwave Survey scans the sky for traces of extraterrestrial intelligence. This search should prove more fruitful than scanning the U.S. Capitol for traces of terrestrial intelligence.

Meanwhile, we beam out *The Brady Bunch* and *My Mother the Car* to the universe. If there is somebody out there listening, I only hope they catch an episode of Star Trek.

Now, remember those one hundred and fifty billion stars we were talking about? Listen, this is a great little theory. (I didn't invent it, but I can't remember the name of the guy who did. I saw it on TV so I can't even look it up.) Suppose only one out of one hundred stars has planets. This is supposed to be an extremely conservative estimate. Next, suppose only one out of a hundred of those is earthlike. Then suppose only one out of a hundred of those developed life. Finally, suppose that out of one hundred of those that developed life, one evolved intelligent life.

Calculating all those supposes means there are 1,500 civilizations in our galaxy. One thousand, five hundred societies that the Enterprise could visit and explore—conservatively.

Now, one last mathematical formula. On the average, twenty-six episodes of Star Trek were produced each year during the run of the original series. Therefore, if the Enterprise were to visit all the life-forms and civilizations in our galaxy, we could look forward to 57.6 years of new adventures. And that doesn't include reruns.

Advertising presentations are often called "dog and pony shows." They are little pieces of theater designed to build anticipation and excitement. The enthusiasm of the presenter shows that the advertising agency believes in the work they are presenting. If done correctly, this is a high-energy ritual that culminates in the client buying the ads that the agency presents.

Each client is different. Singing and dancing rarely achieve the desired result if the client is the marketing director for a mortuary.

Even the best presentations can go down in flames. Once,

while standing in front of a client presenting storyboards—thinking I was doing quite well—I was interrupted. "Excuse me," drawled our client as he leaned to the side and opened a desk drawer. "Does anyone else want an antacid?" he asked as he unwrapped a package of Rolaids he had produced from his desk. I hadn't wanted one before that moment. Immediately after, I needed one.

After ingesting the tablet, the client rejected our ideas and sent us back to the drawing board.

Timing is also important. Never give a slide presentation to three hundred dairy farmers who have just finished lunch. The combination of full bellies and a darkened room produces a reaction called sleep. I'll never make that mistake again, I promise you.

Perhaps my most difficult presentation was to Catholic Charities. Catholic Charities does great work. It feeds the hungry, helps get people off drugs and runs AIDS hospices. For this reason, our agency was glad to help them produce a series of public-service announcements.

Our client was no less than the head of the Catholic Archdiocese of Washington, D.C., His Eminence the Cardinal. Having grown up Catholic, I knew that a cardinal was one step from the Pope and the Pope is practically God. Cardinal Hickey is exactly what you would expect of a man of the cloth. He is pious, quiet, gentle and humble. Certain men have a presence you can feel. Cardinal Hickey had such a presence, and it demanded reverence.

My usual presentation style involves a lot of moving around, and I can be very loud. Once I get rolling, I tend to overheat. Hence my dilemma. Should I present in my usual style? Or should I become calm and humble? Most importantly, was there any error I could make that would damn my immortal soul for all eternity?

I looked to the heavens. And found the Starship Enterprise. Dr. Leonard McCoy had been in this exact situation.

Well, not exact, but close. While visiting a planet ruled by seven-foot giants, he discovered the tribal queen was pregnant. Complications put McCoy, the queen, Kirk and Spock on the run.

Naturally, while this group was on the lam, the queen began contractions. When McCoy tried to deliver the baby, the queen told him that none but a royal personage could touch her. He would be put to death if he so much as laid a hand on her.

McCoy would have none of it. He was the doctor and she was the patient. A baby boy was delivered on Leonard McCoy's terms.

So I introduced the cardinal to the dog and pony. I presented the storyboards with as much energy as possible. On one occasion, while describing a scene, I used the expletive "jeez." As it slipped past my lips, I bit hard. I had the good fortune not to follow this syllable with "us" and escaped undamned.

The cardinal loved my performance. He was a lively and appreciative audience. We sold all our ideas and produced a wonderful public-service campaign.

Apparently, most folks are fairly sedate around Cardinal Hickey. He found my presentation refreshing and loved the enthusiasm. A couple of days later, I received the coup de grâce. A priest who is close to the cardinal told me to consider the seminary.

I feel the presentation worked because the cardinal entered my world. Catholic Charities wanted advertising. They needed what the agency could provide.

If I had been there for an audience with His Eminence, a different approach would have been appropriate. But like McCoy with the queen, I was the expert here. And I handled it as I saw fit.

Bottom line? When in Rome do as the Romans do. But when Rome comes to you, do it your way.

I'm not sure how old Mick Jagger is, but it must be somewhere around fifty—a half century. Pete Townshend of the Who is nearly as old. The Beach Boys are the Beach Grandfathers. Elvis is dead, and he's still around. They all keep rocking right along. And they are putting our concepts of age and aging to the test.

Rock and roll is an obvious place to note this phenomenon, but it's evident all over society. For the first time in aviation history, for example, the flight attendants are older than the planes. It has become commonplace for corporations to bribe employees into retirement with special benefits packages. This notion of going docilely into your golden years to rest and relax has been blown to bits.

My father got married at seventy-five years old—not to my mother. She had passed away a few years earlier. He met his new bride dancing. They went bungee jumping on their honeymoon. Just kidding. They didn't go bungee jumping, but that really isn't a far stretch.

I had the honor of giving my father away at the wedding. Officially, I was the best man. As we waited at the altar for the bride, I couldn't hear the music. There was another song in my head—Frank Sinatra singing "Young at Heart."

Growing older has become the heart of the Star Trek movies. In *The Wrath of Khan*, when Captain James T. Kirk faces the finality of death for the first time in his life, it rejuvenates him. He feels young.

As the subsequent Star Trek movies were released, age always played a major role. It had to be. William Shatner, Leonard Nimoy and DeForest Kelley weren't getting any younger. The fact that three older gentlemen continued to be mega–box office attractions makes the point as strongly as any of the movies.

Age even becomes an inside joke. Bones talks of retirement in *The Undiscovered Country*. Yet in that same film, Kirk fights—and defeats, of course—an eight-foot alien, romances supermodel Iman, crosses a glacier on foot and saves galactic peace. Not bad for a guy a couple of months from cashing in his profit sharing.

It is often said, "You're only as old as you feel." But I'm a little more skeptical. If I want to figure out my age, I subtract the year of my birth from the current year. The resulting number is my age.

Plus I don't buy into this youth-culture stuff. Older is better. I know more. I'm more confident. I'm happier.

Youth isn't wasted on the young—they need it. Without their superior physical skills, they wouldn't survive to an age where they could enjoy the superior life skills that I now possess.

A close friend of mine plays in a rock and roll band called Mr. Right. I've listened to the bands he's played in for twenty-five years. This one is the best. He's not quite as old as Mick Jagger, but when he is I'm sure he'll still be rocking right along. Just like Kirk, Spock, Bones and, hopefully, me.

About the time I entered the seventh grade at Saint Joseph's School, Freddie and the Dreamers had a big hit song. It was modestly titled "Do the Freddie." An accompanying dance was imaginatively named "The Freddie."

The words to "Do the Freddie" went a little something like this:

> Are you ready, let's do the Freddie.
> Are you ready, gonna do the Freddie.

The dance was somewhat similar to a jumping jack. However, you would lift your left arm and left leg at the same time, then as they returned to the ground you would lift your right arm and leg. Repeat this motion and you were doing the Freddie.

Which is exactly what I was doing. I was rocking back and forth and humming the hit tune to myself. This was during recess at Saint Joe's. No one else was around at the time. I had found an unpopulated corner of the paved asphalt playground and was content to amuse myself with the new little ditty and accompanying dance.

I could have maintained this state for the entire fifteen minutes of morning recess, but my eye caught a glimpse of something that took me out my trance. It was a nun, Sister Mary Marie. And she was moving quickly toward me.

Back in those days, nuns wore a full-length habit. Long black dresses covered their legs and feet. Because of this, the only way you could tell how fast a nun was moving was the tempo with which her rosary beads swung from side to side. Typically, the beads would beat out a waltz. When she was in a hurry, her beads might tap out a samba.

Sister Mary Marie's rosary beads were playing "Wipeout." They swung wildly with each approaching step. Worse, I could hear heavy breathing from exertion. My God, she was running. As my gaze meet hers, I saw a red puffy face and steel eyes.

I continued singing but began to slow as Sister Mary Marie got closer. As the song slowed so did my dancing. "Are . . . you . . . read . . . dee . . . Let's . . ." I was like a 45 RPM record on 33. By the moment of collision, I had nearly stopped.

For a second that seemed like an eternity, we stood inches apart. Without warning, Sister slapped me hard across the face. It stung. "Don't you ever . . ." Sister began harshly, ". . . make fun of me again."

I was stunned, unsure how to react. Make fun of you? I stood dumbfounded with an aching cheek.

At times like these, my thoughts often travel to Captain Kirk. Surely Kirk would know what to do. Unfortunately, this incident transpired years before the network debut of Star Trek. Besides, I don't recall ever seeing a giant nun attack the ship.

There is, however, a moment in one episode that I believe is relevant. Beaming down to the planet Deneva, Kirk, Spock and Bones are attacked by group of men. As the men charge with murderous intentions, they yell to the landing party to be careful. Their apparent concern is totally contrary to their behavior.

The inhabitants of Deneva, it is later learned, are controlled by space parasites. Their actions are not by choice. They are not themselves.

I think something like this might have happened to Sister Mary Marie. Not that she was controlled by space parasites. But that there was something else happening in her life that made her interpret my dance incorrectly. Her actions had nothing to do with me. I was just there.

In later years, I might have considered that slap across the face as a cry for help. But at the time, I was just confused and did nothing. But I'll never forget what I did after Sister walked away and left me alone in my little corner of the playground. I did "the Freddie."

An old friend of mine once told me a truth about advertising. "A vice president in an advertising agency," he said, "is a person who can come into his office in the morning, find a single piece of paper on his desk and by noon have turned that piece of paper into a dozen problems."

I fear this is the rule in business rather than the exception. It seems every workplace has at least one of these types. This person is easy to spot. Look for an ambitious go-getter who specializes in discovering the downside of any situation. And, of course, someone who is constantly second-guessing the decisions of others.

As terrible as this sounds, most corporations reward this type of behavior. It's sick. Get two of these guys in one room, and decision-making gets so convoluted everyone ends up with their underwear on their heads. If this seems unlikely, go to work for a large corporation. Bring extra underwear.

Yes, I have met this animal—unfortunately, never in season with the proper ammunition. For now, the names will be withheld to protect the guilty.

No wonder I love Star Trek. Each week a problem arises. Each week James T. Kirk uses his talents and the talents of his crew to find an effective solution. Rarely do the captain and crew *cause* a problem.

One of the major reasons for this is that there is little second-guessing on the Enterprise. When Mr. Spock decides to cross circuit to "B" to handle a transporter malfunction, no one sends out a memo recommending he try three different alternatives. When Scotty readjusts the matter/antimatter valves, he doesn't have to follow a Total Quality Management program. Kirk gives his people the responsibility and the authority to get the job done. And they do.

Kirk solves the problems he can solve and delegates the problems that need to be solved by someone else. Simplistic, you say? Why not? Good managers usually know which problems to delegate and which to solve themselves. The real good ones support the solutions arrived at by their designated problem solvers, give 'em the benefit of the doubt and back 'em up.

Kirk does this every week. It's a lesson we can all learn from. Hey, there are already too many vice presidents at advertising agencies.

Star Trek never talks about food. Everybody on the ship eats, but what they eat is rarely mentioned. Most of the meals that are served are for visiting aliens. When we do catch a glimpse of the Enterprise kitchen in *The Undiscovered Country* there is something on the table that looks like bread dough. We never see what it gets made into, though.

I can understand why they avoid the subject. Every few years, all our beliefs on eating change. Not long ago, granola was considered the height of health food. Today, it's just another high-calorie menace.

Captain Kirk has a fondness for coffee. In one episode, his coffee is drugged with a substance that moves him into hyperspeed. Interestingly, coffee has the exact same effect on me even when it isn't drugged. In another episode, Captain Kirk orders a chicken sandwich and coffee from the food machine. Aside from reinforcing the captain's love of caffeine (he can't possibly drink decaf, can he?), it also means he's no vegetarian. I'm sure there are vegetarians on the ship. Enough hints have been dropped that it is fairly certain that Spock is one.

The only other big eater on any of the shows is Counselor Deanna Troi of *The Next Generation,* who is nearly a chocoholic. It's no surprise chocolate survives through the centuries. I'm sure as long as there is humanity, there will be chocolate. It does strike me that chocolate is full of caffeine. So Troi and Kirk are kindred in an odd way.

One thing the Enterprise never does is pull up to the drive-through window at a fast-food restaurant. We can speculate on the reasons for this. Size alone would dictate sending a shuttle craft or some smaller vehicle capable of getting close to the take-out window. Eating out may not be a reimbursable expense on Starfleet trips. The food synthesizers on board might replicate Big Macs and Whoppers. Or just perhaps there isn't any junk food in the future.

Can the latter possibly be the reason?

Lord knows, if we were to remove junk food from our society our civilization would probably collapse. Aside from important contributions to diet, culture as we know it would cease to exist without Arby's or Kentucky Fried Chicken. After all, most first dates include a trip to a fast-food restaurant. Interfering with the mating ritual at this basic level could have serious effects on the future of humanity.

So, what culinary lessons can be drawn from Star Trek? Stay hopped on caffeine? Vegetarians are aliens? The chicken sandwich will be the food staple of tomorrow?

When I was a kid my father would say, "If you eat too much watermelon, you're going to turn into a watermelon." It didn't happen. If such a metamorphosis were possible, by now I would have turned into a pint of Rocky Road.

Pretty much anything you eat will keep you alive. In college I knew a girl who managed to subsist on popcorn and ice cream sandwiches. Maybe that's all Star Trek implies. It isn't what you eat, it's that you eat. Just make sure you have a little something. Like my Auntie Emma used to say, "Mangia. Mangia."

When I was a teenager, I had a bad habit. Actually, I had more than one bad habit. Then again, that's the nature of teenagers.

Let's start this again. When I was in high school I would answer every question with the same one-word answer. I would say, "What?"

Most of the time I had heard the question clearly. My "What?" was just a way to give myself more time to think of an answer. I did this unconsciously. A grownup pointed out my little habit when she become annoyed at repeating every question.

"I know what you're doing," she said. I was glad someone did, because I didn't have a clue.

What I was doing unconsciously is something James T. Kirk does purposely on many occasions. I was stalling.

James Kirk is the master of stalling. (Actually, James Kirk isn't the master of stalling. Any parent of a five-year-old at bedtime knows the real virtuoso of this art. But back to Kirk.) When the Enterprise gets into a hopeless spot, the Captain will usually find a way to buy a little time, putting off the inevitable until the very last second. And by then, he's figured out a way to make the inevitable avoidable.

He deceives and distracts while Scotty makes the necessary repairs to the phasers or the warp drive. By the time his adversary realizes what's going on, Kirk has the upper hand.

There's an innate problem with this behavior. While stalling may occasionally save your skin, it's a terrible habit. It shouldn't be used indiscriminately, or it will turn into a pattern of procrastination. While this is a great advantage if you're seeking employment at the post office, in most parts of life it causes problems. I know. It happened to me. The trick is to apply this skill only when absolutely needed. And to buy time only for a known purpose.

When Kirk stalls to give Scotty the chance to repair the transporter, he knows why he is stalling. He also knows how much time he must buy, because he gets an estimate from Scotty of how long repairs will take. This gives Kirk the parameters for working out his strategy. He knows exactly what he is doing. The action isn't open-ended.

This is different from telling your spouse, "I'll be ready in a minute," when you haven't even decided what you are going to wear.

On the other hand, if you are buying the time to finish a report, to double-check a fact or to sneak out and buy an anniversary present, use any possible resource. Kirk would.

Hey, you can't buy love. But you can buy time.

One of my first jobs after college was as a mental health specialist for the state of Illinois. In this job I ran a home and supervised development programs for mentally retarded adults. I also supervised the mental health technicians who carried out the programs.

Mentally retarded adults meet with a lot of frustration in their lives. Like any group of people, some handle it well and others cope poorly. As I was young and agile, the home I ran became a popular place to transfer the more aggressive cases. While this made the job more interesting, it also made it less safe.

Complicating my task was the fact that my section also became a dumping ground for problem employees. Many times, working with the employees proved more difficult than working with the retarded residents.

Although there were prescribed procedures for handling problems, this environment constantly produced new challenges. Bad behavior was contagious. When one resident would act up, it would upset others. The situation would snowball unless stopped. Confining a misbehaving resident to his room didn't seem fair to me. This would have the effect of punishing the roommate. As I said, the job was very interesting.

I developed my own solution to stop small problems from growing into larger ones. In the house was a large living room. Almost no one ever went into this room. It functioned mainly as a visitors' room. As we rarely had visitors, we rarely used the room.

I turned this parlor into a cool-down area. The small corridor that connected the living room to the rest of the house became no-man's-land. Or as I liked to think of it, the neutral zone, a buffer between the person who was acting up and the rest of the residents.

This concept was taken directly from Star Trek. The neutral zone is the buffer zone between the United Federation of Planets (Kirk's side) and the Klingon Empire. It also separates the Federation and Romulan space.

The neutral zone on Star Trek kept the peace for hundreds of years. In my case, a couple of hours of peace was the most I could ask for. But it worked. This little cool-down area gave folks time to chill out.

After I left the institution, I took this concept with me and applied it to other parts of my life. When I moved in with my girlfriend, I kept an apartment nearby, a kind of psychic neutral zone. I think it helped both of us from feeling too much pressure. I'm sure it helped me.

When I worked at J. Walter Thompson, the neutral zone was a Cantonese restaurant called Louie's. The king-sized drinks served at the small Rush Street establishment provided the necessary buffer.

If my mother had used this concept, it might have eased much pain and suffering. My sister Barbara and I are two years apart in age. I'm older. We fought like cats and dogs from the moment she was born. This drove my mom to distraction. Finally she came up with what she believed was the solution.

She tied my sister and me together at the wrist and pronounced, "Now you two are going to have to learn to get along." While this technique worked with Sidney Poitier and Tony Curtis in the movies, at 14 New Street there was a different outcome. The experiment ended in failure when my mother removed the bloody stump that had been my sister from my arm. Instead of learning to get along, I just dragged my sister into all the furniture. It was a massacre.

Mom untied us, tanned my bottom and sent us to our rooms. What we needed was a buffer to keep us apart. I'm positive my sister would agree.

We all need a neutral zone to keep our problems at bay, a place where we can cool down. I owe that revelation not only to Star Trek but to a group of retarded men who taught me an important lesson in life.

As a young man, I tied my mattress to the top of my 1962 Mercury Comet and headed to Chicago to find my fortune. My dream was to become a stand-up comic. Back in those days there were few comedy clubs and no cable television. To get the opportunity to perform in one of the few venues, a comic—unlike comics today—actually had to be funny.

Arriving in that Toddlin' Town I learned of a place called Second City. Many big-name comics had started there, and they ran improvisation workshops. It sounded right to me, so I went to Wells Street to sign up for classes.

Second City was set up like this: At the bottom were the first-year students. Second-year students were allowed to participate in the Children's Theater. After your third year, you became eligible for the Chateau Louise Company, a road company permanently stationed at a dinner theater outside of Chicago. Or you could make it all the way to the resident company. Resident company members were gods.

These deities had their pictures hung over the box office of the Wells Street theater. Never had I seen such humans. What I didn't know was that all these portraits were airbrushed. Every flaw and imperfection was removed. One of these portraits was of Shelley Long, who went on to fame and fortune in *Cheers*. I had never seen anyone so perfect in my life. Her airbrushed eyes looked down on me in all my insecurity. That picture scared the hell out of me. Later, when I discovered that Shelley Long actually had moles, I was the happiest man alive.

So I wrote a check and began classes. Standing onstage before an audience, even if the audience is only your class-mates, is one of the few places in life where you can experi-ence tremendous fear without being in any real physical danger. People's responses to this fear are illuminating. I watched a guy totally lose it, insult everyone and run into the Chicago winter without a coat. He could be still running.

Improv turned out to be the best thing I ever did for my-self. I could always think on my feet, but the classes taught me to think *calmly* on my feet. I gained poise and confi-dence. I met new people, made new friends. I did not, how-ever, become any funnier.

My career in comedy would end almost before it began. But improvisation became a skill that I carried with me for the rest of my life. Any business where conditions quickly change or unanticipated questions arise is a business where improv is an important tool. Advertising is such a business. So is commanding a starship.

James T. Kirk is the greatest improviser I've ever seen. Mr. Spock ain't bad himself. To this day, I am amazed at Kirk's ability to create favorable circumstances in the worst situations.

His battle with the gorn is a good example. He is locked in mortal combat with a creature that possesses many times his strength. The thing is nearly indestructible.

Kirk grabs a bamboo shoot, mixes together powdered car-bon, sulphur and a little saltpeter, shoves a diamond down the shoot, puts one end of the shoot against a rock and aims the open end at the gorn. KABOOM, instant cannon.

The real strength of improvisational ability is its applica-tion to almost any situation. It is an attitude. The skill is understanding how to approach a situation looking for an advantage. It is recognizing and moving quickly to exploit opportunity.

While I studied improv at Second City, I became aware of other opportunities in my life. A friend introduced me to the world of advertising. I quickly realized that this was a world where I could prosper.

With a little help, I found a way through the door and got a job as a copywriter at J. Walter Thompson. I perceived an opportunity and took advantage of it. My improv lessons didn't turn me into the next Steve Martin. They did help me find a career where I could succeed.

We're getting kind of near the end here, and we still haven't talked about the most basic question of all. What is the meaning of life? For what purpose are we here? How does Star Trek address the largest issue of our existence?

Lots of philosophers have tried to answer that one. Lots of regular folks, too. Monty Python made a film called *The Meaning of Life*, and while it was very entertaining, it left much to be desired in terms of a definitive answer.

The Baltimore Catechism also tackles this issue. In response to the question "Why did God make me?" it reads, "God made me to know, love and serve Him in this world and the next." That tells you what to do, but it really doesn't say what life means.

At the opposite end of the spectrum, nihilists believe there is absolutely no meaning to existence at all. Eat, drink and be merry, for tomorrow we die. There are advantages to that point of view, but I see a huge downside.

A giant single cell attacked our galaxy in the Star Trek episode "The Immunity Syndrome." By the time the USS Enterprise encountered it, the cell had already destroyed one starship. Worse still, the cell was about to divide. If this was allowed to happen, the whole galaxy might perish. Kirk, Spock and McCoy came up with a plan to kill the cell. The plan worked and the galaxy was saved.

On the bridge, after the destruction of the cell, Kirk made an observation. The cell was like a virus invading the body of our galaxy. The captain and crew of the Enterprise had acted like antibodies and fought off the disease. Wouldn't it be funny, mused the captain, if the purpose of their entire existence had been this one moment in time? To protect the existence of the galaxy, just like our antibodies protect our existence.

When Kirk pondered the meaning of his life, he saw the big and the small. Protecting the galaxy was put on an even plane with the work of the smallest microorganism in his body. His existence and the existence of the galaxy came into balance. But more important, he saw a defining moment in his life.

Well, why not? One great moment can give a life meaning. Meaning, like gold, is where you find it. For many, this purpose can be found in family, in giving one's children a better life or in being there for someone you love. For some, it's collecting a complete set of refrigerator magnets from every state. Others find completion in giving comfort to the less fortunate. Some find it in duty to country.

Not everyone finds that moment or inspiration. But I think most of us do. It can be a monumental event or something small. It may come in an instant or slowly become clear over a lifetime.

Whatever meaning a person finds in life comes from inside. We each define our own purpose in life. Perhaps all our purposes are not as grand as saving the galaxy. But we all certainly have a reason to be.

There is a new addition to the Star Trek family. Unlike *The Next Generation,* there is no USS Enterprise in this spinoff. Instead, the location of this series is a space station near a stable wormhole deep in space. Created by many of the same people who now produce *The Next Generation,* the series is more a cousin than a direct descendent of the original series.

The show is called *Star Trek: Deep Space Nine.* I prefer the name a coworker came up with. Star Trek Lite.

Because there is no ship, the occupants of the space station cannot seek out new life and new civilizations. They cannot boldly go, or even go boldly, where no one has gone before. Basically, they hang out in a mall and hope that aliens show up. Hey, if you think about it, that's exactly what we're doing on earth right now. We spend a lot of time in malls, and many of us are hoping that aliens show up. Maybe that makes *Deep Space Nine* the Star Trek for the nineties. It just seems a little less filling.

I do, of course, watch *Deep Space Nine* and will continue to do so. Like a good steak, the show could use a little aging. It could also use a little more meat. Still, there's time for that. The lesson of *The Next Generation* should be applied here. Let's show a little patience.

There are some interesting characters on the series. The best news is the return of a Kirk type. *The Next Generation* broke Kirk into pieces—Picard, Riker and Troi are all fragments of James T. *Deep Space Nine* reassembles him as Commander Sisko. Sisko runs the space station like Kirk ran the Enterprise.

It's hard to believe this is the same guy who played Hawk on *Spenser: For Hire.* Then again, I never watched an entire episode of *Spenser: For Hire.* But whenever I was zapping by and would stop for a moment, this big, brooding, bald guy would be menacing someone. Now he's cool, intelligent, commanding, dignified and cut from the same cloth as my favorite captain. I'd love to see him take command of a ship.

In a way, *Deep Space Nine* is the real next generation of Star Trek. Gene Roddenberry and Gene L. Coon are gone. Roddenberry conceived the original series and *The Next Generation.* Coon created the Prime Directive and helped define the Star Trek universe. They were the Marx and Lenin of Star Trek. Maybe Marx and Lenin are the wrong guys to draw a comparison to. Communism was a bad idea. Star Trek is a great one. Besides, I don't believe Star Trek will ever fall. It's even possible Kirk, Spock and McCoy might outlive Lenin, Trotsky and Stalin.

Graduating high school seniors sometimes choose a class motto. At Enfield High ours was, "We do not know what the future holds, but we do know we hold the future." I know it's kind of lame, but we were only in high school. I favored the motto a friend had used all through our secondary education. It was a line borrowed from a popular TV commercial: "Better living through chemistry." In the case of my friend, it certainly was more appropriate.

So it is with *Deep Space Nine.* Who knows where it goes from here? With a little luck, maybe the show will develop the right chemistry to enthrall future generations of Star Trek fans. A little time and seasoning will tell. I wish them luck.

My favorite Star Trek ending was Kirk on the bridge in *Star Trek: The Motion Picture.* Millions of us had waited years for the return of Captain Kirk and his crew to the Starship Enterprise. And finally, there he was, bigger than life, sitting in the captain's chair, smiling at the successful conclusion of a brand-new adventure.

Sulu, sitting below at the navigators' station, turned and asked the captain for a course for the ship. "Out there," Kirk replied as he waved his arms. "Thataway."

With that, we knew there would be more. There would be a Star Trek II, maybe III. The adventure would continue. And we could all come along for the ride.

It was also a symbolic passing of the torch. Before Star Trek, the great America morality play had always been westerns. Gunfights, frontier justice and bandits who went "thataway" were the canvas for the philosophers of the twentieth century. When Gene Roddenberry sold Star Trek to NBC, he sold it as *Wagon Train* to the stars. *Wagon Train*, a popular sixties western, proved to be the vehicle that set the stage for the metamorphosis.

I believe science fiction will continue to be the vehicle of choice for American screenwriters and authors.

Back in the first few pages, I spoke of an observation that

set me on the course to write this book. I don't know when I started applying Star Trek to my life. It just happened.

I know I'm not the only one with this relationship to Star Trek. Millions of people across the planet have been affected, or infected.

I don't consider myself a Trekker, although whenever I see Trekkers they seem to be having a great time. I just happen to think that Star Trek was a terrific TV show.

When I've heard "experts" talk about Star Trek, they credit the hopeful, optimistic outlook of the series for its longevity. Maybe they're right. But I think it's more than that.

There are millions of folks just like me who relate Star Trek to their lives. I know this is true because my friends frequently work Star Trek into the conversation to explain their life experiences. The only difference between us is that I wrote down what I felt. Who can guess all the ways we've been touched? If you've read this far, I'm sure you've felt the same things. I've only scratched the surface.

But while the surface is the place where many episodes of Star Trek begin, this is my place to pause.

This isn't an ending. There's plenty more out there, thataway. Next time, I don't have an earthly clue what I'll tell you about. Hey, every day is a new adventure. Maybe I'll tell you the story of the time the planet was on fire when they beamed down on it.

If you believe that Star Trek has had a significant impact on your experiences, please relate your original tale to me at P.O. Box 53178, Washington, D.C. 20009-3178. Don't forget to include your full name and address. We'd love to hear from you.

ACKNOWLEDGMENTS

Thanks to Mike and Jim. Tessa. Terry and Cary. All the Marinaccios, especially David, Beth, Justina, T.J. and Amber. Michael Brennen, too. Most of the Muscos. Paul. Andy. And, of course, Jane.

The

REMARKABLE
INVENTIONS
of
WALTER
MORTINSON

The
REMARKABLE
INVENTIONS
of
WALTER
MORTINSON

QUINN SOSNA-SPEAR

Simon & Schuster Books for Young Readers

NEW YORK LONDON TORONTO SYDNEY NEW DELHI

SIMON & SCHUSTER BOOKS FOR YOUNG READERS
An imprint of Simon & Schuster Children's Publishing Division
1230 Avenue of the Americas, New York, New York 10020

SIMON & SCHUSTER BOOKS FOR YOUNG READERS
is a trademark of Simon & Schuster, Inc.
For information about special discounts for bulk purchases, please contact Simon & Schuster
Special Sales at 1-866-506-1949 or business@simonandschuster.com.
The Simon & Schuster Speakers Bureau can bring authors to your live event.
For more information or to book an event, contact the Simon & Schuster Speakers Bureau
at 1-866-248-3049 or visit our website at www.simonspeakers.com.
Jacket design by Krista Vossen
Interior design by Hilary Zarycky
The text for this book was set in Fournier.
Manufactured in the United States of America
0319 FFG
First Edition
2 4 6 8 10 9 7 5 3 1
Library of Congress Cataloging-in-Publication Data
Names: Sosna-Spear, Quinn, author.
Title: The remarkable inventions of Walter Mortinson / Quinn Sosna-Spear.
Description: First edition. | New York : Simon & Schuster Books for Young Readers, [2019] |
Summary: Against the wishes of his mortician mother, Hadorah, twelve-year-old Walter
and classmate Cordelia take a hearse on a road trip to meet legendary inventor Flasterborn,
who once mentored Walter's long-dead father.
Identifiers: LCCN 2017060162 | ISBN 9781534420809 (hardcover)
ISBN 9781534420823 (eBook)
Subjects: | CYAC: Inventors—Fiction. | Automobile travel—Fiction. | Mothers and
sons—Fiction. | Single-parent families—Fiction. | Undertakers and undertaking—Fiction. |
Death—Fiction. | Humorous stories.
Classification: LCC PZ.1.S682 Rem 2019 | DDC [Fic]—dc23
LC record available at https://lccn.loc.gov/2017060162

My mother's name was Shelley Spear.
She was born with a lump hanging over one eye, an
ear folded in half, and hair the color of an old man's,
and she happened to be the loveliest woman I ever
knew. She liked reading books, writing stories, and me.
(She also liked my brother, but this isn't about him
right now.) There's nothing that would have made her
happier than knowing I had written a book of my own.

Unfortunately, my mother was very sick. She died
when I was about your age, maybe. But that's all right,
because she was wonderful while she was here, and I'm
so thankful to be able to give her this story at last.

Now—would you mind doing me a favor? I need you
to read something aloud for me. It needn't be more
than once, and you can whisper it if you'd like:

Did you hear that, Shell? This one's for you.

CHAPTER 1

· · ·

WALTER MORTINSON

W alter" is no kind of name for a boy. "Wally" perhaps, but it's well known that Wallys don't normally
become Walters until they sprout their first ear hairs.
No, "Walter" is a name for a man—one with a woolly wal-
rus mustache that tickles his buck teeth, stained from cigars,
whiskey, spinach, and whatever other hogwash adults waste
their time on. "Walter" is the name of a man who harrumphs
instead of saying hello, a man who is big, gray, and terribly
ordinary. So it's rather an odd happenstance that our Walter
was the exact opposite of all of these things.

Walter Mortinson was undoubtedly a boy. His wiry pipe-
cleaner frame was unique to a twelve-year-old, and his wide
brown eyes were still too big for his round face, pillowed
with baby fat. But Walter, as many boys and girls are, was
much cleverer than a man.

His brain wasn't hardened with age, bloated with useless worries about expenses, timeliness, and the desire to eat leafy green things. No, Walter's brain was still wonderfully soft and squishable. This was convenient, as it allowed Walter to squeeze the entire universe—all of her stars and possibilities—between his ears. Most Walters cannot manage such feats, but this Walter, Walter Mortinson, could, which is important because he had vast things to think about: Walter was an inventor.

Odd ideas occurred to him. He imagined beasts that didn't exist and contraptions that could do things that hadn't yet been done. Why, just a week before, he had wondered if fingernail clippings could be turned into tiny scissors to trim toe hairs, and the answer is yes, with a strong enough magnifying glass and springy enough toe hairs. While many people have such thoughts, Walter had the tenacity and the nimble fingers to bring his ideas to life.

On this morning he was doing just that. He had awoken far earlier than the birds (or the worms, for that matter) and had gotten to work on his newest idea. It had required him to sneak into the neighbor's yard early that morning and dig something up, but no matter. They hadn't been using it anyway.

For hours he sat hunched over his prize, its once-white form marred by dirt and soot, his walnut knuckles twisting their way skillfully around it. Walter could see the final product in his mind and had nearly achieved it. It was show-and-tell day. He just *had* to finish his project; he would stay nose-to-his-desk until then.

And while Walter was correct—he would complete his task—this wouldn't happen until five minutes after the school bell had rung, which meant Walter would be late. Again.

Walter was always late.

CHAPTER 2

. . .

THE HAWK ON THE HILL

The Mortinson home was just between the town, to the west, and the junkyard, to the east. While once the house had been exactly between the two, as time had gone on, the town had kept its distance, and the junkyard had grown larger and closer.

And if anyone in the town of Moormouth had been curious, they might have noticed Tippy Tedesco, a tall woman, standing atop one of the spindly junkyard heaps. A particularly curious person might even have seen the whirring gold mechanism in her ear. But no one paid Tippy any mind. I suppose that's no surprise; no one in Moormouth paid attention to much at all.

If you didn't notice the mechanism in her ear, however, it's possible you might see the glint of her strange gold goggles instead. They fitted over her glasses, and the lenses of the goggles spun as they automatically focused on whatever she spied. All at once they were able to cut through the town's overbearing smog and magnify anything for a good mile.

Tippy herself made quite the hawkish impression: squinting past her twice-broken nose, hunched at the shoulder, perched high above the town. Fortunately, no one cared to look. They were too busy with their daily routines.

Moormouthians streamed from their dull houses and, like clockwork, trudged to their even duller schools and businesses, where they were supposed to be. Not one man, woman, or child looked out of place or, as it happened, happy.

Tap-tap-tap . . .

Tippy drummed a code into her earpiece: "Like goldfish in a bowl, they have adapted to their surroundings with empty-headed indifference."

No wonder, the lady thought as she pinched her beaky snout, trying to stem the smell of burned rubber. Her eyes glazed as she watched what could only be described as human cogs in a foggy factory town machine—for that's what the town was, a great factory.

Boys and girls were raised to believe that they should care about nothing more than doing what they were told. What they were told, of course, was to "be quick about it and just grow up already." So that's what the children did. Boys and girls became men and women. Men and women then went on to do what *they* were told: work in big square buildings that puffed out smoke like snoring grandpas. The men and women, who probably would have been better off just staying boys and girls, would stand in front of conveyor belts all day long, making dreadful things like itchy woolen socks and rigid white toothbrush handles. For their whole lives they'd slouch in assembly lines, twisting sock hairs or trimming brush bristles—never wondering what lay beyond the concrete walls of their cold, colorless town, because, after all, they'd never been told to wonder.

If each place had a personality, something to be most known for, Moormouth was the place where people worked sunup till sundown until the very day they died.

The beaky woman shook her head as her gaze shifted to the only house she cared about, the one unique fixture Moormouth had to offer. The slouching building squatted a good distance from the rest of the town. The space between gave the impression that either the house was running away from Moormouth or Moormouth was running from it. There was a long mismatched chimney chugging away, an old chestnut tree (with one fat turkey sleeping in its branches), and a shining black hearse parked out front.

Tippy watched from her place overlooking the entirety of the town. The junkyard marked the city limit, which gave her the perfect view.

Her eyes, however, were fixed on the young man bounding down the porch steps. He was lanky in a way that only twelve-year-olds can be, with a lollipop head and oversize feet (to keep him upright, of course). He wore a black-and-gray suit, his school uniform, with a hound's-tooth tie and bricklike shoes. He was easy to see even from a distance. His thicket of pumpkin-colored hair contrasted with his dark skin and made him stick out, perhaps even more than his stumbling feet or wide eyes.

Then again, the boy didn't need any help sticking out.

As if feeling her stare, he glanced over the hill at the junkyard; because of the fog, all he saw was the hazy outline of someone, but before he could determine who it was, Walter was pulled once more into the unforgiving rhythm of Moormouth. He turned and hurried toward the one-room schoolhouse a mile the other way. When he chanced a look back, the shadowy figure was gone.

Meanwhile, the woman continued to watch, now from the cover of a dilapidated refrigerator. She was crammed onto the bottom shelf, peeking through a crack in the door until the loping boy was a safe distance away.

No, it wasn't worth thinking twice about Moormouth, but Moormouth wasn't why she'd come. She had started this mission with little hope, but it had steadily grown over the past few years as she'd made her regular check-ins.

On this occasion she had been watching him for the past five days, sleeping in a claw-foot bathtub. She had seen Walter create the most marvelous contraptions. He had truly become something rather special.

Now it was time, at long last, to set into motion something most exciting.

Tap-tap-tap: "Yes, he's ready."

CHAPTER 3

THE BUMBLING BULLY

Walter had made the same walk to school every day since he was five years old. It was fortunate that he didn't have to look where he was going anymore, for Moormouth's ever-present, swirling fog made it almost impossible to see where he was anyway.

Instead he played a game called Kick the Rock that he'd devised seven years before. Walter would find a rock and kick it. Though this wasn't his most creative invention, it was surprisingly fun.

He had found a perfect pebble that morning as he'd raced out of the house. He kicked the stone between both feet, punting it up above the mist and watching it dive back down. On today's walk Walter was doing his best to ignore the boy walking only a half step behind him.

Alexander Grooblan was the kind of child who was

probably half-ogre. As a result of this, he had never learned how to speak without spitting. Walter did his best to avoid him.

It was difficult, however, on days like today, when Alexander adamantly refused to mind his own business.

"Mortinthon."

Walter ignored him, kicking his little, round rock. He silently repeated in his head: *Right, left, right, left, ri*—

"Mor-*tin*-thon."

Alexander pushed him with all his might. Walter stumbled, gangly limbs windmilling. He fell face-first but was able to stop himself with his hands—nose just above the pebble.

Walter stood up, brushing himself off and pretending as though nothing had happened. When Walter had been younger, his mother had told him not to feed the pigs that Mrs. Eggerley dragged by every spring, in case they came back for more. He had taken the advice to heart. Walter continued to ignore the big pink boy behind him, even when he could feel and hear the brute's snuffling on the back of his neck.

"I didn't want to haff to do that, but you were being rude. Didn't Mommy ever tell you not to be rude?"

Walter was vigilant about not stepping on a daisy, the only splotch of color for a half mile. Alexander trampled it.

"Or was she too bithy killing Daddy?"

Walter walked faster. He didn't know how long he could put up with this. Fortunately, they were much closer to the school than he thought. Unfortunately, he didn't know that.

"Don't run away, Wally! Everyone knowths ith's true. Itty baby Mortinthon and evil Mommy Mortinthon alone in their houth—oopth, I mean their corpth mutheum."

Alexander snorted up a wet chortle while Walter distracted himself by fiddling with the elegant gold pocketknife that had belonged to his father. He slowly pulled out each tool, admiring them one by one: a tiny screwdriver, a magnifying glass, a slide with a pressed mechanical flower (shining a brilliant cobalt), a wrench, and a blowgun.

"What? Noffing to thay to me? Noffing? Too thtupid, I gueth."

Alexander stomped on Walter's heel, forcing him to trip over his pebble. By the time Walter spun around to retrieve the rock, however, Alexander was gone. Walter's squinty gaze swung up to find him, only to see that he'd cornered new prey, a waifish girl walking a few paces behind. She had sunken cheeks and a patch over one eye. Her name was Cordelia, and Walter liked looking at her.

"Hey, thyclopth. Thee anything interethting thith morning? I mean, bethideth your own fathe?"

"Leave me alone, clodpoll," her thin voice rasped back.

Walter quickly scooped up the rock. Although Cordelia looked like she could hold her own in spirit, she was easily dwarfed by Alexander's massive form.

"You're the uglietht girl at thchool. Probably even in all of Moormouth. Mutht feel thpecial."

The smog in front of them parted as the pebble zinged through the air and nailed Alexander in the temple. Cordelia gasped. The huge boy reeled backward, furious.

"WHAT THE—"

Another rock shot into his open mouth, forcing him to sputter it back up with machine-gun hacks. He looked up just in time to see a third, smaller rock come hurtling toward his eye. Out of his other he could see Walter, blowgun to his lips.

Alexander stomped toward his relatively minuscule nemesis and, as an afterthought, pushed Cordelia as he went. She fell, papers flying out of her bag in a messy storm. Still, she couldn't tear her eye away from the scene unfolding in front of her.

Walter was frozen, gun poised at his lips, a fourth pebble already in place. Alexander snatched him up by the neck. Walter, face already purpling, desperately spat into the blowgun. The rock plopped against Alexander's bulging forehead vein.

Alexander swung the red-haired boy up by his neck scruff, to just short of Alexander's own face. Walter looked back in fear, his whole body quivering.

Hopefully Alexander isn't too mad—

But Walter was soon disappointed when the bigger boy wound his meaty boulder fist up and sank it into the softest part of Walter's belly. Walter's eyes bulged as the remaining puff of air escaped his lungs. He couldn't breathe. Smirking, Alexander plonked Walter onto his knees and lumbered off toward the school.

"Thee you in clath!"

As Walter tried to regain his breath, Cordelia eyed him, crouching by her spilled bag. Finally the wind rushed back into his throat, and then Walter crawled over, inhaling deeply, just happy to have control of his lungs again. Regrettably, that also meant he was free to ramble all he wanted or, rather, didn't want.

"Are you all right? He's wrong. Your face isn't ugly; it's nice. I mean—it's okay, but also nice, and I think all your papers are still here. It's not like there's much of a breeze to blow them away. Actually, the weather has been very mild, hasn't it? And . . ."

He trailed off, looking down at the papers he was scooping up. One was a drawing of a circus, another of a sunflower, and the last was covered in words, written in every direction. Walter scanned the words quickly, unable to stop himself. His eyes lit up when he saw a name. Not just any name, however. A famous name.

Automaton, the Mad Scientist. Little was known about him other than the fact that he was, unlike most people, a robot. What's more, he wasn't just any robot; he was a doctor (which, if you ask a great many people, is far harder to become than a robot). Dr. Automaton had the unique distinction of being in charge of the Flasterbornian Immortality Center and Laboratory—or FICL, if you happen to be too lazy to say "the Flasterbornian Immortality Center and Laboratory." FICL is, as you probably have already heard, the most glorious hospital in all the world. Why shouldn't it be? It, along with the doctor, was created by Flasterborn himself. And, as the whole world knew, if anyone could accomplish the impossible, it was Flasterborn.

Seeing Dr. Automaton's name made Walter especially excited because he knew more about Flasterborn than most, which is quite the feat, because *everyone* knew about Flasterborn. About half of everything in people's houses had his name on it, for Flaster's sake.

"You like Flasterborn?"

Before he could read any more, however, Cordelia snatched the stack of papers away. She glared at him, adrenaline still rushing through her wispy frame.

"There's drool on your chin," she said. With that, Cordelia pushed herself up and rushed off without a second glance.

Walter flushed, rubbing at his chin as he trailed behind her. Drool was an unfortunate side effect of the blowgun.

He watched Cordelia disappear into the smog, and sighed. He was going to be the latest person to class. Being the latest wasn't a problem anymore. It was more off-putting to those around him, he found, if he wasn't.

CHAPTER 4

. . .

WICKED MS. WARTLEBUG

Magda Wartlebug had wanted to be a teacher from the age of four, when she would capture the prettiest ladybugs, stick her prettiest hatpins into them, and then fasten them to the ground so that they had to listen to her lessons about the importance of kindness.

She graduated early and rushed to Moormouth in order to replace the town's only teacher, Ms. Croat, whom she vowed to never be like. (Ms. Croat had died the previous May due to an overdose of despotism.) Ms. Wartlebug was ecstatic as she looked forward to accomplishing what she had always known she could.

Then she met the children.

Ms. Wartlebug had thought children would be more like ladybugs—quiet, puny, and easy to nail down. Alas, she learned, they were far louder, slipperier, and spittier than she could have imagined. This made her realize that her role as a teacher was far more important than she'd ever known. It was her duty to make sure the children never learned anything. That way they would never reach their dreams. If they never reached their dreams, then they wouldn't do anything important.

It was crucial that children never did anything important, Ms. Wartlebug decided, because children were *silly*. They laughed, and they imagined, and they played make-believe. Ms. Wartlebug could not allow them to spread such nonsense, so if she couldn't pin them down, then she would have to stop them from thinking.

This morning she was doing her best to accomplish just that. Behind her on the slate chalkboard (which was still cracked from when Ms. Croat had disciplined a student for sneezing out of turn) was one word: "Gravitee." This, of course, is not how "gravity" is spelled, but that was the point.

Ms. Wartlebug's gaze roamed the room, her chest swelling with pride. No one even seemed to be paying attention. Elliot, the miscreant who she hoped would one day fall into a large, deep hole, was burning long strands of hair belonging to the sleeping blonde in front of him. He collected the ashes in a little toast box.

The students, ranging from six to sixteen years old, were utterly useless (she reminded herself for the fifth time that morning).

Nicolette, a kindergartner in front, raised her hand so high, it hurt her thin, shaking arm. Ms. Wartlebug groaned, "What do you want?"

"But how does gravity *work*?"

"I already told you."

"Yeah, but are you sure my feet is full of rocks? They don't *feel* full of rocks."

The teacher sighed, lurching to Nicolette's desk. Ms. Wartlebug had a large hump in her back that caused her to bend over at the waist, which meant she was already nose to nose with the girl. "First of all, it's not 'feet.' It's 'feets.' You have two of them."

"Yes, Ms. Wartlebug. Sorry, Ms. Wartlebug."

"And for anyone with half a brain, it's obvious that your feets are full of rocks."

Nicolette looked at the teacher blankly. The girl very much wanted to have at least half a brain, but she just couldn't understand. Ms. Wartlebug rolled her eyes, slinking back to the board.

"Then I guess I'll have to explain it again—"

But before she could continue, the door burst open. And she knew exactly who it was.

"I'm sorry. I—"

"Sit, Mortinson."

Walter scurried in, his head hung low. Ms. Wartlebug

didn't bother recording him as tardy. She had already marked him so for the rest of the year.

Walter Mortinson was odd, and she didn't trust him.

"Now, where was I? Oh yes. Let us see if the *other* children have at least half a brain, shall we? Elliot!"

The boy quickly blew out the match in his hand, dropping a final ashen hair into his toast box. "Yeah?"

"Where do rocks belong?"

Elliot scratched his head, looking out the window. "On the . . . ground?"

"Exactly. And, Ms. Primpet, where do your feets belong?"

Walter spun to look at Cordelia. She glanced back at him in a moment of shared truth, before she turned to the teacher and said, "I'm sorry?"

"Apology not accepted. Now tell me, where do your feets belong?"

After a second's pause Cordelia answered, "On the ground."

Ms. Wartlebug smiled her peculiarly sharp-toothed grin and shook her hump in glee, turning back to Nicolette. "That's right! Now, little girl, what does that mean?"

"My feets is . . . rocks?"

"Close enough. Gravity is when everything's filled with rocks. And things that aren't filled with rocks fly off into space. Now, class, that's your homework for tonight. Write three essays on things that aren't filled with rocks. I'll give you a hint: balloons, birds, and astronauts. You're welcome."

Ms. Wartlebug coughed, hobbling toward her desk. She couldn't wait to throw the essays into the fire and grade the students on how well each paper burned, but Walter's voice destroyed her reverie.

"But that isn't how gravity works at all! Gravity is the force that pulls us downward. Things with more mass, bigger things, have more—"

"Shut your trap!" Ms. Wartlebug clapped her hands loudly. "There will be no nonsense, balderdash, or poppy-cock in my class, or *else*—"

An alarm blared on her desk. The students covered their ears in pain.

"Saved by the bell, Mr. Mortinson. It's time for show-and-tell. Who wants to bore me first?"

She saw Walter's hand shoot up, the only one in the room.

"Amelia, I'm sure you will."

The blonde snorted awake. "Wha' happened?"

"Show-and—"

"Oh!"

She flung her wiry frame up and tossed her long, luxuri-ous hair over one shoulder.

"This is my hair. I've been growing it since I was born. Sometimes I talk to my hair about its dreams so that it may one day reach them. Right now its dreams is my knees. Thank you."

Amelia bowed and strode back to her desk, grinning triumphantly. Nicolette clapped.

"Well, Amelia, thanks for that rousing speech about your hair. *Again.* Next up—" Ms. Wartlebug made it a point to scan the room, making brief eye contact with Walter, her sole volunteer, before moving on.

"Elliot."

The miscreant stood. He carried up the toast box full of ashes. Then, in a voice like sludge, he said: "This is the ashes from when I burned off the back of Amelia's hair and then put 'em in a box."

He poured the ashes out, the black specks fluttering to the ground. As soon as Ms. Wartlebug saw Amelia's horrified reaction, she vowed not to punish Elliot for the mess. The girl gasped, smacking a hand to the bald spot on the back of her head.

A few more students applauded. Perhaps there was hope for the boy after all.

"Excellent teamwork, Elliot. Who's next?"

Walter raised his hand yet again. Ms. Wartlebug sighed, dreading the inevitable.

"All right, Mortinson. Get it over with."

Walter shakily grabbed the brown paper package at his

feet. As he walked up, he looked over his shoulder at Cordelia. However, he pulled his gaze away just in time to avoid tripping over Elliot's foot, which had snaked into the aisle.

Walter closed the gap between himself and the front of the room, quivering as he watched the other students watch him. He willed himself not to glance up at the girl as he took a deep breath.

Ms. Wartlebug shouted, interrupting his concentration, "Now, Mortinson! No funny business this time!"

He set the package down and pulled gently on the bow. It came undone, falling with the butcher paper around it. Inside was his invention, the one he had worked on all morning.

It was . . . a rabbit?

Oh yes, it was a rabbit all right, but it was just the skeleton. Walter had turned it into a windup toy, a crank wedged in the back.

"This is Ralph."

He twisted the crank. No one could say anything, all holding their breath. Rigidly the skeleton creaked to life and hopped along the table. Nicolette shrieked as it reached the edge and made a nosedive for her. Walter cradled Ralph before he hit the floor.

Then the room exploded with sound. The students were wide awake, squealing:

"Holy Flasterborn!"

"Is it dead?"

"He's a freak!"

"MY HAIR!"

Walter's eyes darted across their horrified and confused faces. He finally met the eye of the girl in the back. She squelched a small smile as she looked down at Ralph.

"Enough!" Ms. Wartlebug snatched Walter by the ear and dragged him out.

"Shut your traps. Mr. Mortinson and I will be taking yet another trip to see the principal."

Sideways, Walter watched the crowd of children cheer.

He sighed. Mother wouldn't be pleased.

CHAPTER 5

. . .

FLASTERBORN THE FANTASTIC

Tippy Tedesco had been working for Horace Flasterborn for precisely twelve years, eleven months, twenty-nine days, and eighteen hours. She was desperately hoping he wouldn't forget their anniversary.

Tippy had donned her best sports coat, had slicked back her poof of tendrils, and wore the glasses she thought made her nose look only once-broken.

So far he'd only asked for a cup of hot molasses . . . but the day was young!

She had reported to him about the Moormouth boy as soon as she had returned. The journey had taken a day in the strange vehicle Flasterborn had built for her. It had many legs that had scuttled with such incredible speed that Tippy's hair had thrown itself loose from its tight bun, the curls battering her cheeks until her face was puffy and red. But that was per-

"I've finished my letter to the boy."

"You'd like me to send it?"

"Please."

He handed her a sealed envelope, black with gold ink. She was careful not to let his gloved hands meet her sweating ones.

As she held the letter, she tried not to let her fingers tremble too much—lest they shake away the magic he'd certainly embedded in it.

She turned to leave just as a little blue bubble popped and filled her nose with the warm smell of salt water and summer.

"Tippy, wait!"

Kerthunk, kerthunk, ker— She willed her heart to calm, lest it shake her fingers.

"Yes . . . sir?"

"I'll take another cup of molasses when you get the chance."

"Of course, sir."

Twelve years, eleven months, twenty-nine days, eighteen hours, and ten minutes (give or take), but it felt like the first day.

She quietly shut the door behind her, locking the magic back in, and went to the little rectangular window in her sparsely decorated but quite nice (if she did say so herself) office.

fectly all right with her. Tippy didn't think such silly things as her hair or her health were as important as getting back to her boss. He seemed to agree, because as soon as she'd burst in that morning, hair standing straight up, he'd first asked her what had taken so long and then had promptly locked himself in his private office.

Tippy didn't like calling his room an "office," however. No, for her it would always be the "Room of Wonders." Nearly thirteen years ago she had christened it as such, partly because of the many wondrous inventions inhabiting it. She wasn't sure what they all did, but that alone made them at least twice as wonderful.

She would sneak in some afternoons (during his third nap of the day) and poke around. The guilt had been overwhelming at first, but she'd decided that anyone else would have done the same. Who would be able to resist peeking in on a living legend, the greatest inventor of all time?

Tippy didn't like calling Flasterborn an inventor either, though. Deep down she thought he must be a bit magic. That, of course, she never told him. No, she kept her suspicions to herself, but they were bolstered every time she was brave enough to scavenge the Room of Wonders.

Her favorite was a curious device shaped like an old perfume bottle that plopped out little bubbles filled with smoke. They radiated every color imaginable (and even some yet unimagined). The bubbles would drift around a bit, not exactly upward, just wandering. Then, suddenly, one would pop, and from the little firework-burst of smoke would waft a smell, either peculiar or lovely.

Tippy had sat there for the entirety of one naptime about nine years before. She'd watched as the globs had eased out of the pinched gold spout and swum around her head.

One, she remembered, had been an apple green and had released a smell that had reminded her of a pie her mother baked only on the snowiest days. Another bubble had followed, this one the rosy brown of an earthworm, and it had exploded with the aroma of what was definitely the dirt she used to pound down and throw at her older brother. The last bubble had been metallic, though what shade, she couldn't decide, and when it had popped, it had made her head swim and her skin flutter. She didn't know what the smell was, exactly. It had reminded her a bit of burned sugar mixed with . . . something sweaty? Or an animal, perhaps? Whatever it was, she'd been disappointed when it had disappeared.

Yes, she'd decided, Flasterborn *had* to be magic.

That invention was one of many. The room was like a miniature carnival, full of all the most marvelous things, things that only existed in dreams, and yet somehow Flasterborn had brought them to life. It was no wonder he spent all his time in there, Tippy thought. If she could have, she would have too.

The other reason she called it the Room of Wonders was because that was all anyone ever did about it. They *wondered*—about how it had come to be, what secrets it held, if they'd ever know for certain what—

"TIPPY!"

Her knees practically buckled as the man himself shouted excitedly through the gold device in her ear. She smoothed down her jacket, hair, and nose, then flew to the door and, with a deep inhale of anticipation, pushed it open.

Inside, the room was brought to life, with little zaps, whirs, and thunks. A twisting maze, built from tiny gold train tracks, snaked through the room. Tippy was so enthralled by the sights that she forgot to duck when the miniature train racing by hit a jump in the track, soared right over her head, and dashed across her freshly flattened hair.

Tippy quickly smoothed it down as she stuttered to her boss:

"Y-yes, Mr. Flasterborn?"

He grinned at her from his seat in the middle of the madness, and she had to stop herself from grinning back. It was particularly difficult, seeing as Flasterborn's enthusiasm was the most infectious she'd ever seen. His round face was perfectly jolly, his eyes were alight with fire, and his little beard curled whenever his patented ear-to-ear grin appeared. Right now his goatee was doing a full loop-de-loop.

Tippy pulled a small black disk from her pocket and brought it to her lips. She blew into it until it inflated into a box with helicopter blades that spun wildly as soon as they popped free. She flicked up a small button pad on the box and punched in the location, then dropped the letter into a slit on its side. Without any more direction, the little box zoomed out the window and disappeared behind a cloud.

CHAPTER 6

· · ·

MOTHER MORTICIAN

To see anything in Moormouth was a task. The town was stuffed with smog, like an overburdened teddy bear. The smog forced you to squint past the layers of gray until the equally colorless buildings came into view. This squinting was widely believed to be the reason why even baby Moormouthians had tiny crow's-feet. There were some things, however, that no one bothered squinting at.

The Mortinson home was one such place.

Even the braver children who would scamper toward the outskirts of town knew to avoid the crooked house. They would take the long way around, so that they didn't have to run into the Mortinsons.

After all, in Moormouth it was commonly accepted that it was far better to be alive than be adventurous.

What the few folks who did pass the house saw wasn't all that impressive. The first thing they noticed was the sign out front:

THE MORTINSON MORGUE

Curiously, the sign looked like it had been broken in half, and the bottom piece jaggedly sawed off.

What the missing piece had said, no one could guess. The sign seemed to tell you all that you needed to know: this place belonged to the Mortinsons, but, unlike most houses, it wasn't only the living who were welcome.

The two-story building buckled in the middle, as though the thick thatched roof were attempting to return to the sunburned grass below.

The house used to be a brilliant blue, but you could hardly guess it from the soured gray it had become, with its chipped, bleached paint.

The only living greenery was a little vegetable garden lining one wall of the house. In the front yard was the only living brownery: a sprawling leafless tree that had usurped the entire lawn.

Out back was a thicket of wild bougainvillea that had long since laid claim to an old mechanized carriage, with two metal horses slumbering at the front. The vicious vine grew in and around the vehicle in such a way that made everyone too afraid to chop it down—just in case it decided to lay claim to them too.

It might surprise you, but inside the house wasn't much better than outside.

There wasn't even a facade of comfort. The oak floors seemed to curve upward into the pine-paneled walls. The furniture was sparse and unkempt, rotting with the dead grass outside, the flowers in the vase on the dining room table, and the dreams of the home's inhabitants.

Hadorah Mortinson, the woman of the house, had considered replacing the old furniture for the sake of the business nearly five years before, but had then thought better of it. As the only mortician in town, she was never lacking for customers. People died whether they wanted to pay you for it or not. Because they never had visitors, there was no one to impress.

The Mortinson Morgue was practically a coffin—just how Hadorah liked it. That also happened to be a large part of the reason why her son, Walter, dreamed about anything and everything else.

Hadorah worried that Walter's dreams were at best foolish and at worst perilous, so she tried her hardest to get him to dream about something a bit more reasonable.

This concern was only reinforced as she read through the school note for the third time in a row. Walter had managed to hide the note from her for the entire night before, but after twelve years of practice, she'd learned to sniff out a disciplinary letter even when he'd hidden it in his dirty socks. If you happened to know the smells that arise from Walter Mortinson's dirty socks, you'd be quite impressed.

But Walter was not impressed. He was too focused on trying to work out what the note said. The night before, he'd cobbled together a monocle that would allow him to look *through* paper when he shook the monocle's chain. At least, that was what it was supposed to do. Really, he'd made the light embedded in the monocle too bright, and the first time he'd tested it, it had burned a hole straight through the paper he'd been testing. He never quite got the kinks worked out, something he was terribly frustrated about now, as he sat across from his mother reading the dreadful note.

Walter squinted at the letters through the paper. It didn't help that they looked backward to him from this angle. All he could make out was:

ɴǝʇʇǝℲ lɐqᴉɔuᴉɹԀ ɟo ǝɔᴉℲℲO ǝɥʇ ɯoɹℲ

After twelve years he'd come to hate those words.

"A rabbit?"

"Admittedly, he was already dead when I found him."

The rabbit in question sat on the chair between them and

seemed not to care that they were talking about it (whether this was because it was dead or a rabbit was unclear).

"A *dead* rabbit?"

Walter fidgeted; this wasn't going as planned.

"He can move now."

Though, again, the rabbit made no effort to prove it.

"Walter, we've talked about this."

"No, we talked about the projector, and the lamp, and the—"

"Inventing."

He stuttered for answers, though he knew from experience that none was sufficient. He then looked to the rabbit, hoping perhaps he had something to offer. He didn't.

"But I—"

"No excuses! The last time you brought one of those blasted creations to school, I told you what would happen, and I meant it."

Walter gulped. Apparently some words were worse than "nɘʈʈɘꟻ lɒqɿɔniꟼ ʇo ɘɔiꟍꟻO ɘʜʇ moɿꟻ" after all.

Walter sat in the dirt of the vegetable garden, wondering how he could turn the trowel in his hands into an aircraft that could fly him away from there. He constructed three potential possibilities, but none seemed feasible with his mother hovering over him.

"Get it over with, Walter."

"No, thank you."

"Now!"

Hadorah pressed her shoe onto the top of the trowel, Walter's hand still wrapped around it. The point sunk easily into the earth. Walter hesitantly complied, mounding dirt to the side of the growing hole. Hadorah dropped the windup skeleton into the ditch. Walter looked up at her as she stood directly above him, blocking out the sun.

She growled, "Walter—"

Startled by the twitch in her eye, he quickly shoveled, burying the rabbit deep below the cabbage roots.

"Thank you," she said.

As he continued to dig, her voice cut into him, one jab at a time.

"Only three days until you're old enough to start taking over for me. You really must stop inventing and get to work in the morgue. It's time. I won't always be around, you know."

He braved a last look at her, but was absorbed by something else.

Floating down from the clouds was a tiny black box, with even tinier helicopter blades spinning round and round. What a strange little thing.

"What are you—" Hadorah turned to look. Walter wanted to distract her, but it was too late.

He knew she wouldn't like it. Hadorah rarely liked anything—especially anything interesting. Still, he couldn't stop her from snatching the box just as soon as it was in reach. With a pitiful whine, it popped, leaving her grasping only a letter that had been hidden inside.

Eyes wide, she flipped the letter over and looked closely at a wax seal on the back. Walter jumped up, going to peek, but before he could see anything, she strode to the house with purpose.

"Wait! What is it?" he called after her.

"Nothing."

"But you have to read it. What if it's for me—"

"Forget it, Walter. It's not for you. It's just junk. Finish and come inside."

She raced up the steps and slammed the front door. Brow furrowed, Walter stared after her, then slumped back to his place in the dirt.

It was always like this. He never got to see anything interesting, and there was never anything he could do about it. As strong as his curiosity was, his mother's desire to squelch it was inevitably stronger.

Walter patted the hole and pushed himself up, driving the trowel into the ground for leverage. He stood mechanically, too entangled in his own thoughts to pay much attention to anything else.

A tomato hung from the trowel's blade as he trudged up to

the house. The tomato fell to the ground at the bottom of the porch steps. The spade dripped with red juice.

Then Walter, too, slammed the door.

Hadorah Mortinson sat at the end of her bed, trying very hard not to think of the letter. She'd put it in the kitchen trash can at once, burying it underneath coffee grounds and banana peels to ensure that Walter wouldn't locate it. It seemed Flasterborn had found his way through the fog of Moormouth and was crawling back into her life.

She wished she had someone to talk to about this wretched realization, but there was no one. Hadorah hadn't a single friend in the whole town, and it had been that way since she was only a child.

She'd grown up here, in this place, in this house, in this very bedroom. She surveyed it now. There was almost nothing in it anymore, no pictures, no carpet, no love, just wooden walls and a white bed.

She remembered being a young girl, just Walter's age, how she'd picked out her first-day-of-school coat, a nice pink one with a white collar. Though her uniform had been black and gray, her mother had insisted that Hadorah never wear black. It had been important for their family not to seem like morticians, because people in Moormouth did not like morticians.

But it had hardly mattered what color her coat was. It never stopped the bullying nor the rumors.

When Hadorah was a child, she sat alone in the back of the schoolroom. No one wanted to sit next to the girl covered in "dead-people germs." Anne, with her shiny black hair, sat in front of Hadorah. Her dad worked in the floss factory, and everyone liked Anne because she always smelled minty.

Hadorah had tried to be friends with Anne. But the other girl would say the most horrible things, like that Hadorah "smelled of rotten," and Anne would ask if her hair was red because it was covered in blood. Hadorah soon gave up on Anne, but that didn't mean Anne gave up on talking about Hadorah.

Every day, Hadorah heard the rumors, murmured all around her. People thought her family did dastardly things just because they were morticians. The kids whispered about how Hadorah's family cursed the town with fog because of their evilness, how her parents must have been killing people to keep their business intact. Some even claimed that Hadorah and her parents were dead themselves . . . pale ghosts continuing to walk the earth.

Hadorah wasn't a curse, nor a murderer, nor a ghost, but no one would hear it, because no one liked Hadorah Mortinson.

Well, no one liked Hadorah Mortinson until they met Maxwell Mortinson.

When Hadorah first met him, he was just Maxwell. You

see, Max came from an island on the other side of the world, a place where people had only one name. When Hadorah and Max got married, he added the Mortinson on.

Maxwell Mortinson was the first Mortinson that Moormouth liked. Oh, and did they like him. Max was different. He was sunny, and he was kind—nothing like what the town was used to. In fact, just as soon as Max arrived in Moormouth, he began to make it a more pleasant place.

First he devised big vacuums that looked like elephant trunks. They sat on people's roofs, sucking up the smog. For the first time in a long time, Moormouthians could truly see the sun, and it gave them hope that, perhaps, not everything was so hazy after all.

Then he put together robot arms that worked in the factories. Moormouthians now had to find things to do other than stand by conveyor belts all day. It was frightening at first, but they discovered that they truly . . . enjoyed some things. There were restaurants, and playhouses, and even a door-to-door kazoo salesman (who found he really loved kazoos).

Yes, everyone in Moormouth came to adore the Mortinsons—or, really, one in particular. Life for Hadorah wasn't nearly so hard then. Anne still didn't want to be her friend, but at least she had stopped whispering horrible things.

Then Max died, and suddenly the town's rumors bit back with a force they'd never before known.

People said Hadorah had to have been jealous; she was a witch, a murderer. They had always known she was one, and now there was proof. Though no one could quite link Hadorah to Max's strange death, she had been there at the scene of the crime and refused to explain what had happened.

She knew something, but she kept it hidden. That wouldn't do.

Then the elephant vacuums became clogged up and no one knew how to fix them. The smog returned, causing everyone to become gloomier than ever.

The robot arms slowly went on the fritz, falling limp and useless. People had to return to the factories to keep the businesses running.

Shops closed, theaters were demolished to make way for more factories, and all the kazoos were thrown out.

Things were never the same in Moormouth after Max died, but for Hadorah the town felt just like it always had.

CHAPTER 7

. . .

PUSHING UP PRIMPETS

That night was long and restless for Walter, who could never shake the dreams that plagued him. Though he had a hard time really remembering his father when he was awake, somehow Walter couldn't stop thinking of him when he was asleep.

Then, when morning came, Walter was reminded of what the true reality was. The disappointment was never worth the fleeting moments of reminiscence.

A series of bangs and rattles made Walter's eyes shoot open. The sound was caused by the jingling locks as Hadorah rapped on the door. He launched upward, slamming his head against his desk. He liked to sleep under it, in the hopes that he might dream up new inventions. Usually this sleeping arrangement only resulted in a rather large bump on his noggin.

His head throbbing, he whipped around, trying to

remember where he was. With a steady breath he realized it was his own room.

His mother's voice was no-nonsense as it pierced through the door. "Time to get to work!"

Walter slid himself out from under his desk and shot an annoyed glance at the offenders of his alarming wake-up: fifteen varied locks on his door. (They had seemed reasonable at the time.)

He then surveyed his room, if you could call it that. Really it was one huge, constantly moving pile of contraptions.

There were thousands of inventions, and their various parts, scattered about, littering the floor to the point where it could no longer be seen. Everything was there, from a butterfly made of butter knives to a shoe-spoked wheel that constantly ran in circles.

Like an expert alligator hunter, Walter honed in on the pile. He stuck one hand deep in and a moment later pulled out his prey: a palm-size grandfather clock. The hands of the clock were those of an old man, and the pendulum a cane. He read the wrinkly face: five a.m.

"You have fifteen minutes, and then we're leaving!" his mother yelled.

With a tortured groan Walter dropped the clock back into the mess.

Somewhere, deep in the pile of junk, something mooed.

. . .

Hadorah and Walter stood outside the Primpets' house, squinting. On the outside it appeared to be perfect in every way, from the doily curtains to the pansy-pocked garden. The idyllic scene was interrupted by shouting from within. Indistinguishable insults were slung back and forth with a viciousness Walter had only ever heard once, the time Ms. Wartlebug played the video reel of a brutal fight between a hippo and a lion (in celebration of her birthday).

Walter and Hadorah stood stock-still out front, wearing identically slack jaws.

Then the side door opened. A ducking spindly figure raced out, screaming voices following her from the house.

"Don't let her go into the—"

But Walter wasn't listening, because he was too busy staring at the girl. He'd know her shuffle anywhere.

It was Cordelia.

She stared at him for only a moment. She was clutching a book in her arms, as well as something hidden under her clothes, which was trailing the end of a long rope.

When their eyes met, she darted off into the woods. Walter couldn't help but stare after her.

Hadorah wrapped her iron grip around his arm, drawing his attention back, her eyes never wavering from the front door. Only a moment later it swung open, causing the mother and son to jump. Standing in the doorframe were two of the smiliest humans Walter had ever seen.

These were the Primpets.

There are some people who smile no matter what, even when their left foot has been bitten off by a hungry, toothy thing. They just hold up their bloody stump, plaster on a big grin, and say, "Well, isn't that unfortunate? Would anyone like tea?"

For folks like the Primpets, the very worst thing in the entire world is when people suspect that they're odd.

"Ms. Mortinson! How silly of you to stand outside. Come in! Come in!"

Walter shot a questioning look at Hadorah as the beaming woman shuffled them inside.

"Thank you, Mrs. Primpet."

Walter knew not to take his eyes off Mrs. Primpet's. The toothy grin reminded him of something. . . . Oh, yes. It was the very same look the lion gave the hippo before she pounced.

The Mortinsons and Primpets stared down at Arlo, the ninety-two-year-old patriarch. He looked worse off than he was, which was quite a feat, seeing as he was dead.

Walter traced Arlo's wrinkles with his gaze, wondering what must have happened to this man that had made him so scrunchy.

Walter was startled out of his pondering when Mrs.

Primpet's still-beaming face looked up suddenly from the body, staring directly into Hadorah.

"So! Need anything else from us?"

Walter was surprised when the voice of his usually unflappable mother wobbled. "We can, uh, wait outside if you two have any last words."

Mrs. Primpet continued to beam. "Nope, not necessary! Anything else?"

Happiness had rarely frightened Walter so much.

"I suppose not," Hadorah replied.

With that, the Primpets flounced away, snapping the door shut. Their hurried whispers permeated the walls, just too quiet to make out.

This was a curious place, but Walter decided he would rather keep these curiosities than have them answered.

He turned to the photos that circled the room. They were all of Arlo and depicted each stage of his life. There was a black-and-white one of a baby Arlo wearing some kind of frilly dress (fashion was much odder prior to the invention of color, Walter surmised), and even one of the man as he looked now . . . though noticeably less deceased. Walter was drawn to one photo in particular; it was of Arlo, not too young, not too old, handling a marionette. He looked to be in a state of complete bliss. Next to the picture hung the very same marionette. Walter reached for it—

"Walter!"

He knocked the photo over, causing a domino effect, each picture toppling into the next, all the way around the room until the crashing resulted in a final bang. The last picture smacked to the floor in front of him. The frame shattered, and the photograph floated out—Arlo and his marionette. Walter snatched it up, shoved it into his pocket before his mother could see, and kicked the remnants of the frame under the bed.

A tiny voice rose up through the floor below. "Ms. Mortinson?"

"Everything's fine!"

Walter's mother shot him a withering look. "Help. Me."

Walter glanced back at the frames littering the floor before he hurried over to her. She already had Arlo maneuvered up onto their Flasterbornian Self-Rolling Gurney. Walter was glad for it. He didn't mind dead bodies so much anymore, but he didn't fancy getting overly personal with one. He watched the gurney roll from the room, then stop a few moments later.

They'd have to carry it down the stairs.

Walter looked on, uncertain, brow furrowed. His mother stared down at him, a lip curled in poorly restrained amusement at her son's horrified face.

"Welcome to the family business."

• • •

46

Arlo lay on the table, naked save for the sheet draped from his waist down. He didn't mind his nudity so much. There were more pressing matters at the moment, like the woman pressing a needle into his skin.

Hadorah worked slowly, careful to ensure perfection. She hunched over the long, curved needle and thread, sewing with great precision. Walter looked on, the process reminding him of making a teddy bear.

The whole thing made him a bit uneasy, but not for the usual reasons.

He eyed the boring suit hung on a nearby chair. It would be Arlo's final outfit, and it didn't seem appropriate. Arlo hadn't been wearing a drab ensemble like that in any of the pictures Walter had seen. Arlo hadn't been just a gray old man, so he shouldn't be destined to lie in a box in a gray old suit.

"He liked puppets."

Hadorah paused her suturing to look up at her son, an eyebrow raised. "What are you talking about?"

Walter shrank a bit, uncertain now. "I-I-I saw it in pictures; he liked puppets."

"I see. Good for him."

Hadorah shrugged it off, returning to her work, but Walter couldn't help himself.

"Don't you think it might be nice to give him a puppet or dress him like a puppet or . . ."

Hadorah heaved a sigh, removing the little, round glasses she wore when she worked. "It's just not how things are done here."

"Shouldn't his funeral be about *him?* What he liked? I don't think he'd like this at all!"

Hadorah's voice grew firmer and louder. "No, Walter. We are doing what we always do."

"But why?"

"Because."

"But that's not an answer—"

Hadorah held up a hand, grimacing. "That's the end of it, Walter. We do it how I say. Do you understand?"

He looked from Arlo to her, grappling internally, before giving a timid nod.

Hadorah lips turned up. "Good. Now, why don't you try?"

She passed the needle to him. Walter took it, looking less than enthused.

"If I do, can I go to my room?" Walter asked.

"When you finish, sure."

Walter nodded again. Then, clearly less cautious than his mother, he bent over the body. The boy barely looked as he went to work.

"See? They have to be very close. It's not easy, so don't . . ."
Hadorah trailed off, watching her son do a much better job than

she ever had. Like a sewing machine, he completed a perfect zig-zag stitch without pause, cut the needle off, tied the loose ends, and turned to look at his slack-jawed mother.

"Good enough?"

Hadorah had to remember to close her mouth before croaking out an answer. "I suppose."

That was all he needed. Walter took off, straight up the stairs and toward the workroom door (which was, conveniently, also the basement door of their house).

"But, Walter!"

He hesitated, hand on the doorknob, eyes squeezed shut in frustration. He was so close to freedom.

"No more of your shenanigans. I mean it."

Walter let the gravity of her tone sink in before ripping the door open and hurrying back into the house. Hadorah waited for the knob to click before inspecting his work. She trailed a finger down the eerily identical stitches, releasing a low whistle.

She smiled, cracking anew the dimples that had long lain dormant. It seemed he wasn't naturally skilled at only his father's work; he had the spark for hers as well.

CHAPTER 8

. . .

THE BEAN

The many clocks in Walter's room ticked, for some reason, out of unison.

Walter sat on his bed, legs crossed, the way he always did. There was nowhere else to work, as the entire room was an ocean of inventions.

Just now he was adding to the ocean as he tinkered on a small white mechanism that fit perfectly in his hand. It was a tiny frog made of petrified wood, held together with springs and screws.

Gently he placed it in one palm and pressed down on the back legs. When he released, the frog sprung off and jittered straight across the sea of junk. It leapt against the window and then ricocheted off another invention (what appeared to be a lamp containing either fireflies or highly agitated stars). The frog clicked back and forth against the pane. Walter waded over carefully to retrieve it.

Timing it perfectly, he shot a hand out to catch the frog midjump. He grasped it, holding the fiend still as it tried to break free of his hand. Once it was subdued, Walter turned to look out the window . . . and saw something rather curious.

A pale finger of moonlight managed to burst through the Moormouth smog and point straight at the ground. The spotlight shone directly on the vegetable garden, where Ralph the rabbit's grave was still fresh and visible.

Walter believed in coincidences only when it suited him. Therefore, this light, he decided, was no coincidence.

It was a sign.

Mischievous children develop a condition early on. This condition is the result of a squishy little bean that grows in your brain somewhere between the lobe that tells you, *Eating paste will result in a tummy ache* and the lobe that says, *Jumping off a building will result in something slightly worse than a tummy ache*. This bean is that tiny thought in between that says, *Yes, but doesn't it look fun?*

Mannerly children, on the other hand, have perfectly plain brains, and so this thought never crosses their minds. Polite children don't have to worry about what paste tastes like, because they don't care. Their heads are so full of the things that adults have told them that they simply can't make room for a squishy little bean.

Walter had fallen ill to the bean; in fact, it had thoroughly taken over at least a sixth of his entire brain. This meant that he not only knew what paste tasted like (in several varieties), but he also knew that despite being told he was not allowed to go outside at night, he had decided to do it anyway.

A well-behaved, beanless child would never do this. Walter had never been all that well behaved.

Anyone with "the condition" can tell you what it feels like to sneak out, how your heart catches fire and desperately tries to beat the flames away, how your hands shiver because all the heat is now in your chest, how your ears can suddenly detect sounds you never before realized existed.

Walter peeked out from behind his door, listening. When he was satisfied that the house was sleeping, he tiptoed out into the hallway. In his hand quivered the trowel, so polished that it reflected the moonlight from the window.

He slunk down the hallway, knowing to avoid the squeaky fifth floorboard, until he got to the tall spiral staircase between him and freedom. He eased his way down, cringing, aware of what was about to come. On the fifth stair, he heard the dreaded creak slip out, before he quickly hopped onto the sixth, which only creaked more loudly, and onto the seventh, which creaked the loudest.

Terrified, heart threatening to burst out his ears, he jumped up onto the banister and slid down. It was perfect, silent, but he was going too fast. At the last moment Walter swung himself off course and leapt onto the ground, scarcely avoiding disaster.

He paused, waiting to see if he'd been heard. . . . The coast was still clear. He hurried, excitement renewed, out of the house.

In his haste, he failed to notice that his mother's hearse wasn't parked in front as usual.

Once at the grave, Walter dug, his hands quaking and his eyes darting back and forth between the garden and Hadorah's bedroom window, willing the light to stay off. After a few uneasy jabs with the trowel, his curiosity and confidence built, and soon he went at it with gusto. His sweat dripped down as he glimpsed a glimmer of bone white. He dug more furiously. Ralph was waiting.

He was distracted from his feverish digging by the crackling of car tires pulling into the gravel driveway, mere feet away.

Like a thunderstruck cat, Walter sprang upward, flattening his body against the house's side. Wide-eyed, he watched as the headlights flicked off.

Hadorah clomped up the driveway to the porch, weariness clear in her heavy gait. If she had glanced at the corner of the house, on the shadowed side, she would have seen him—sweat dripping in rivulets down his hair, chest heaving.

Walter watched her and hoped desperately that she'd be too tired to look over.

She was.

Hadorah passed him, no more than five feet away, going for the first step. Walter let out a quiet sigh of relief. He could sneak back in when she went to bed. But instead of the click of her clog meeting stone, there was a most terrible squish.

"What the . . ."

The lobes on either side of the bean screamed at Walter to stay put—begging him not to crane his neck and look, but he couldn't help himself. Walter peeked around the wall and saw the second most terrible thing: the deflated tomato he'd dropped the night before, dripping from his mother's heel. Then he looked up to see the first most terrible thing: his mother.

"WALTER!"

Without thinking, Walter shot from his place, ashen and trembling. He knew not where he was going, only that any place was better than this. Unfortunately, the direction his bean-diseased mind chose was straight toward her. She closed the gap, flying at him in a rage.

"How dare you disobey me!"

Walter winced as she stepped close to him, but then swiftly moved past . . . toward the hole. Horrified, he watched as she sank down, shoved a hand into the dirt, and emerged, standing, with Ralph gripped between her fingers. With gritted teeth, she threw the rabbit onto the ground.

"No!" Walter took a step toward her, but it was too late. Hadorah stomped hard, cracking the thing into pieces.

Breathing quick, heavy breaths, she stared down at the sad mess of bones, screws, and springs that littered the ground. After a few moments of silence, she looked up at Walter, to see tears forming at the corners of his eyes, and she suddenly deflated.

"Oh, Walter. I didn't mean . . ."

She walked toward him, reaching out a hand, but Walter flinched away. He strode toward the house. Hadorah followed, hesitant.

"I didn't want you to—"

He punctuated her shout by slamming the door.

Hadorah stopped at Walter's room just in time to hear the clanging of fifteen locks.

"Walter? Please. Let's talk about this."

She waited, attempting to listen through the thick door, in vain. After a minute she sighed. Her shoulders slumped, making her look much, much older.

"I'm just trying to keep you safe."

Walter listened from the other side, stick straight and stony faced. He waited to hear her footfalls leading her away.

When she was finally gone, he released his own sigh, letting his shoulders drop too.

Walter wiped at his face, smearing the two tears that had escaped, and then waded toward his dresser. He knocked behind it until he found the hollow place, then pulled the back panel off. Inside, it was surprisingly well organized, nothing like the rest of his room. He looked at the contents— first Maxwell's gold-plated pocketknife. It was the closest to the opening and clean of the dust that lingered on the rest of the shelf. Walter often snuck the knife to school but was careful never to let Ms. Wartlebug or Hadorah see it. He didn't want either to take it away. Then, when he got back home, he would quickly put it back, right on the edge of this secret compartment. Behind it were several other strange things: a video projector attached to an old cream-colored rotary phone, a stack of books he thought his mother might not like, and a small photo album. Carefully he pulled the album out. It was worn but well cared for.

He plopped down onto his bed and began flipping through the book. The first few pages were pictures, mostly of young Walter. Then came the articles; they were stained with age. Each one featured the same grinning man.

Walter was clearly a blend of him and Hadorah. The boy had Hadorah's untamable red hair and spattering of freckles made. The rim was a thin bronze circle, with what appeared to be an ordinary glass lens in the middle. A delicate chain hung down from the rim, and when you shook it enough, a light blasted through the center of the glass, so bright that it lit the entire basement.

Walter pried the lens out of the rim—revealing that it was actually two circles of glass with a little bulb in the center. He then pulled from his coat a small foil figure he'd made, one of an old man. He gently slipped it between the layers of glass in just the right position. Step one was completed.

Walter then stood to grab the next tool, the tiniest screwdriver he'd ever seen, but, unfortunately, it wasn't hanging on the wall where it was supposed to be. This was particularly troublesome, because, as small as it was, it was rather hard to see anyway.

Walter had to scour the room to find it, opening every cupboard and drawer, peering into even the nookiest of nooks and the cranniest of crannies.

As he sifted through the very back of a drawer, he found something strange underneath a stack of receipts: a map.

Walter had to pull it out gently, for it looked old and worn. He then blew a layer of dust off the face and discovered that it was a map of the surrounding area, from Flaster Isle way in the west to Moormouth in the east. Between the two was a red line drawn in fat marker. There were cities circled along the

but also the rich, dark umber of this man's complexion and the same scheming glint in his eyes. Walter stared at the pictures, his gloom only growing.

The first headline read: INVENTOR BRINGS PROSPERITY TO FACTORY TOWN, over a photo of the man smiling in a much brighter Moormouth, cutting a big red ribbon.

In the photo under the headline MORTINSON WOWS WORLD WITH INVENTIONS, the man stood, laughing, as children on winged tricycles (emblazoned with the name "Flycycle") lifted off the ground around him.

The last headline said, MAXWELL MORTINSON: HEIR TO THE FLASTERBORN EMPIRE. The man, Maxwell, stood with Horace Flasterborn, who had his arm around Max's shoulders. Both looked positively gleeful, the older man's goatee in full curl. Behind them, where the ink of the photo had smeared from thumbprints, was the shadow of a young, hawkish Tippy in the crowd, whom Walter might have recognized if he could ever have looked away from the man.

Alas, he could not, for this was his father.

Walter had read every newspaper story ever printed about Maxwell Mortinson but was rarely ever told anything else. There hadn't even been a funeral for Max, a decision Walter simply could not understand. Everyone deserved a final goodbye, didn't they?

He stared, absorbing the pictures, something building inside of him. After a few moments he snapped the book shut, then tucked it safely back into its place behind the false back.

The boy shakily stood. He was embarking on a new mission.

CHAPTER 9

• • •

THE NEW MISSION

Walter was tired of sneaking. He'd filled his furtive quota. By now his heart had given up caring, and he tromped down the stairs, daring them to squeak.

When he passed his mother, asleep on the couch, he didn't bother to check to see if her eyes were open or closed. Perhaps, had he been slightly more cautious, he would have seen the newspaper cutout fall from her sleeping fingers and drift under the sofa.

But, no. He failed to see any of it as he strode straight toward the basement door and down out of sight.

Once in his mother's workroom, he hurried over to Arlo, now dressed and preserved. Walter pulled from his pocket the photo showing the old man with his marionette. Walter sat down and leaned the picture on the shelf above the worktable. He then extracted something else—the monocle he'd

way, places called "Honeyoaks" and "Shrew's Borough" and other silly things like that. Walter had never heard of these places, let alone been to them. He hadn't been anywhere outside Moormouth, actually.

Fascinated, he pored over the parchment, memorizing every circle and divot along the journey. There were far more places out there than he'd ever realized.

When his eyelids grew heavy and he realized how little time he had left, Walter rolled up the map, tucked it into his pocket, and went back to work.

As he sat on the bench again, he was stabbed by something and instantly leapt up. He looked down to see that the smallest screwdriver was sitting right where he had been.

Shaking his head, Walter picked it up with the tips of his fingers and began working on the monocle, having forgotten all about the strange map and the stranger places on it.

The map, of course, had once belonged to Hadorah, who had been the one to mark it up with the fat red marker.

She and Maxwell had stood beside each other in their tiny apartment on Flaster Isle. It had been the size of only half a room. Hadorah had rented it because she'd liked how smart the building looked. Maxwell had moved in with her because he'd liked how smart Hadorah was.

The two had looked down at the map as they'd planned

their adventure. They hadn't known where they would end up, only that it had to be far from the island they'd been stranded on.

Hadorah had appraised the map, overwhelmed by how many places there were.

"But where will we go?" Hadorah had asked.

"Where we're supposed to be," Max had answered.

She'd rolled her eyes. "But how will we know where that is?"

"I guess we'll just have to explore to find out, won't we?"

He'd taken the marker from her hand and capped it. They wouldn't open it again for quite some time, not until they had traveled far away. Instead of planning where they'd go, they would record where they had found themselves, marking their journey with a red line.

They had hoped for the trip, from Flaster Isle to wherever they were supposed to be, to take years, as they explored and marveled and learned. Then, after less than one year, Hadorah's father had died, and Moormouth had needed a mortician. The two had returned just in time for Walter to join them.

The morning after Walter's mission, Hadorah was careful not to wake her son up, lest he see the gleeful smile she couldn't quell. Her eyes took in every last inch of the scene, which filled her with so much pride, she feared she might burst.

She had really gotten through to him, and now he was actually doing it, following in his mother's footsteps. She had always hoped Walter would take on the family business, and he finally had. There he was, fast asleep with a pair of forceps in one hand and a tiny tin of pale mortuary makeup in the other. That could mean only one thing: Walter was well on his way to becoming a mortician.

Her smile faltered when his head shifted. His eyes looked puffy, from lack of sleep? Tears? Without thinking, Hadorah leaned her face close to his, frowning.

Walter snorted awake. Hadorah reeled back, steadying the plates of eggs in her hands. Walter fought back the heavy tentacles of sleep as they tried to claim him again.

"*I didn't*— Mom?"

"I brought you breakfast."

Walter cautiously took the plate. The last time his mother had made breakfast was the day after his fifth birthday, and that was because all she'd had to do was slice off a piece of cake. He didn't trust her intentions, nor the eggs, which were strangely black and crispy.

The two ate without speaking, Arlo laid quietly in the middle, until Hadorah couldn't take it anymore.

"I'm really proud of you for listening to me. Don't think I didn't notice."

He nearly choked on a particularly crunchy yolk, nodding

politely. He had no idea what she was talking about, but he didn't dare let *her* know that.

"You'll see, Walter. Morticianing is a very respectable profession. Not like inventing."

Walter's chest felt hot; he couldn't stop himself. "So Dad wasn't respectable?"

"No, of course I didn't mean it like that. . . ."

"But that's what you said."

"Your father was a wonderful man, Walter, but he's gone. And if it hadn't been for his inventing, he'd still be here." Her voice became stuck in her throat. She cleared it, turning her eyes away from Walter. "This isn't something we should talk about."

"You never want to talk about him."

"Now isn't the time."

"It's *never* the time."

Her face whipped up to his. "To talk about your father's death? No, it isn't."

Walter sat rigidly, and the words he had been trying to keep locked away tumbled out, faster and icier than he'd intended.

"How did he die?"

"I told you."

"That you don't know."

"I *don't* know."

Hadorah stood abruptly, nearly knocking her plate over. She was frazzled. Hadorah wasn't good at being frazzled. She grabbed the plate, her hands unsteady, and stormed from the room.

Walter refused to look, not even when the door slapped shut behind her.

CHAPTER 10

• • •

YET UNREIMAGINED

Tomorrow came far too quickly for Walter's taste.

The entire town was packed into the tiny church around him, sardines in a can. Unlike most sardines in cans, however, everyone was wiggling.

The women, young and old, wore their finest mourning attire: collars up to their chins and sleeves down to their knuckles. The men donned their most solemn bow ties and oiled their mustaches. The children pulled on their itchy black robes, woven from wool, coal, and something intentionally scratchy. Men, women, and children alike watched the gloomy display with varying degrees of boredom.

Funerals in Moormouth were the biggest events all year, but, as it happens in any place where ceremony rules over sentiment, Moormouthian funerals were awfully serious, cumbersome affairs. No one truly enjoyed them, if people were to be honest, least of all the person of honor.

Only Walter and the slight girl in the front row (fiddling with her eye patch) actually listened to every word.

Preacher Chernbog looked rather close to death himself, if Walter were to say so. And Walter was among a line of experts on the matter, including his mother and the town doctor. Hadorah was quite good at her job, and the doctor was terrible at his, which meant they saw about the same number of dead people.

But neither Hadorah nor the doctor, nor anyone else, for that matter, could remember a time before Chernbog, who was as gray as a human could be. His sermons were equally monotone, only shaken up by his quavering voice. In front of Chernbog was Arlo, lying quietly in his open coffin.

Suddenly, and with a surprising amount of vigor, the preacher hit the side of the plain pine coffin with the heel of his hand. Arlo, inside, shook from the force. Walter, watching, nearly hopped out of his seat, his gaze glued to the monocle sitting over Arlo's right eye. Arlo had worn a monocle for the last twenty years of his life, but no one seemed to notice that this one was a different color.

"And let his life have been grand."

The whole town followed, repeating as though schoolchildren.

"And let his life have been grand."

The old man hit the box harder. Walter flinched again, never tearing his eyes away from the jiggling glass perched above Arlo's cheek.

"And his family be blessed."

The droning chorus continued.

"And his family be blessed."

Walter chanced a look at the girl in front, sitting with her family. Cordelia was the only one not smiling. While her parents seemed to *always* be smiling, Cordelia rarely ever was. And though Walter had seen Cordelia without a smile nearly every day for as long as he could remember, today she looked even frownier than usual. She had loved Arlo, her grandfather, more than just about anyone.

Chernbog hit the coffin for the third time. This man must have been a boxer in his day.

"And his crossing be peaceful."

"And his crossing be peaceful."

In a final attempt to hammer the message home, Chernbog smacked the coffin with both hands. Walter's eyes went to the monocle, which slid slightly down the side of Arlo's nose, jolted from the blow.

"Amen."

The old preacher gave the coffin a final good-bye whack, which normally wouldn't have been an issue, but this wasn't a normal funeral.

The first sign that something was off was when a light blinked up from inside the coffin. Those in the front row sensed something and leaned in to look, whispering. Then, not a moment later, a ghostly figure shot from the box, a projection that looked exactly like Arlo. Those watching from the pews, however, didn't know anything about a projection. To them it looked as though the bright light of his spirit were hovering just above his body and he was . . . dancing?

Chernbog stumbled backward, hand to his heart. "Mercy."

The specter's long, ghastly limbs swung this way and that, into unusual, inhuman positions that made him look almost like a puppet. Yes! He looked exactly like a puppet, and if one looked close enough, they might even see the shadows of strings pulling up each of his arms and legs. Arlo paid no mind to the shocked looks before him. Instead his ghost continued to jig merrily, head lolling one way, then the other.

It was a rather good show. But like most good shows, it went unappreciated.

The congregation were on their feet, overtaken by uproar. Children jumped onto the benches to get a better look, tripping on their robes; wives shielded their husbands' eyes with their long sleeves; and grandmas sat sobbing into black hankies.

Then something shot from the coffin. It was a spring that sprang right off the forehead of Cordelia's father, George— "Ay!"—who snatched it up and could only stare as he twisted it around. Struck by suspicion, he strode to the coffin and peered in. After a moment he yanked Arlo's monocle free. George's eyes squashed shut as the light beamed into his face. He dropped the monocle, and it shattered on the ground, finally extinguishing the ghostly figure.

Mr. Primpet rubbed his eyes, looking down at the broken invention. "Ms. Mortinson? What is the meaning of this?"

Walter thought it a shame that the question was directed to his matriarch, who was still as gobsmacked as everyone else. Walter had a brilliant answer that had something to do with an analogy about his philosophy on life and the buoyancy of ghost tummies. His analogy was never heard, however, because, on cue, Hadorah snatched him by the ear and dragged him straight out of the church, with every eye, all six hundred and thirty-one, following him, one more closely than the rest.

Hadorah didn't bother with any words as she threw Walter out. She shot him a single withering stare that was worse than any other he'd ever felt. She then returned inside, straightening her skirt, leaving him alone.

The wind whistled behind Walter, causing him to shake harder than he already had been. Tears of humiliation and fear threatened his eyes, and so Walter did what he always did when he wasn't sure of his next move. He ran to his favorite place in the world: the junkyard.

• • •

Pratt the cat had lived in the junkyard since kittenhood. While his brothers and sisters had all left to join various street gangs or take up in some fancy Dumpster, he had stayed. He was a junkyard cat through and through.

He'd been born at the tippy-top of the tallest tower of garbage, in a heaping lint-filled bathtub. His mother had told him that that was why he was gray. He'd just assumed that everything from Moormouth was gray.

The junkyard, to some, was different. It was a mishmash of every color imaginable, thrown here in a great mound of forgotten promises and misplaced dreams. Someone who didn't know how to look at a junkyard might blend it all together and see a colorless, hilly mess, but unlike Pratt, Walter knew how to look. For him, this place was a glittering paint palette of opportunity.

That being said, there are some places, like people, that seem downright ugly. As if the universe thought, while being created, *Well, someone has to be the knee wrinkles.* But the most amazing thing about such places and people is that when hit by the right light at just the right time, they look more beautiful than anything else.

The time of beauty for the Moormouth junkyard was half past dinner, and a quarter to bed—or, as it were, when the funerals let out. The dying rays of sun burst between piles of junk, reflecting off all the many surfaces of odds and ends. Ten to fifteen feet tall, the junkyard towers loomed over the flat factory wasteland of Moormouth beyond.

This place was a haven for broken things, from one-eyed dolls and cracked dishware to floppy tires and forgotten footstools. That night Walter stood right in the middle of it all.

He, however, preferred not to think of these sorts of things as "broken," per se. For him they were just yet unreimagined.

Walter stood atop a spindly pile and bashed the shiny bits and bobs with a broken chair leg. At one time the leg had probably been quite lovely, embellished with a floral design and a clawed foot. Now it made a great blunt object for swinging.

Teacups exploded like fireworks. A defunct piano screeched. He struck harder and harder, as if trying to shift the pain in his heart to his hands, where he might send it careening into the trash pile. With the frustration he'd built up living in Moormouth, Walter could have done this for hours.

Gravity had a different plan.

Walter swung hard against an old icebox, causing a patchy gray cat to howl as he darted between Walter's legs. Walter tripped and rolled right down the hill after him—and crashed in a tangle of limbs at the bottom.

Hot, salty tears leaked from Walter's eyes. He didn't even

bother to wipe them away, too overwhelmed by his own exhaustion.

He lay there for minutes or hours—for once, without his many clocks, he couldn't tell. But Walter knew he couldn't stay, for fear of becoming part of the junk that was trapped there forever.

No, it was time to go back.

Walter willed himself to stand and clomped his weary way home.

Walter trudged down the dark lane toward his house, nose flaring like a bull as he breathed heavily through his fatigue, when, out of the blackness of night, a white wooden frog danced up to him. It had come from the front yard. Walter stopped to look, cocked headed and confused, at the spring-loaded amphibian. He picked it up and cradled his invention in both hands as he stared into its dull bolt eyes.

"How did you get here?"

The frog tried to bound from his fingers. Walter, just nimble enough, stumbled to catch him. When he looked up, he saw a trail of inventions leading around the old tree and out of sight.

The frog scrambled desperately in his hands. It seemingly knew, in its inanimate and immaculate mechanism, that something was not right. Walter had the same feeling and numbly shoved the frog into his sock for safekeeping, just in case.

Carefully he trod to the tree and peeked around, and was shocked by what he saw.

The entirety of his room, save for the desk, dresser, and bed, sat in a grand mound in the middle of the browned grass between the front yard and the backyard. The pile was still alive with movement and sounds, sparking here and barking there. It undulated with the effort of hundreds of inventions, all doing what they were meant to do. It was they, the products of Walter's hopes and imagination, that sat before him. And in front of them was Hadorah holding a very large sledgehammer.

"I warned you, Walter. No more funny business."

A small frog, just like the one scrambling to escape Walter's knee-highs, hopped toward him. Hadorah's foot shot out and stamped on it. The frog crumpled with a pitiful whine, and though Walter was too stunned to pay attention, he would swear later that its identical brother in his sock stopped moving as well.

"You've left me no other option. In six hours you will be thirteen, and I'm done, done with all of this. So, you have a choice."

She picked up her foot to reveal the remains of the collapsed frog. Walter pushed down the lump in his throat.

"You do away with all of these . . . monstrosities. And agree to take up morticianing, or continue inventing and face the consequences."

She drew a crumpled flyer from her pocket and spread it out for him to see. It showed a picture of a gloomy estate looking over a barren hill. Above, in cheery red writing, it read: "Clawson's Correctional Institution for Uncorrectable Children."

Behind her, silhouetted in the moonlight, was the same building as the one in the picture. Lightning didn't crack behind the building, but it really ought to have.

"I can't save you from inventing, but maybe *they* can."

Walter pressed his fists together behind his back and willed his anger down. His face became blank, and his voice flat. "What do I have to do?"

"It's simple."

She snatched up an invention, a small metal hand that opened and shut on its own. Walter had originally hoped it could be used to hold pieces of paper together, but the hand much preferred snapping to grasping. Hadorah gingerly placed it, palm side up, on the cracked slab of rock in front of her. The fingers wiggled in hello before suddenly shooting apart as Hadorah raised the hammer above them. She then heaved the hammer down with a great crunch. Walter gasped. The hand was pulverized.

"Destroy them all."

"And if I won't?"

"Then you will spend two years locked away on the hill." (Again, lightning didn't strike, but it definitely thought about it this time.)

Walter had trouble keeping his rage at bay. Tears threatened his eyes as he looked upon the remains of his hard work. With every last bit of strength he had, he smooshed the feeling deep down into a place inside him that he was very familiar with. This was the place where he always locked away troublesome feelings that didn't belong.

His mother then passed the hammer to him. Its stone head met the ground with a *thunk*, his hand still wrapped around the handle.

She appraised Walter, eyebrow arched. He looked only at the pile, quaking in front of him. She nudged an invention out with her foot: the grandfather clock.

He looked to her, to the clock, and then to the hill. There was nothing he could do, nothing to invent that could save him from this, so he turned the lock inside himself, silencing his emotions squirming to be free. Then he did his very best impression of a robot.

"No more inventing?" his mother asked.

He nodded.

"Then do it now," she said.

Walter lifted the hammer just above the clock, then let it fall; the clock smashed. He cringed at the horrible sound. Hadorah pulled the next invention out: a singing bird made from browned dandelions. Hadorah went right back to the pile—over and over again—an assembly line of horror. The next out was a humming candle, permanently lit. Forcing back the ache in his chest, Walter closed his eyes.

He pretended to be an invention with only one function, and in a perfect display of his own machinery, he performed, dropping the hammer onto the candle.

There was another great crash, and the candle's light went out.

CHAPTER 11

. . .

EXACTING ESCAPE

As you know, to see anything in Moormouth was a task, but if you squinted hard enough, you just might have seen the Mortinson home lined with trash bags, their guts spilling out.

A close investigator might also have noticed that the contents of these bags were rather unusual: springs, screws, bits, bobs, and every other thing that had once been part of Walter's collection. Now they sat in the ultimate ruin of a black plastic bag.

Inside the house boded little better.

Walter's room had been transformed. While it had once been alive with the squeaks and squiggles of marvelous wonders, it was now bleak and cold. The only movement was the swaying curtain, unattended to for years and half-eaten by voracious smog. The floor—unseen for nearly a lifetime—

turned out to be a tightly woven, off-green carpet. Who knew?

Little light poured into the room, because of both the midnight hour and the dense haze. But Walter didn't need it. He moved as a boy who knows just what he's looking for and has no time to spare.

He needed an invention, just one, just something.

Walter had forgotten the frog in his sock because it had stopped moving entirely. This was a horrible shame, because an hour prior, Walter had been so desperate that he'd even tried to dig up the vestiges of Ralph's bones, hoping to put them back together. But the ground had been picked clean of them.

Then he remembered: only a few days before, he'd tried his hand at a comb that would change one's hair color. After tinkering on it for days, his curls had been *supposed* to turn dandelion yellow. Instead the comb had made them glow in the dark. He hadn't wanted that, and it had taken quite a few showers to stop his hair from attracting moths at night.

After that, he'd dropped the comb into the trash can beneath the kitchen sink.

The comb had been a failure then, but now it was all he had. He hoped it was still there; it had to be.

Walter dug through the trash. By the bottom, it seemed that there was no comb after all. Heart sinking, he made one last push. Below a pile of banana peels and coffee grounds, he felt something stiff and square.

He pulled it out of the mess and discovered that it was a letter. The envelope was black, and the seal was gold. Walter's breath quickened when he recognized it as the letter from the helicopter box. Then, upon closer inspection, he realized that the seal belonged to Horace Flasterborn. He flipped the envelope over. His breathing stopped entirely. On the front was his own name: Mr. Walter A. Mortinson.

With shaking fingers he picked at the edge of the seal on the back. Time went treacherously slowly as he, as carefully as he could, pulled the little wax circle off, leaving only one small tear in the paper.

Walter gasped as the tear grew larger, branching off into more strips that instantly curled up. He dropped the letter, as if burned, and continued to gawp. The black envelope split violently into ribbons, twirling into gold curlicues. With a final audible pop, the letter was spat out of the glittering mess.

That's one way to put confetti in a letter, he thought. Despite the fact that Walter could dream up at least one hundred easier ways, he didn't much care. Nothing he imagined could top that.

Still quivering, he bent over to grab the innocuous-looking parchment. He couldn't imagine what it said.

Mr. Walter A. Mortinson,

As a colleague and friend of your father's, it is
my great pleasure to invite you to join me as an
apprentice. You are welcome to stay with me on Flaster
Isle upon your reaching thirteen. Should you show even
a fraction of your father's ability, it will be well worth
both our time. Let us create the impossible.

Yours,

Flasterborn

And Happy Birthday.

Flasterborn. *The* Flasterborn? Walter could hardly believe it. A million and two thoughts were running through his head, and yet only one bubbled above the rest:

This had to be a horrible mistake.

Flasterborn didn't know him. Of that, Walter was certain. How could he? Walter wasn't entirely sure that everyone in his class knew him. The inventing legend, Walter's only living idol, must have assumed that the boy was like his father.

How wrong he was.

Walter may not have remembered his dad, but he had seen the pictures and read the news stories innumerable times. Maxwell Mortinson had been a legend, universally loved, an absolute genius.

Walter was none of those things.

He'd heard the stories about himself, and all he could conclude from them was that he was as different from his famous father as he could be. He, Walter A. Mortinson, was a goober. And no one likes goobers, least of all a world-famous inventor like Horace Flasterborn.

But just as Walter prepared to shove the letter back to the bottom of the trash can, a thought occurred to him: he had nothing to lose.

With a startlingly renewed vigor Walter rifled through his dresser, emptying it of his clothes. Then, back behind it all, he knocked a few times until he found the hollow place. With a fierce yank he pulled the false back panel off, then dug inside. From the cavern he pulled out Max's pocketknife, the double-stuffed photo album, and the old map from the workroom.

He stretched open his knapsack, dropped the keepsakes inside, and buried them with an odd assortment of clothing. (If only he'd paid attention, he wouldn't have packed two pairs of long johns and a pair of swim trunks.) After struggling with the old zipper, he finally ripped it closed.

Then he sighed, staring at the gutted carcass of his childhood—a room that didn't feel like his own. It now felt like a horrible place, and as he stepped out, he didn't even want to look back.

. . .

Once outside his room, Walter stopped and took a few steps toward the forgotten, shadowy corner of the upper floor. He didn't bother going over very often, since the punishment for doing so had been fiercer than any other.

He looked around, cautious, before peering up into the very darkest corner. There had been an opening up there once, clearly, but it had been boarded up long ago. The hatch had led to the attic, Walter knew, but Hadorah had banned anyone from so much as thinking about it since Max's death. Walter couldn't remember what the attic held, but his curiosity had always been outweighed by fear. Tonight Walter no longer feared the punishment. He just no longer cared to know what was inside. This house had nothing for him anymore.

The floorboards moaned in the way that they only do past dark. The stairs squeaked, as if in cahoots with the floorboards. His old boots slapped the floor, laughing along with all the rest . . . and then Walter saw the light at the end of the staircase.

He stood in the living room, which was lit only by the flickering candles that were slowly dying on the dining room table. Hadorah's room, to his left, was dark, but a sliver of light escaped from the basement door ahead, which had been left ajar.

He cautiously closed the gap between himself and the basement, then poked his head in, just enough so that he could hear the sharp whir of a drill echoing up the stone staircase within. Hadorah must have been working on something, but he had no interest in learning what it was.

Instead he backed away and slunk right out the front door. He eased the knob, twisting carefully until the door clicked softly behind him.

Once outside, Walter ran. He skidded over the gravel to his mother's car, all the while fiddling with a stolen key ring.

He fumbled at the car door, eyes plastered to the house while his nervous fingers shook the key against the lock. He finally fit the key in and clambered into the driver's seat.

He felt a pang of nervousness as he considered the fact that he'd never driven a car, exactly. He'd built quite a few drivable things, certainly, but never anything with wheels.

He'd be fine, he reassured himself. How hard could it be?

He jerked forward after throwing the car into reverse, and then clunkily led the long black automobile out of the driveway.

When he reached the fork at the end of the road, he took off in the opposite direction of the old house, not daring to look back.

Meanwhile, back in the workroom, Hadorah toiled away through the evening and into the night. The bags under her eyes proved she'd much rather have been elsewhere, but the wrinkles in her brow spoke to her stubbornness.

She scrubbed hard at something, trying to make it look fresh. She was doing a darn good job too.

There. She approved of her work, sitting back, satisfied.

In front of her was a gleaming white rabbit, as good as new, or as new as a skeleton rabbit can be. Ralph would have been happy to be back, but really he was just happy not to be in the ground anymore.

Hadorah had painstakingly puzzled the many little bones back together with tweezers and paste. Finally she tied a shiny black ribbon around its neck and wearily stood to deliver the present. She was so tired, she didn't even notice when something clonked her mailbox outside.

Hadorah trudged up the stairs, being as light-footed as she could so as not to wake Walter, then placed the rabbit gently against the door so that he'd find it when he woke. To her shock, however, the door gave way.

She peered inside . . . only to find the room empty. Walter was gone.

Hadorah rushed out and in her haste dropped Ralph outside Walter's door.

Hadorah had nearly tripped while running down the stairs and was now staring into the inky blackness of her driveway, where the hearse should have been parked.

Her jaw went slack, and her thoughts sped several light-years a minute. . . . Her mouth caught up only in time to utter a single word.

"Walter."

When Walter had been four years old, he'd made his first friend.

Maxwell had been horribly excited and had soon informed Walter of all the wondrous things to do with your friends: you could hop on rocks or skip in puddles or even share a nice chocolate!

Hadorah hadn't been as excited as Maxwell, because Walter hadn't made just any friend. He'd made friends with a Primpet—Cordelia Primpet. From what Hadorah knew of Primpets, this couldn't end well. Yet as she watched her husband swing her son in circles, hollering at him about stones, mud, and candy, she couldn't bring herself to call the upcoming playdate off.

She insisted, however, on being the one to drive Walter to the Primpets' house.

They arrived in the long black hearse, earning an upturned nose from Mrs. Primpet and downturned lips from Mr. Primpet, both standing outside with a protective hand on their daughter's shoulder. Cordelia stood in front of them, her blue eyes shining out from under long black bangs, and she practically jumped out of her frilly white socks when Walter leapt from the car and frog-jumped to her.

"Hello, Mrs. Primpet. Hello, Mr. Primpet!" he sang, approaching them.

Hadorah heaved an uneasy sigh as she followed (though with less jumping). She nodded to the Primpets as she drew near. "George. Anne."

Mrs. Primpet's face curled into a wide smile that didn't reach her eyes. "Hadorah, so nice to see you. Where's Maxwell?"

Hadorah gritted out her own fake grin. "He was busy."

"Shame. Come along, Cordelia."

Just as Walter leapt forward to engulf the small girl in a hug, Mrs. Primpet pulled Cordelia into the house.

Hadorah thought that perhaps she shouldn't leave him there, but when she saw the two children look to each other and clasp hands, she knew there was no other choice.

The playdate proceeded in an equally unusual manner. First Walter tried to show Cordelia how to balance on rocks, but Mrs. Primpet, forever hovering over the children, was quick to yank her daughter away, informing both tots that rocks are horribly unsafe and not to be touched.

Walter then tried to skip in mud puddles, but the second his toes dipped in, Mrs. Primpet sprayed him down with a hose. "Germs are dangerous," she snarled.

Finally, Walter brought out a little chocolate bar he'd pulled from the cupboard at home. He offered a square to Cordelia, but Mrs. Primpet snatched it away and dropped it into a trash can.

"Chocolate gives you cavities, you know."

Walter had never heard of cavities, but they couldn't be that bad if they lived in chocolate.

Mrs. Primpet had then relegated the two to Cordelia's room. It was so horribly dull, Walter thought. There were no toys, no costumes. Why, she didn't even have a single wrench! The room had nothing but a bed and books.

Walter sat, bored and confused, until Cordelia pulled down her favorite book to show him. It had pretty pictures of a circus. Cordelia told Walter that she liked books, which made Walter think he might like books too.

After they looked at five picture books, Mrs. Primpet decided it was safe to stop watching them from the window, atop her ladder outside.

Once the scowling lady was gone, Walter gave Cordelia the present he'd asked his father to make for her: a little metal rabbit, painted a lovely bright orange. That was her favorite color, she had told him. And he had remembered. How wonderful. Walter's favorite color, he had told her, was periwinkle. She'd never heard of periwinkle and asked him what

"That's a letter from—never mind. I'm going to Flaster Isle, and I know that you're interested in Dr. Automaton, and I was just wondering if you would, you know . . ."

She stared at him from high above, and it made it hard for him to think.

"I mean, I can get you there. Fast. You could maybe even see him. Flasterborn was friends with my . . ."

"When are you going?"

"That's the thing. We don't have much time. So I was thinking, if you wanted to go, that we could—"

She interrupted him, voice forceful. "*When* are you going?"

"Now."

Cordelia disappeared into the darkness of her room, and Walter's heart sped up again as his chest filled with dread.

"Cordelia? *Cordelia?*"

Nothing. Just the swaying curtains in the breeze. Walter, no time to spare, hurried back to the car. He hustled in and jabbed at the ignition. Just as he fit the key in, the passenger door swung open.

Cordelia stood before him, out of breath and still in a white nightgown that hung to her shins, her knapsack now clutched to her chest.

"Let's go."

Walter couldn't keep the smile off his face as he jerkily

it looked like. Walter didn't know, but he liked the sound of it. That was good enough for Cordelia. She decided she also liked periwinkle.

Cordelia's mother would never have let her have the orange rabbit. It had gears that could pinch, and sharp ears that could scratch, and little nibbling teeth that could bite. But Cordelia loved it, so after a long day of winding it up with Walter, she stuck the rabbit on top of the curtain rod by her bed.

Her mother would never look there, because her mother didn't know Cordelia could climb the curtains to reach it. Cordelia's mother didn't know lots of things.

This would be the first and final playdate for Walter Mortinson and Cordelia Primpet, for not long after, everything changed.

Walter, now nearly thirteen, tried to remember that day as he sat in the front seat of the hearse. He was attempting to convince himself to get out of the car and finally approach the Primpets' house (after, of course, rehearsing nearly fourteen times what he was going to say).

Once he built up the courage, he stumbled out and stood below the highest window, the only one outfitted with metal bars. He could do little but stare at the drawn curtains.

He breathed in a bit of courage and tossed a pebble up at the window. It hit expertly, making a slight *ping* before clattering to the ground. He waited for a reaction, skin atwitter—but no response came.

After a moment he decided he ought to try again. This time he picked up a slightly bigger rock, figuring that would do the trick. Walter lobbed it up, and it struck the window with a resounding *thwack!* That must have woken her, he concluded, smoothing his hair as she undoubtedly came to check who was below. . . . Alas, the curtains didn't budge.

Slightly confused, mildly frustrated, and quite impressed, Walter selected his next attempt. This one, which could only be described as a palm-size boulder, would really do the trick. It was the kind of stone that Walter thought would definitely wake him up if it were thrown at him. He chucked it at the window, hoping his aim wasn't off.

It wasn't. The rock made a congratulatory *crash* as it sailed right through the glass.

Walter could hardly move as his terror rose. His eyes, however, did shoot to the front door, where he was certain the elder (and far more sinister) Primpets were about to barge from. This was a door-barging moment. He nearly jumped when, instead, the high voice of an annoyed girl pierced through the air above him.

"What are you doing?"

Walter's head whipped back to Cordelia's window, only to see her inspecting the demolished pane.

Walter thought fast to answer. He was an excellent answerer. "I broke it."

She sighed. "I see that. Why?"

This was a much harder question to answer.

"I, uh . . . I wanted . . ."

Cordelia uneasily backed away from the sill as her mind concocted ever more unlikely scenarios explaining the late-night visitor.

"Look, I don't know what you're up to, but I'm going to go get my parents—"

"No! I just came to . . ." He bolstered himself before continuing. "I'm leaving."

"I'm glad."

"And I want you to come with me."

She stopped in her tracks. "What do you mean?"

Walter's practiced speech had ended there, and he struggled to find the words.

"I, well, I can't explain it all now. We have to go. But . . . I'm going to Flaster Isle!"

With a burst of inspiration, he held up the gold-and-black letter, slightly crumpled now. Cordelia just stared, not near as impressed as he'd hoped she would be. He flushed, tucking the letter away again.

pulled the car out of the driveway and careened into the night.

He remembered just in time to flick off his headlights as a police car stalked around the bend, lights illuminating the now-empty driveway.

CHAPTER 11 ½

· · ·

THIRTEEN YEARS AGO

Once upon a time two lovely newlyweds stood before their brand-new home. The paint was brilliantly blue, the grass was violently green, and the birds in the gently swaying trees were probably chirping about love—or something equally nauseating.

The husband was handsome in a way that wasn't like chisel-jawed movie stars; he instead had the kind of smile that infected you. He was special—doubly so, in fact, because he truly didn't know how special he was.

The woman on his arm knew all too well. She was his wife and looked the part, with her rosy tendrils and umbrella-skirt summer dress. Her eyes, however, were a bit too crow-footed even for a native Moormouthian. She was a fretter, and that was unfortunate.

Some people only worry when there's a monster afoot or

when they are trapped in a very small space where they can't reach their own nose. Some people, like this pretty, crow-footed lady, just worry about worrying.

Worries are dastardly little things that can't do anything but twiggle your mind and make your heart hurt. They feel like evil beetles eating you from the inside, but really they're no more dangerous than a bit of extra sticky toffee. That's what they are, you see—extra sticky. They trick you into believing they're something much scarier, and that's why they are so scary. It's a horrible, tragic affliction because unlike monsters or small spaces, the only way to defeat a worry is by not worrying about it—but just try to tell that to a fretter.

Still, this poor lady was special too. It was just harder to see because she unequivocally believed she wasn't. Today, however, was their first day in the bright blue house. Today was sparkling. Today smelled slightly of honeydew. Today was too wonderful for her to worry about anything, so she, too, smiled an infectious smile and glowed just short of being jaundiced.

"Haddy?"

She turned, hugging her ballooning nine-month-pregnant belly. "Max?"

"Welcome home."

The two smiled at each other in such an adoring way that it happened to cause an onlooking chipmunk to suffer from indigestion.

The newlyweds then looked in unison at the sign on the front lawn.

THE MORTINSON MORGUE

AND INVENTORIUM

Maxwell kissed Hadorah. Today was wonderful.

CHAPTER 12

. . .

ONCE AFTER A TIME

That day thirteen years later was not nearly so nice. Hadorah stood outside, a crumbling shell of the bubbling-over bride she'd once been. She hunched, withering into the fog. The veins on her hands were prominent and crawled up her arms as if escaping for higher ground. Her once-fiery curls had frizzled and fried, and were silvering. The pretty white sundress she'd once worn had given way to something that rather resembled a deflated potato sack.

There's nothing more curious than a woman stuck in a perpetual potato sack race of one.

The man standing across from her on the hole-strewn lawn seemed to agree. Officer Culpepper remained at Hadorah's house only because he felt so sorry for her. None of the other cops had been brave enough to speak to the old widow. His antsiness was evident in the clenching of his jaw and the way his fingers twitched, a stress habit he thought he'd cured ages before with the help of a lotion his mother had made from sour grapes and mushroom dew.

Alas, no stress was greater than that of a missing not-quite-teenage son, and it was Officer Culpepper's job to deal with it before his patience wore too thin. He would have to find some disagreeable grapes and wet mushrooms later to keep the twitch in check.

"I'm not quite sure what you want us to do, Ms. Mortinson."

"He's a child. He . . ."

"He's nearly thirteen. You know how those monsters are."

Officer Culpepper chuckled; Hadorah did not. Officer Culpepper stopped to write a quick reminder in his journal, accompanied by a doodle of Hadorah's scrunchy face: "Do not make fun of losing a child when the parent is very frowny." He continued, trying to make his voice sound gruff and policelike.

"Give it some time. Could just be out with his friends—I wouldn't even say he was really missing until tomorrow."

He hoped this would be a helpful point. Then again, he didn't have any missing sons. The woman balled her fists yet again.

"If he isn't missing, then where is he?"

Instead of answering, Officer Culpepper struggled with his twitching fingers to write another reminder note: "Find the biggest mushroom in town." Officer Culpepper was rather proud of his happy mushroom doodle and nearly forgot all about Hadorah, who was already tromping back into her house.

Job well done, he thought.

CHAPTER 13

• • •

WHERE WALTER WAS

Rows of bare trees caged Walter and Cordelia into a one-way road. The mist was so dense, it sank below the hearse, only for its silky tendrils to be kicked back up by the wheels, toward the rising sun. Sharp-fingered branches twisted down as if to grab the car right into the air.

The hearse ambled forward, seemingly floating along the empty landscape.

Walter craned forward in his seat, nose nearly touching the steering wheel. He tried his very best not to look at Cordelia again. Walter had been looking at Cordelia approximately once every three minutes—which is far too many times to look at someone who hasn't spoken to you in three hours. The last words Cordelia had said to Walter still swam in his head: "Could you move your arm, please?"

He *had* moved his arm—too fast, incidentally. He'd accidentally knocked the car into reverse, which had been a sticky bit of a situation.

Cordelia hadn't talked after that.

Walter hoped she wasn't having a bad time. He was turning to look at her again—to check if she looked like she was having a bad time—when he remembered he wasn't supposed to do that.

Walter then tried so hard to focus that he hopped right out of his seat when the girl (you know, the one he *definitely* wasn't thinking about) spoke for the second time in three hours.

"Where are we?"

Walter scrambled to regain his composure; he certainly didn't want to look unobservant. "Huh?"

"Where. Are. We?"

Walter dug through his bag to grab the map. He whipped up just in time to avoid slamming into a blackened trunk.

"We are . . . uh . . ."

He stared at the map, knowing every inch but still not clear where he actually was on it. He considered the bright red line he'd been trying to follow. It was more than five hundred miles long. He drew his finger along it aimlessly.

"Somewhere along here."

Cordelia sighed. Sighing was Cordelia's specialty. She had perfected it in school (when Ms. Wartlebug rambled on about how superior ladybugs were to children), at home (when her mother would chastise her for daring to do anything fun), and even at the grocery store (when curious children and their less forgivable mothers would point at her eye patch and whisper).

After a particularly good sigh, Cordelia returned to the journal that had claimed her nose since the beginning of the journey. Walter couldn't help but peek over. He was intrigued by what he saw—a mess of mysterious scribbles.

If you were to ask Walter, he'd say that there's nearly nothing more intriguing than a mysterious scribble.

He turned his head this way and that, trying to decipher the scribbles, but was only able to make out a doodle of Dr. Automaton before the book snapped shut.

Walter was so immersed in the mystery, he didn't notice Cordelia's second specialty—a one-eyed glare.

"So why are you so interested in Dr. Automaton, then?" Walter asked.

"None of your business. Just drive."

"I only wanted—"

"WALTER!"

"I'm sorry. I—"

He leaned away from the screaming girl, snapping his head back to the road. That's when he saw the swarm of butterflies flittering past. They had been disturbed from their place inside a hollowed tree by the bright headlights, and they'd raced out as one and now blocked the hearse's path.

Walter didn't mind dead things so much anymore, but he desperately hated making them that way. Why, he'd walk a good twenty feet out of the way just to avoid tromping on a trail of ants.

Walter was thinking this as the car continued to careen down the road straight toward the swarm.

He promptly slammed into it.

Walter's scream and hundreds of tiny splotches followed.

Cordelia had never seen a dead butterfly before, let alone a *gazillion* of them, and certainly hoped not to repeat the experience. She and Walter stared at the unmoving insects (and some smushed remains) littering the windshield and ground. They were as bright and patterned as quilt squares.

"Do we just drive over them?" Cordelia asked.

"No. They should be given a funeral."

Walter sounded so professional that Cordelia didn't think to question this.

"So . . . what do we do?" she wondered.

"I could bury them," he replied.

This wasn't an ideal situation for her—it would take too long—but at least it would make the dead things less visible. Cordelia didn't care for dead things. "How long will it take?"

Walter scratched his head. "With or without the proper tools?"

"Do you have the proper tools?"

Cordelia's hopefulness was dashed as Walter inspected the empty forest. "I doubt it, and it would take an awfully long time to build so many tiny coffins."

Cordelia allowed herself an annoyed sigh. "Can't we just leave them here?"

"I think that's probably rude, after killing them."

A staring contest ensued, but Walter was doubly as equipped as Cordelia. She sighed again. "Fine."

Walter sat perched at the wheel. He whistled as he drove, a little lullaby on a loop that Cordelia was quickly growing tired of. It was a simple melody that sounded either very old or very made up.

Trying to block the boy out, Cordelia had condensed into a ball in her seat. She was staring behind her, into the back chamber of the hearse. There, in the back, was a large stuffed body bag, inside of which hundreds of dead butterflies shook with every bump in the road.

She couldn't stop thinking about evil butterfly zombies wrapping her in their wings, like a terrified human burrito— when Walter's chipper voice broke Cordelia from her horrible daymare.

"Fortuitous, if you think about it."

Cordelia was glad to be distracted. "What is?"

"That if someone needed to transport dead things, we're particularly well equipped."

Walter proudly tapped the dashboard, where a REST IN PEACE! sign popped out. He pushed it back in, continuing to hum.

Cordelia suddenly wondered if this trip was a very, very bad idea. At least, she thought, it couldn't get worse.

One should never dare think such things.

Moments later Walter hit a large bump in the road.

The ensuing events occurred practically in slow motion. Cordelia saw them before they transpired, but couldn't react fast enough.

The car hit a bump, and a lone loose butterfly jolted up and managed to glide, caught on a wave of wind, straight into Cordelia's gaping mouth.

Cordelia tasted, for the first and last time, a postmortem butterfly.

She screamed and did what any reasonable lady might do.

Cordelia spat that butterfly right out of the car.

There was a silent pause as Cordelia and Walter took in the moment; then Walter spoke.

"That's probably rude too."

CHAPTER 13 ½

. . .

THE LITTLE BLUE TOWN

Elverpool was the kind of bayside town where people forgot both their responsibilities and the importance of wearing shoes.

In this strange society, the inhabitants wore fish scales pressed into their skin as a form of tight-fitting clothing, and they strode barefoot down the muddy streets, like fish with nowhere particular to be. They wore lures in their ears, starfish in their hair, and fins on their nails.

Nearly every Elverpudlian had stringy green hair, dyed from the algae, and cracked, scaly skin, from the sea salt that coated them. Their eyes were extraordinarily round and sat quite far apart. Their noses were thin and stuck against their faces, so flat that most could hardly detect the fishy odor that overwhelmed the town.

Men and women alike had sharp, high cheekbones that

sloped into thin mouths, with teeth that had become smoothed from nibbling on bumpy coral.

Elverpudlians were usually shorter than Moormouthians, with squat limbs and squatter fingers and toes that wiggled out of their hands and feet, forming flippers.

Elverpudlians were very good swimmers, but terrible runners. This hardly mattered. Elverpudlians rarely ever had a reason to run.

They were perfectly tranquil, as is every person unburdened by too much thought. What worries are there to worry about if you'd rather not think?

Those too old to flop into the water and find tasty coral nibblings sat on the pier that encircled the entirety of the town, save for the single road leading in and out.

Right in the middle of town, between Ye Olde Worme Shoppe and the Sand Castle Realty office, was the kind of place you'd remember.

Sturgeon's Rowhouse Gill was just too fishy to forget. First there was the décor (which was a bit sink-or-swim, to be honest).

The restaurant itself was shaped like a massive treasure chest, with real barnacles, as big as beach balls, sucking at the sides. The restaurant's sign was wedged into the split of the chest, keeping it forever ajar.

If you looked closely, you might notice a little silver

sturgeon-shaped jewel that almost seemed to weave between the letters as it glinted in the sun.

Plunged through the top of the building, through a large hole in the roof of the restaurant, was a boatless anchor, seemingly thrust down by an angry god who perhaps had eaten some bad shellfish there once.

The inside was even more chaotic than the outside. From hooks on the ceiling hung wide fishing nets; the paneled walls were held together by melted sea glass; and the booths were rowboats, stranded all over the main floor.

A tired but still optimistic Hadorah sat on one side of a rowboat. A life preserver was squeezed around her very pregnant stomach, boasting FISHING FOR TWO!

Perhaps the most amazing thing was that she had allowed it to be put on her.

The preserver was soon sullied, when Hadorah was sprayed by a thin rain of soup. She looked up, miffed, to see a man more beautiful than every lure in town.

Hadorah felt the frustration melt away, much to her annoyance.

Max's bright yellow soup was being trod by a small mechanical duck he'd just made. It had forks for feet and spoons for a beak. As it happily flapped in its squiggle around the bowl, it emitted mechanical quacks that sounded nearly like the real thing.

Max plucked the little duck from the bowl and plopped it smack down into the middle of the slab of salmon sitting in front of her. Hadorah watched for a moment as the duck out of water attempted to continue its swim. Obliging its attempts, she cut a chunk out of the center of the fish and tipped Max's soup into the basin. It filled quickly, and the duck was swept back into the stream. It swam, quacking once more.

Max shimmied out of the booth and pecked Hadorah on the head as he trotted off. As soon as he was out of sight, however, Hadorah looked down, and her smile vanished.

With two dainty fingers she fished out the duck and held it up to her eyes as it struggled.

Hadorah brought a perfectly polished pinky nail to a tiny screw in the duck's neck as he squirmed. She gently turned twice.

The duck suddenly stopped moving, dangling between her fingers. She dropped him back into the soup. He floated lifelessly. Hadorah then took her first bite of fish as she waved down the waitress.

"Check, please."

CHAPTER 14

SOMETHING FISHY

By now Cordelia had nearly forgotten about their earlier mishaps. She was too consumed in the world of the book she was reading.

Cordelia loved books; she particularly liked the fact that the story had already been written. The ending was entirely unavoidable, which tended to make it easier to swallow; if nothing could have been done differently, then it happened the way it was supposed to. Cordelia always worried about doing things the right way to make sure that nothing bad happened, so this whole "already written ending" thing was a huge relief.

She was the kind of person who liked to read the ending first, in fact, because that way she knew what she was getting herself into. Books, Cordelia had long decided, were much better than real life. So as long as she sat reading, she was thoroughly distracted and thus pleased.

Walter was also preoccupied, but not with stories. His eyes flashed between the girl and the road, now only once every five minutes. He congratulated himself. He hoped she didn't notice.

She did, in fact, but she certainly didn't want to let him know that. Instead she turned the page.

"So . . . ," Walter started. He hadn't yet thought far enough into the future to know what else to say. "I really, uh . . . like rabbits. They have wonderfully sharp teeth, don't they? D-do you like rabbits?"

He then turned to her with a lopsided grin that she ignored. If there was anything Cordelia hated more than cabbage, raisins in cookies, and cherry-flavored medicine, it was people who talked to you when you were reading.

Walter's Adam's apple bobbed as Cordelia curled further into her seat, away from him.

"I like cabbage," he said. He still didn't know what to talk about. This was not the right thing. "Looks like brain. Feels like brain if you cook it. Doesn't taste like brain, though."

He laughed, hoping Cordelia would as well. She didn't. He suddenly felt the need to reassure her. "I've never tasted brain."

He waited for her response. Cordelia turned a page. He took that as a good sign and decided to try his next move, placing one hand in the ashtray between them, hoping to bridge their divide if even by a few inches.

"I'm going to just leave this here, if that's okay."

She turned another page. Walter continued. "So, do you like—"

"I'm reading."

"Oh! Sorry."

That was a cue Walter understood. He turned bright red and rubbed at his neck, muttering to himself in the way he always did when he couldn't quite figure something out. Cordelia cut in, her glance sharper than her tone.

"What did you say?"

"Uh—I was just asking how it is."

There was a pause. Walter waited, breath caught in his throat. *Nothing good can come of this.*

She waved him off. "It's fine."

Or perhaps it can. "What's it about?"

"A girl."

"Oh! That's nice!"

"She dies."

Then again, perhaps not, Walter realized.

Eyebrow quirked, Cordelia turned back to her book, glad to have finally shut him up. She quickly read the last page and closed the book with a sigh, then tossed it onto the pile next to her. Just as she snuggled in for a bit of a break—

"Did she die?"

"Yes."

"Was there a funeral?"

"No."

"That's too bad. No one deserves to—"

"Look, Walter. I may have agreed to accompany you, but I never agreed to be your friend. There's a reason we don't talk at school."

Cordelia waited for a moment to see if he would respond. For the first time all trip, his eyes never left the road.

Nodding to herself, Cordelia curled away again.

Then a very frustrating thing happened: her stomach rumbled, quiet but audible. Walter refused to look. She drew her knees up, hoping to dull the sound, but her stomach groused again. He glanced over as she stared out the window. As he looked away again, she shifted—a big mistake. Her tummy roared, and not like roaring wind, or a roaring sea, mind you. No, it was a lion's roar. Cordelia could no longer keep her face from going bright pink.

Without looking away from the windshield, Walter veered off the main road, right past the sign reading ELVERPOOL CITY LIMITS.

Cordelia anxiously looked at the highway in the distance. "Where are you going?"

"I'm hungry," Walter replied.

Cordelia sighed, thanking her luck as she loosened her grip around her legs.

"I suppose we have time," she said, "but we have to make it fast."

Walter nodded, keeping a small smile off his face. He still wasn't brave enough to look over, but if he had, he might have seen Cordelia's sneer slip for just a second.

The hearse slid onto gleaming streets made of abalone, a pearly shell that washed up often on the Elverpool shore. The duo was in momentary awe as the late-morning sun reflected off the road and lit the sparkling buildings with dancing shadows.

From a distance the ground shimmered in blues and greens, as if the car itself were floating on water.

Walter couldn't help but feel unfortunately conspicuous, a black smudge in a blue town.

His fears were solidified as the townspeople stopped swimming and sunbathing to stare.

No one in Elverpool had ever seen a hearse, as it was a long-held tradition that the deceased were lovingly tossed to sea, with a quick fly-fishing session to follow. Furthermore, no one in Elverpool had a car. There were only boats and feet. No one ever needed to hurry.

To Walter's relief, however, the Elverpudlians had soon had their fill of worrying and turned to their friends to talk about where they would eat or how they had learned to blow bubbles with their spit.

Walter, Cordelia, and the hulking automobile were all but forgotten. Cordelia's hunger, however, was not.

"There. Let's just go there." She pointed to the massive treasure chest that sat in a lump in front of them.

Walter nearly thought to argue, before he remembered whom he'd be arguing with. This establishment didn't look like the kind of place one should be eating at. The open-mouthed chest looked more ready to eat them, in fact. Still, he swiftly parked the car, but staring up at the restaurant, muttered, "I don't—"

"I'm sure it's fine. Come on."

Cordelia barreled out of the vehicle and tromped toward the restaurant. As she pushed past the seaweed hanging in the doorway, Walter watched, too shocked to say anything, as a large barnacle shot a tendril out to grab her—only moments too late. It curled back up in its shell and waited.

Walter had never eaten in a treasure chest before and was already nervous about the dangers that loomed ahead.

Staring at the hungry barnacle, he figured he ought to at least go in through the back.

The interior of the restaurant hadn't changed in thirteen years; neither had the waitress.

As Walter and Cordelia pored over menus, Ria Trout-sputter approached.

She was the single most unhappy person in the world, for good reason—she was wearing her work uniform, a fish costume that looked as though it had swallowed her whole. It was bulbous, rubber, and orange, with scales made of recycled life vests and eyes made of lure bobbles. It hung around her with a perpetually shocked look. With it she wore matching toe rings that squeaked when she walked.

Ria had once had dreams of being a famous actress who made people of all ages sob and sigh, or perhaps being a marvelous chemist who discovered the cure for aging and all of humanity's woes.

Instead she'd grown up to be a halibut, and now everyone was to pay.

"What do you want?" Ria asked.

"I'm sorry?" Cordelia replied.

Ria responded helpfully, as halibut do, "To shove into your faces?"

Cordelia snapped back, as Cordelias do, "Just give us a second, all right?"

Walter offered a smile in place of Cordelia's brush-off. Ria wasn't paying attention anyway; she was too busy setting her watch alarm. A second later it blared.

"Second's up. What do you want?"

Walter, always ready to appease, said the first thing that came to mind—despite having no idea what it meant.

"I'll have the special."

Ria gritted her words through a rehearsed smile. "That shore is an ex-shell-ent de-sea-sion. You?" She turned toward the unamused girl.

"The cod." Cordelia snapped her menu shut and shoved it toward the woman.

"Oh my cod, good choice. If you need anything . . ." Ria trailed off as she trudged away.

Walter's eyes gleamed as he prepared a joke, and for a second, though neither he nor Cordelia would ever know it, he looked quite like his dad. "Well, someone woke up on the wrong side of the seabed."

Cordelia, unimpressed, turned her attention to the bowl of tartar sauce packets, reading the back of one.

Walter may not have been able to stop his blush of embarrassment, but he also couldn't help the giggle that slipped out. *Seabed.*

Meanwhile, the cogs of Moormouth had never stopped turning. The entire town flooded out of the church doors Sunday morning. Hadorah bobbed along with the mob, still wondering where her son was and quietly hoping he didn't end up on her table next.

Behind her, Mrs. Primpet fought through the crowd, keeping pace with the mortician. She shouted to be heard over the yawns and grumbles. "I hear your boy's missing too?"

Hadorah couldn't quite meet the other woman's prying eyes as Mrs. Primpet matched her shuffling gait. "Sorry we haven't had time to talk," Hadorah said, just loud enough for the other woman to hear.

"It's funny how they can't find them, isn't it? A whole police force and just two children."

"I'm not sure 'funny' is the word I'd use."

Mrs. Primpet beamed her curious clown-lipped smile. "And I'm sure you would have said something, but you haven't an itty-bitty inkling of where they might be?"

Hadorah anchored herself to the ground, causing Mrs. Primpet to nearly bump into her.

"No, I don't."

Their uninterested and unconcerned neighbors parted around them, merely glaring at the inconvenience.

"Odd that our kids are together. I didn't realize that they were close anymore," said Mrs. Primpet.

"Neither did I."

Mrs. Primpet smiled. "Well, you'll let us know if you hear something?"

"Of course."

"See you next Sunday, dear!"

With that, Hadorah breathed all the tension out of her body

as she watched Mrs. Primpet disappear into the gloomy crowd like a lighthouse swallowed by the smoke of a wreckage.

Though the sky was clearer a couple hundred miles north-west, the tension was equally thick. Cordelia had, by now, surrounded herself in condiments and was finally on to sugar, her final distraction. Walter, meanwhile, had pried all the prongs off a fork with his pocketknife and was moving on to bend the defenseless spoons.

"So . . . Flaster Isle?" he asked.

Cordelia actively wasn't paying attention. She was, instead, reading the ingredients on the back of a packet. Hm. Apparently there's sugar in sugar packets. She tossed that one aside to read the next. Unfortunately for Cordelia, Walter didn't seem to care that she wasn't responding, as he continued, "To learn more about . . . Well, you know, a lot to learn about in a place like that. Flasterborn asked me to—I mean, I wanted to go see . . ."

Cordelia tried not to sound too interested when she remembered the letter Walter had showed her. It was from Flasterborn? But how? She had been trying to contact him for years, with no response. How had Walter gotten one?

"Is that what the letter was about?" she asked.

"What letter—oh! Uh . . ."

Walter wasn't used to having Cordelia respond to him and had to pause and gather his wits before replying, "Yeah. My dad was, you know, and I am, well . . . Never mind, it isn't important."

"I understand, Walter. You don't have to tell me. I didn't mean to pry." Her voice slinked like a cat, but Walter, who'd never had a cat, didn't know how dangerous that could be.

"No, that's all right! I'll tell you!" he shouted, a bit too loudly. His voice broke as he continued, more quietly, "When my dad worked with him, Flasterborn, I guess . . . I guess they were friends. So Flasterborn has asked me to, possibly, come work for him—sort of."

"Wow! That's amazing." Cordelia surprised both Walter and herself with her genuineness.

"Yeah, well. We'll see. He hasn't actually met me yet."

Walter's tone sank, but Cordelia either didn't notice or didn't care. She barreled forward. "So, he knows you're coming?"

He nodded, causing her grin to ignite as she bubbled in her seat, strategizing. "Fantastic."

"What about you? Why do you want to go to Flaster Isle?"

And just as quickly as Cordelia had opened up, she shut down again. That was not a question she was willing to answer.

She pushed the plate away, not bothering to look up at him. "I'm not hungry anymore."

Ria, with her ever-perfect timing, squeaked up. "From the bottom of our carps, we hope you had a swimmingly good time." She dropped the check onto Cordelia's nearly untouched food, adding, "Gratuity's not included," before flouncing to another table.

Cordelia grabbed a hunk of cash out of her journal and peeled off a few bills.

As the runaways disappeared out the front door, Ria sneered, waving her lolling fish tongue at them. She picked up Walter's bowl and panicked when it wiggled.

The kids turned to look back at the restaurant after hearing the older woman shriek. Then, with a mighty pop, soup splattered across the window in a lovely explosion of yellow and fish guts.

Cordelia's face was blank as she turned to Walter. "What was that?"

"Oh, I managed to put together a little exploder. It's made of octopus, Fizzy Pops, and soda water. Dastardly little thing. She won't get that smell out for weeks."

He turned back to see Cordelia smiling, which made him smile too.

"Who doesn't want to go there? Everybody loves Flasterborn."

"You must really love him if you came all the way here with me."

"I must." Cordelia picked up her third sugar packet, and that was that.

Walter gave up, shoulders sinking. He had never been very good at talking to people who were alive.

Ria returned balancing a bowl and a plate in one hand, while scratching her wagging tail with the other.

"If you need any kelp, drop me a line." She unceremoniously dumped the dishes, and Walter dared a glance up.

"Actually, I would love . . ."

But she had already squeaked off.

He stared into his bowl, a yellow broth littered with swimming bits of fish and the like. A tiny octopus surfaced. He spooned it up and lifted the little thing to eye level—a tentacle hanging limply off the silver edge.

Cordelia looked on, aghast, pushing down a gag. Walter looked up, meeting her disgusted eye.

"Whoops . . ." He dropped the octopus back into the soup, accidentally sending a splash across her white nightgown.

She gasped, wiping at the stain.

"I'm so sorry. Here, let me . . ."

"I'm going to the bathroom."

Walter reached over with his napkin but was too late. Cordelia was already scampering away.

"Cordelia, wait. I can fix—"

But she was gone, trotting through the restaurant, fumbling blindly through her backpack.

Finally she found what she was looking for and pulled out a pill bottle. She spun the cap off expertly. Without thinking, she dropped a pill into her hand and swallowed it dry. Tossing the bottle back into her bag, Cordelia found herself at the end of a promising hallway. She peeked around, making certain it was empty, before proceeding in.

There was a bathroom door on either side of the dead end. On the doors were pearly plaques, one with the word "Cow" and the other with the word "Bull," accompanied by identical silhouettes of manatees.

Between the rooms was a phone in a water-filled glass box mounted to the wall. For this phone, "grimy" was an understatement. It was dusted with a smattering of tiny barnacles sucking away and other bottom-feeders that had, somehow, beached there.

Cordelia pulled a handkerchief out of her pocket and gingerly submerged two fingers into a hole in the top of the box, in order to retrieve the receiver. She had to bat away a curious anemone with her pinky along the way.

After pulling the phone out, she held the speaker a good

six inches from her ear as she dialed a number she found written on the most-opened page of her journal.

"I'd like to be connected with Dr. Automaton. I need an appointment."

She paused, listening to the woman on the other end.

"No, you don't understand. There isn't much time—"

Her whisper was interrupted by heavy footsteps.

"I have to go." Cordelia tossed the phone back into the box, splashing herself, before spinning around, desperately hoping that Walter hadn't caught her.

As the scummy water, mingled with soup, dripped fr∘ her dress, she was both annoyed and relieved to see that intruder was only a cook. He crooked a brow at her b∘ entering the "Bull" side.

Cordelia sighed before pushing open the "Cow∘ already wondering how she was going to scrub th∘ green spot off the white nightdress.

She had been in far too much of a hurry ∘ thought to bring any other clothes. This was so∘ would soon come to regret.

Cordelia returned to the table, looking mor∘ upset than ever before. Walter peered over a∘ with concern.

"Didn't you want to eat something?"

CHAPTER 15

FLASHBACKS AND FANFARE

Hadorah arrived home unsure of what to do. Hadorah *always* knew what to do. But this was a catastrophe. No one would help her find Walter. So she did what she always did when she felt afraid and unsure: she cleaned.

Hadorah clutched the trash can in one hand and a broom in the other as she swept. She tidied the whole house twice.

As she swept the kitchen, she took extra care to get beneath the little crevice under the counter. Amid the dust bunnies was something unexpected. It was small, gold, and circular.

Hadorah stared with instant recognition at the familiar curling letters imprinted in the wax. There was only one *HOF* she knew of: Horace Odwald Flasterborn. Somehow Walter had found the letter. And if Hadorah knew Flasterborn, she knew exactly what it said.

"That no good . . ."

But the rest of her thoughts were lost as she rushed from the room—a new energy rattling in her bones. This was the energy of a mother ready to catch her son doing something he shouldn't be, and catching her son doing something he shouldn't be was something Hadorah knew she could do. Not even fear would stop her.

Walter was driving again and this time had kept his mouth shut. He'd done such a good job, in fact, that while Cordelia wrote the last of her thoughts in her notebook, she secretly hoped to be bothered.

Just as the hearse chugged around a bend, the thin gullet of road opened into the belly of a wide desert. It was the sort of desert that graced the pages of picture books about genies and knights (not the silvery dragon-obsessed knights, though—the Arabian kind). The sands looked like shaved gold, with swirls of heat dancing off the surface. There were no plants and only one rock, under which sat a very grumpy lizard.

Cordelia and Walter both loved this place, if only because they loved picture books. They didn't dare voice these opinions out loud, however, for fear of being judged.

From end to end the landscape was empty, just a vast, glittering sprawl of sand. Walter picked up the pace, sending grains shooting around the tires and behind them in a cloud.

Soon, however, they realized they weren't nearly as alone as they had thought. A group of hazy, colorful blobs took shape ahead in a long line across the plain in front of them.

"What is that?" Walter asked.

Cordelia prepared to respond in an uncaring and slightly annoyed way, only to look up at the mysterious shapes and become curious as well. "Maybe it's a . . . a . . ."

As they squinted into the evening dust cloud, they saw something unsettlingly peculiar.

"It's a parade," she said.

Cordelia was right. The shapes came into view. They were floats. One was a massive, shining sun; another was a roaring lion's face; behind that was a peacock with vast rainbow tail feathers. Now that Walter was close, he realized that the parade was as long as his two eyes (or Cordelia's one) could see, and he was now blocked by its path.

"What do we do?" Cordelia groaned.

"Enjoy the show, I guess."

"Can't we pull around or something? This could take all night!"

Walter chewed on his bottom lip as he tried to see the end of the parade, but it was just too long. He finally shook his head and tugged a thin knitted blanket out of his bag and tossed it onto her. She glowered, before throwing the blanket over her feet and curling away from him.

Walter thought he ought to sleep as well, but he couldn't tear his eyes off the bright floats in front of him. They looked familiar, but he couldn't figure out why.

Four hours later, and the parade had finally let up. The last float was a giant jiggly watermelon.

Walter watched the watermelon bounce after the parade, which had turned in the direction they were moving and was advancing parallel to the road.

Walter could finally drive again, which was wonderful because he'd waited so long. It was also terrible because he was now very tired.

He yawned as he eased the hearse back to life, driving alongside the parade, passing float after float.

He failed to see that Cordelia, still wrapped silently in her blanket, had her one eye wide open. He slurred, trying to keep himself awake and out of his thoughts, "Cordelia? You up?"

Her eye snapped shut. She was hoping not to be caught. It worked. Walter yawned and said more quietly, trying not to wake her:

"I just wanted to say that I'm . . ."

As he trailed off, her heart sped up. . . . *That he what?*

"I'm sorry for staining your dress."

Oh. She feigned a deep breath to cover up her sigh. *Good,* she thought.

"I didn't mean to, and this whole trip . . . I . . . I . . ."

She waited, but the answer never came. She curiously peeked over, becoming concerned . . . just as the car began to swerve.

Cordelia saw that he'd fallen asleep—and was directing the car headlong into one of the floats. She shot up and dragged the wheel back on course, narrowly avoiding disaster.

Walter jerked awake. "Mom, what—!"

His face suddenly became hot as he coughed to cover up the words he's already let slip. When he spoke, he made his voice sound much deeper than it naturally was.

"What's going on?" He took over for Cordelia, nudging her hands away.

"You fell asleep," she said.

"No I didn't. When?"

She shrugged. "The car's veering woke me up."

"Sorry; thanks. I'll pull over at the next stop. Don't worry. You can sleep."

"But if I don't talk to you, you might fall asleep too!"

"It won't happen again."

Cordelia mulled over her limited options, assessing the risk of sleeping and letting the boy certainly follow suit (and probably kill them both), versus the risk of staying up and having to talk to him.

She didn't particularly like either.

"Well, I don't think I can sleep anyway," she said. "This blanket is awful. It's itchy and it has big holes."

"My mom made it."

Cordelia scoffed, hiding a half laugh, then regretted it. "Really?"

Walter refused to look at her, making the girl feel all the worse.

"Sorry. I just didn't see her as the knitting type, is all."

The smile was soon wiped off her face.

"Why? Because of the whole dead-people thing?"

"I didn't mean it like that."

"Or because she's not like *your* mom?"

"She *isn't* like my mom—"

"Or is it because you think she killed my dad?"

There it was. The silence she used to wish for, yet now it felt deafening.

Walter inwardly cursed as he got ahold of himself again. Unfortunately, there was no invention that he could think of that would let him go back in time; he'd spent years trying.

"Sorry. I'm just tired." His voice betrayed a weariness that went beyond that night, and Cordelia wasn't foolish enough to pretend she didn't recognize it.

Her voice was even quieter than his. "I don't think she did it."

"Did what?"

"Killed your dad."

"Yeah, well, you're the only person in Moormouth, then, I guess."

He finally cracked a smile that she returned, despite neither of them thinking it was particularly funny.

"I think it's . . . nice that she knits. My mom doesn't knit."

"Neither does mine. Can't you see? It has big holes."

Now they both smiled, big honest ones, as Cordelia observed the brightly colored woven mess.

"It's nice."

Walter smiled even wider. He found a bravery deep within himself that was reserved for when he was feeling particularly senseless or sleepy. "Would you mind grabbing something out of there? It's a brown book."

Cordelia looked around, before realizing that he was pointing to his bag by her feet. With a previously unknown urgency she sought to please him.

She rifled through the clothes, deciding not to question the choice of two pairs of long johns and a pair of swim trunks, and emerged with the little leather album. On the cover was an intricately etched flower. One side looked light, while the other was in shadow.

"It's . . . nice?"

"Second page."

She fumbled with the plastic-covered sheets, cracking the book open. Then she faltered, staring at the first page, where an image had been pasted of young and beautiful versions of Hadorah and Maxwell, holding baby Walter outside their house . . . the same house that Cordelia had been told to avoid as a child. It struck her just how sad it was that they looked so happy. Realizing she was being watched, Cordelia flushed and flipped to the second page.

It was a faded photograph of toddlers in a line. They wore uniforms nearly identical to the black-and-gray suit Walter had on now.

Three-year-old Walter, with a mess of orange curls and a slate-colored hound's-tooth tie, stood at one end. He looked utterly terrified as he stared at the camera. Next to him, however, was a smiling schoolgirl—cherubic with two blue headlights for eyes and curled ribbons in her hair. She was only just recognizable as a miniature version of the girl holding the book between her shaking hands. Cordelia looked closely to see if it was as she had remembered . . . and it was. The two toddlers' fingers just touched.

"Is that you?" she asked.

Walter nodded. "Maybe we were friends?" He waited for the response, a second too long.

"Maybe," Cordelia finally replied.

She snapped the book shut, controlling her breathing as

best she could. Cordelia shoved the book back into the back-pack, careful not to bend it. She waited a moment to let the air clear, but found she couldn't stand the silence anymore.

"So what makes them go?"

His eyes followed her finger pointing to the unmanned peacock float ahead.

"Could be lots of things."

"That's all you've got? Aren't you supposed to be some kind of genius?"

He smiled to himself in a way that she found utterly infu-riating, and said, "Not everything is so complicated."

"What, is it magic?"

"Mechanics *aren't* magic?" He side-eyed her, but she was yawning. He looked away quickly so as not to be caught staring. "We can stop soon . . . even though you aren't tired."

Cordelia stifled a second yawn before nodding slightly. Her eyes had already begun to droop against her better judg-ment. "I'm not, but I might sleep a little bit . . . just until morning or so."

"Me too. We have places to be, right?"

Cordelia nodded again, curling up in the seat once more. She jolted back awake when Walter hit the brakes.

"I'm not asleep!" Cordelia declared.

"No. Look . . ."

The float ahead had stopped in the middle of the waste-land. Small beings, lemurlike, with long noodley limbs, trudged out of the bottoms of the floats. They were only two feet at the tallest. The massive floats deflated as the creatures marched out, hundreds of them, stretching after a long day's work. They made no sound but gestured to one another as if speaking. It was almost as if they could read one another's thoughts.

How very strange.

Suddenly, as the tiny beings departed and the colorful skins of the parade lay motionless, Cordelia and Walter came to the same bizarre conclusion.

The little beings were what had made the parade go.

Walter's voice was practically a whisper, but Cordelia still heard him when he said, "And some things are more compli-cated than you might expect."

Cordelia stretched her neck out the window, staring as the parade creatures disappeared into the night. "Where are they going?"

"Maybe the parade is over."

As Cordelia looked at the floats, she suddenly remembered the last time she'd seen them, as a little girl. With a pang of reproach she spat, "It doesn't go through Moormouth any-more, but it used to. It's the Summer Solstice Parade."

"But it isn't summer."

"Exactly. The parade goes until the solstice. I don't think it ever stops moving, really."

"But what about when the summer solstice is over?"

"It becomes the Winter Solstice Parade."

Walter was too tired to think about the never-ending parade. The desert was wide and strange, and now felt unnerving without the sun to make the sand glitter or the floats to brighten their way. They had to get off the road and find somewhere safe to sleep, so he pressed his foot on the gas and went faster now than ever before.

Hadorah knew where Walter had gone, but she had no way to follow. He had taken her only means of transportation.

She stopped in her tracks, just short of the porch.

Or had he?

Hadorah circumvented the house, heading for a place she had let vanish from her mind for years.

Going into the backyard wasn't easy. She fought with the coils of overgrown weeds and hiked through the hip-high grass. (If Walter had been there, she mused, he probably would have been concerned about hippopotamuses, or whatever else he was always getting on about.) She banished the thoughts as she stared at an old mechanized carriage, gears covered in dirt, dust, and whatever else, the metal horses at the front wrapped in vines. Hadorah had blamed this vehicle for many things, and now it was going to have to be put back to work. She desperately hoped it wouldn't disappoint her again.

She pulled away one of the bougainvillea creepers to get a better look at the condition of the contraption. The once-shiny silver iron had been eaten away by rust and inattention. The idea of driving it once more was terrifying, but it had to be done.

Hadorah nearly tripped. She was surprised to look down and see the vine she had detangled, now wrapped around her leg. What an unfortunate coincidence, she thought, stepping out of it. Walter would have imagined that the vine had a mind of its own.

Hadorah just saw a plant, and as with anything that got in Hadorah's way, she knew just how to fix it.

"Now, where did I put that hatchet?"

Hadorah tromped off, not bothering to look back—for if she had, she might have seen something that her son would not have missed: the slight quake that ran through the bush as it considered its imminent demise.

CHAPTER 15 ½

• • •

THE BEARDED BABY

H adorah sat beside Maxwell. She was already pregnant but not yet bursting at the seams. Her rotund belly pressed up against the carriage door as she considered the peculiar landscape. The dusty dirt road had morphed into something muddier and cobbled. The massive mechanical horses lead the way, hooves chattering as they plonked from stone to stone.

The dirt beyond was pocked with hundreds of pits, as if a great colony of moles had had their fill of it. Maxwell, humming to himself, nearly drove right into one.

"Whoops! Sorry, Haddy."

Hadorah ignored him, and squashing her nose against the window, she realized these were no mole holes at all—they were much, much too wide, and dreadfully deep. They were man-size. Hadorah suddenly thought this trip might not be a good idea.

The cobbled lane branched into a smaller path, just wide enough for the carriage. Hadorah and Max followed it, deeper and deeper into this strange place. Still, she saw no signs of life save for the trees that were growing ever more frequent. These were the tall, fluffy variety of trees that looked like they might house a nice squirrel family or a wise owl that solved riddles (you know the type). In fact, Hadorah was to learn, they bore a very different kind of life.

She gasped when the houses came into view. Instead of being built on the ground, the log cabins were plopped right on the trees themselves, perched all the way at the very tippiest-toppiest of the frothy green branches.

Shrew's Borough was a city in the sky.

This odd little place was evidently trying to keep out of the way of other people, or else keep other people away from it.

The buildings crowded together, the spaces between crisscrossed by rope ladders that led to the ground. Hadorah watched, bewildered, as the branches shook. When she refocused on the inner workings of the trees, she saw Boroughers climbing from door to door. They were miners, all of them, with headlamps and plaid shirts. They were bearded, too, even the women and the children. Their facial hair was groomed into braids and curls and coifs—the pride of everyone who grew them.

Hadorah was particularly mesmerized by a baby miner,

cheeks as big as her eyes, helmet nearly sliding off her head. She was strapped to her mother's burly chest, and the older woman swung through the trees. The baby had a wide grin stretched under her wispy handlebar mustache.

Having spotted some of the tree-dwellers, Hadorah now noticed the whole of them, hundreds scampering through their airborne colony with ease.

Hadorah wouldn't have liked living in a tree, she thought, nose scrunched. For one thing, there were too many people for such a small place, and not nearly enough land to live on. As a consequence, Hadorah realized, they had to build up . . . and certainly these trees were very, very far up, past even the clouds coursing around the town.

Wait. Clouds?

Hadorah peered out the window and then promptly shrieked. Shrew's Borough was hundreds of feet in the air, perched on a perilous cliffside.

Why, of all the places, had her infernal husband brought her to this one?

"Because someone needs my help."

Of course, she thought. *Someone always needs his help. He's* Maxwell. Her face grumped into a deep grimace. Sometimes she wished she were the only one who loved him. It hardly seemed fair that she had to share him, especially when no one except for Maxwell seemed to want to share *her.*

As the horses plonked their last plonks, Max and Hadorah came upon a band of miners carving a cave into a molehill. One miner, a man with big floppy earlobes and a bigger, floppier beard, could just be seen in the back of the dark cave, manning a massive automated drill. The thing sparked and fizzled, chugging through the mountainside with furious growls. But as soon as the floppy man had started making headway, the drill sparked, lighting some green substance in the dirt. The green stuff abruptly burst into flames. Two miners nearby leapt onto the fire, suffocating it with blankets as the floppy miner yelped, his beard ablaze. The helper miners then leapt onto *him*, smothering his beard and smacking him to the ground in one brave swoop.

The monstrous machine continued chugging, causing havoc as it spun. Hadorah just managed to make out a gold *F* emblem on the side of the drill as it barreled into a group of onlookers. A meaty fist grabbed the handle, just in time.

Hadorah's gaze traveled up the burly arms of the hero and rested on the woman's stern face. She was missing a front tooth. Hadorah simply didn't trust people who were missing their front teeth. She was prejudiced like that.

But that didn't much matter to the woman. Her long mustache was double braided into her longer beard, which swept in the wind behind her as she squinted at the carriage. Hadorah couldn't meet her hard glare, piercing through the windshield. She sunk into her seat, hoping to disappear.

Maxwell didn't feel the same, jumping out, instantly shouting, "Good rummage, Galena?"

"Better tomorrow, Mortinson."

Galena was at least one and a half Maxwells tall and three wide. They shook hands firmly, then grasped each other in a half embrace, Max quickly lost in the folds of her body.

Galena pushed him away finally, shouting, "Awful nice of you to inventerize a replacement. Now, where is it?"

Hadorah could feel the carriage shake underneath her as Max stepped up onto the side, to untie the invention on the roof.

"Well, lookie here!" Miners surrounded the device.

It was a massive spinning top, painted a brilliant sky blue, with green swirls twirling down the sides. Hadorah watched but couldn't hear as Max brought the group of miners, led by a fascinated Galena, back over to the mine. They huddled around him as he wound a long rope through a hole in the top, then handed the rope over to the floppy-lobed gentle-miner. Floppy grabbed the rope with one hand and held the handle on the top firmly with the other. He then closed his eyes as he yanked the rope out. The crowd gasped and parted as the top spun.

Unfortunately, Floppy had never let go, so he spun too.

The top zoomed toward the mountain and barreled easily

into the hole, creating a deep cavern as it dizzied itself. Finally it quieted. Moments later Floppy reemerged, triumphant and wobbly. Miners cheered and converged on him.

But then there was the matter of the old Flasterbornian drill, sputtering and sparking in the middle of the cave floor. Galena parted the crowd, trudging over to it. She grabbed a pickax and thrust the tip deep into the machine. The beast whined and then fell silent for good.

The crowd chanted Max's name as they tossed his tiny frame above them.

Hadorah never got used to being with Max. Of course, she thought, he was wonderful, but it was hard sometimes when she realized that everyone else felt the exact same way. She secretly wished that someone else would one day think she was wonderful too.

CHAPTER 16

• • •

DREG AND THE TERMITONOUS

Walter didn't know it, but he had parked in a town far different from the one his parents had passed through those many years before.

The forest was now gone, leaving dirt flats in its wake. The only surviving trees were skeletons, their thin riblike branches having long ago given up. They could no longer hold up any homes and were now empty. In the dark of night this looked like a sad place.

The main feature that had remained was the massive cave mouth roaring out of the ground. On its rock face had been sculpted a mighty mole, his mouth open wide, pig nose snuffling up, and granite teeth flashing in the moonlight. The cave's giant mole hands, with their big banana fingers, seemingly pushed the earth around them to the sides, creating little hills.

But none of this did Walter know. For one thing, his mother had never told him about her and his father's travels. For a second thing, it had been very dark when he'd clunked onto the cobbled road, and he hadn't seen much other than the skeletal trees lining one side, which had looked more like looming shadows in the night.

He had been desperately tired, fighting the fingers of sleep that beckoned him. He'd had just enough mind to pull off onto the road made of rocks and mud.

Walter hadn't thought it odd at the time, a road made of mud. Perhaps most people, even most sleepy people, would have felt the rough desert sand give way to the slippery stones and would have thought: *Huh, isn't this peculiar? I, a normal person, dislike peculiar things, so I'll find another road.* Unlike for most people, Walter's fear of the abnormal didn't exist. If you asked him, in fact, he'd say that normal was quite a bit scarier than abnormal. "Normal" meant working in a big factory making toothbrush bristles. "Normal" meant the gray people who had whispered behind his and his mother's backs after his father had died.

"Normal" meant not special.

Walter had thought this way often, which meant he had gotten into trouble often—but it also meant that Walter experienced things normal people never do.

He had slipped along the curious road, unaware as the

endless dirt flats on either side had given way to an equally endless drop off the face of a very tall cliff.

In the darkness it had looked as if the landscape were high up in the clouds. Coils of mist had sunk below the rocky edge, sifting with treacherous serenity. Had Walter swerved an inch farther when he'd parked, he would have careened unknowingly over the edge, and, consequently, he and Cordelia would have had a morning involving considerably more dying. Cordelia didn't much like dying, so it was fortunate they hadn't.

Walter had situated the car safely in front of the twelve-foot-tall mole statue (which, if you're not good at measurements, is a bit larger than an average mole) and behind a very large pile of trash. Again, for any normal person, a very large pile of trash would probably have been concerning, but Walter hadn't seen the mound when he'd laid the rumbling automobile to rest.

If we're being honest, it wouldn't have much mattered. Walter loved a good pile of possibilities.

As the sun rose over the odd little place, it shot light skipping across the fading fog. Shrew's Borough, seemingly made of near-black shadows the night before, was starkly different when met by morning. The many tones of rock—from the reds to the yellows to the browns—radiated sunny warmth.

The hearse stood fast on the side of the cliff. No one was

around to notice it, except for the miner sitting on the edge of the crag nearby. He sat wide legged, a fishing pole over the side of the ledge, a large helmet tipped over his forehead. Excited, he reeled the line up through the fog. On the end of his pole was a shoe.

"Dagnabbit, another 'un."

Disappointed, he tossed it onto the slumbering hearse.

He hadn't seen the kids, so he didn't know he was burying them in garbage. They were unconscious, so they didn't know either. How horribly, horribly unlucky.

Unless, per chance, you love trash.

Walter stirred when the moss-encrusted tongue of a boot slapped against his windshield. Befuddled, he rubbed his crust-encrusted eyes. *That can't have been a boot flying by its tongue,* he thought. He had invented those only a month ago. . . . Then a broken lightbulb came flying into view next, interrupting his thoughts.

Somewhere between concerned and intrigued, Walter slipped outside, wading through the growing cover of garbage along the way, cautious not to wake Cordelia, who was snoring in the passenger seat. He didn't think she'd like his plan.

Drat, thought Dreg. *This ain't it neither.* He pulled the open Worm Crunchies bag off his fishing line and tossed it onto the growing rubbish heap behind him.

The young miner, whose beard hadn't yet reached his chest, was tired of near misses. This was Dreg's first job, see. Well, actually, "job" is maybe too big a word. This was Dreg's first big scheme (of many to come). He had been scheming for a while but had yet to get rich. This fact he found very, very confusing.

"It ain't called a get-rich-quick *job*, shoot," he mumbled to himself.

Dreg had devised his scheme in order to buy Opal—who had the most beautiful, densest sideburns in the colony—a new handle for her pickax, one that would match her favorite plaid overalls. To earn money and, consequently, prove his love, he was fishing for trash. Not just any trash, however. Dreg was fishing for *expensive* trash.

All sorts of things got thrown into the Pit—that's what Boroughers referred to the cliff basin as. Rarely, treasured mining ore got lost down there among the rubbish, whether it flew off into someone's shoe while they were drilling or became caught in their mustache, then flicked down the drain—sometimes the ore seemed to even disappear on its own. Boroughers didn't like losing their ore. Dreg was happy to sell it back to them for more than it was worth . . . if he could just find some already.

He knew that if he didn't work quickly, Frazil, who had a freakishly long goatee (that was most certainly fake, if you asked Dreg), would buy Opal a plaid handle first. And then Dreg could kiss those beautiful sideburns good-bye.

Suffice it to say, Dreg took his scheme very seriously.

One of his greatest fears was that others would catch on to his brilliant plan. He hadn't even yet considered that someone might leech off his work. He'd spent so much time and effort pulling the trash up out of the Pit, and some fiend could have been picking through it when his back was turned. This realization occurred to Dreg as he heard a rustle behind him.

"What the . . . Who's that scrambling in there?"

Dreg dropped his big hairy hand into the pile—scratching it uncaringly across buckets, drill bits, and beard combs along the way. Like all Boroughers, Dreg's skin had thickened up and was elephantine, from years in the mine.

Meanwhile, Walter clung to the inner trash as long as he could, desperately trying to reach for his prize. He'd seen a flash of whatever it was when he'd first hopped in, and he just had to find it. In his last few moments he succeeded, extracting his reward from the innards of a rusted tin can. Clutched in his fist was a small, curiously glowing sphere. It reminded Walter of a marble. Walter had big plans for this marble.

Just then Dreg pulled the red-haired boy out with one hand and held him at nose height by the scruff of his collar.

"Who goes there?"

Dreg had read this phrase in a book once and hoped it

had the same effect now as it had on the characters in the story. Unfortunately for Dreg, Walter was more confused than intimidated.

"Goes where?"

"Here—ya know, right here where we is." Dreg scratched his head with his free hand as he surveyed the rubbish. "Who goes here?"

"Where is here?"

"Ya know, in this town—er—in this trash pile! Who goes in this trash pile? Naw, that's not it. I mean . . ."

Walter wriggled out of the fumbling miner's grasp.

"Do you want to know who I am?" Walter asked.

Satisfied, Dreg nodded, smiling widely, before remembering that he should have a serious face. "Yeah. Who are ya?"

"I'm Walter."

Dreg felt proud that he had extracted information out of his prey . . . but he wasn't quite sure what to do with it.

"Oh . . . yeah . . . Walter. Well, Walter, I am Dreg."

Dreg ended the declaration by pounding on his chest. Walter held out his hand. Confused, Dreg engulfed it in his meaty catcher's mitt. Walter guided Dreg's fist up and down, grunting with the effort of it.

"Nice to meet you, Dreg."

"Nice-in-ta meet ya too."

Walter nodded, slipping himself out of Dreg's fist. He

proceeded to brush himself off as Dreg tried to rearrange his wits.

Walter knew his way around a bully and figured he'd do what he usually did and ignore this one. He pretended Dreg wasn't even there as he inspected his new treasure. The marble-thing just fit inside Walter's pinched fingers. It was green, sort of. As Walter turned it in the light, the marble reflected blues and pinks, but when Walter tried to find them again, they were replaced with oranges and yellows. *Marvelous*, he thought.

Little did he know that Dreg was peering to see what Walter was holding and didn't seem to find it wonderful at all. His face puffed up twice its normal size as he bellowed: "THIEF!"

Walter knew that when bullies turned red and screamy, it was time to go. He darted across the pile, trying not to stumble along the way. Years in the junkyard had taught him how to balance on garbage. Dreg was not so practiced, but his massive feet crunched through it with natural talent.

"STOP, THIEF!"

Walter whipped his key out as he made it to the hearse. He tried to turn the key gently so as not to wake Cordelia. He didn't suspect she would like odd miner business. And while he was right—she definitely didn't like odd miner business—unfortunately, Walter didn't even get a chance to enter the car. Cordelia had already awoken, and he hadn't anticipated the fury she'd brewed up.

The poor boy had no idea that one of her worst fears in the whole world was being buried alive.

Just as Walter opened the door, he realized Cordelia was no longer inside. In her panic, she'd swum out, straight into the garbage.

His head whipped around. Where could she be?

He jumped as Cordelia's trash-covered form erupted from the gut of the mountain of stink.

"GRAH!"

One of her hands was lost in a bottle with murky contents, the other in a toilet roll tube; her once-white nightdress was stuck with old newspaper; and her head had become lodged in a rusty radio, covering her face and blinding her completely.

To be honest, it wasn't her best look.

Upon seeing her, Dreg and Walter blanched—but for very different reasons. As Walter tried to think of a way to make her less inclined to scream, Dreg was too busy being terrified.

You see, Cordelia may have been petrified of being buried alive, but Dreg had an equally strong fear of something called the Titanous Termitonous.

Perhaps you have heard of the boogeyman—an ugly, oogley fellow who lives below children's beds and munches their toes when they fall asleep. Moormouth's boogeyman was called Laxidaisyskull, a skeleton that followed you around, knees clacking, if you didn't work hard enough. In Shrew's Borough there was no boogeyman nor Laxidaisy-skull. Instead they feared the queen herself: the Titanous Termitonous.

As Dreg had been told when he was only a nugget, the Termitonous is a woman-size termite, dredged up from the depths of the Pit, who had an appetite for so much wood that she could devour a forest in one buggy bite. Once all the tops of the trees had been eaten, she would look for more food below, in the Boroughers' dwellings, underground. She had a particular fondness, Dreg suspected, for children's flesh.

And while Dreg would swear up and down that he didn't believe in such foolish things as the Termitonous (especially in front of Opal . . . *Frazil* definitely didn't believe in such childish legends), deep, deep down in his belly, he had hoped never to meet the Termitonous.

As Cordelia wailed, radio antenna jutting out of her head at odd angles, hands elongated into points, Dreg's childhood fears came scuttling back.

Cordelia stumbled in a zigzag toward him (admittedly, unknowingly). She even tripped and nearly landed straight on him. But Dreg was too fast; he shot away, unseeing . . . straight toward the hearse.

CHAPTER 17

• • •

MERRY MAD MINERS

It was pitch black in the mine, the only light coming from the headlamp on Dreg's bobbing helmet. Walter and Dreg had been stumbling down a carved rock slope for a while, and Walter was growing more and more afraid of what waited for them at the bottom.

In fact, Walter was worried about a great many things.

Who was this miner boy holding him, and why was he so big? More important, was Cordelia all right? Had she stumbled off the side of the cliff? And what about the car? Would he be able to fix it? Would they ever get to Flaster Isle? . . . Would Hadorah be very mad? This absurd thought stopped his worries in their tracks.

Of course she would.

But he had no time to fear what his mother would say, for

Walter had to dive under the trash again to avoid getting squashed by Dreg's barrel body as he came tumbling by, wailing.

But hold that thought! Remember that Boroughers are approximately a smudge bigger than Moormouthians—a "smudge" being quite large. Dreg was the runt of his family, and the tippy-tops of Walter's curls just brushed Dreg's chest. In Moormouth little Dreg would have been stared at as he trudged through town, because no one in Moormouth had ever seen a man so big . . . let alone a bearded child.

Now, imagine that a massive child like that came hurling at you at a speed so fast, it's only ever reached by people being chased by bears or by children who are very afraid (who are also, sometimes, running from bears). Imagine his flapping boots, the size of toolboxes, stomping inches from your head as you huddle on the floor under a pile of Pit trash. Imagine that very big, very fast boy slamming into the side of your car—parked just on the edge of a very high cliff.

"No!" Walter screamed as he heard the horrible thwack of Dreg's hip meeting metal.

The car creaked ominously, giving Dreg just enough time to fall back safely onto his globular behind. He hadn't been paying attention to where he was running, only that it was away from the Termitonous. Now he could only gawp at the mess he'd made.

The hearse rocked onto the lip of the mountain, before the edge of the cliff below inevitably gave way. The black car dove into the Pit, trash falling behind like fluttering leaves in its wake.

Walter ran to watch as it clunked and thunked down the rocky face and then rumbled to a dusty stop at the bottom. His head now filled with fuzz, his eyes growing hot with fear, Walter whispered to himself, "Mother is going to be very, very displeased."

Walter then glanced at Dreg. Dreg, however, had his eyes trained on Cordelia—who was still blissfully unaware of this whole disaster.

"Argh!" She released a guttural sound as she finally pried her arm free of the bottle it had been stuck in. In a shot, Dreg's face morphed from fear to anger.

When Walter then hurried over to pry her other hand out of the toilet roll tube, Dreg was steaming.

"Y-y-ya tricked me!"

Walter, befuddled and affronted, shouted back, "I did nothing of the sort! You wrecked my car!"

But Dreg was not listening, already shaking his head. As he saw Walter struggle to free Cordelia, Dreg came stomping over. "Ya done shammed me! Pretendered to be the Termitonous just to steal my spoils!"

Walter had stopped listening, trying to tug Cordelia's head

out of the radio. Dreg continued, lacing his fingers easily around Walter's thin arm. "I ain't lettin' ya get away with it!"

Dreg yanked Walter away from Cordelia, who stumbled, falling back onto the trash with a yelp. Walter struggled to get free as Cordelia did the same, her voice echoing inside the radio.

"Walter? What's going on?"

But Walter could only get out a "Cor—" before Dreg carried him off, straight into the mouth of the giant mole.

he was constantly distracted by his captor, who seemed to only want to squabble.

"Quit squirmin'!"

"I can't; that's my arm!"

"Yeah, well, that's my ore!"

"I don't even know what you're talking about! My friend is up there, and I need—"

"Oh, sure, and I bet the Titanous Termitonous means nothing to ya neither!"

"In fact, it doesn't!"

Dreg huffed, having had well enough of the thieving boy. He heaved him into the air effortlessly and tucked him up under one arm. The two continued, Dreg tromping downward.

"If yer gonna act like a sack of worms, might as well carry ya like one!"

Walter could feel the ooze of the other boy's armpit soak into his only shirt. He was too troubled by this to listen to Dreg's mutterings.

"Stupid teeny thieves. Bet this is Frazil's fault, stupid goatee. We'll see what Ms. Galena says about it. Stupid car— shouldn't of even been there, and they thought they could sham me. Well, I never . . ."

Walter was distracted instead by his surroundings. As the

beam of the headlamp cascaded over the walls, Walter saw something increasingly peculiar. While most of the stone cavern was a reddish sort of brown, there were odd streaks through it. These streaks were green and glowed faintly.

As they descended, the streaks became larger and more frequent. The veins gradually wove through the walls, into patterns and braids. In these greater concentrations, the green stone glowed much more brightly, lighting the way softly. What was more, now Walter could see that the streaks weren't all green—when he looked at the stone one way, it appeared to be blue, from another way yellow, even pink.

Just like his marble.

Walter felt in his pocket, fingering the little sphere. He held on to it, pushing all of his worries into it. Cordelia would be fine, he thought, squeezing the marble tightly. The car would be fine, he thought, squeezing it more tightly. Hadorah might be only a little bit mad, he thought, squeezing it tightly-est. It would all be all right—it had to be.

And somehow, having that little green marble in his fist made him feel a bit better. After all, this glowing rock should be impossible, but here it was, all around him. Maybe impossible things *could* happen.

This was what Walter chose to focus on—hope—as they descended, farther and farther, into the depths of the unknown.

• • •

Cordelia, meanwhile, was not nearly so hopeful. No. Cordelia was, to put it lightly, miffed. To put it strongly? Murderous.

She was finally able to rip the radio from her head, along with a small patch of hair. She squealed as it went, tossing the wretched thing right off the side of the mountain.

Wait. Mountain?

She did a double take as she looked back down the cliff-side. Gasping, she stumbled away. As she backpedaled, she tripped, falling to the ground with an awful clatter. She collided with an old, massive drill bit, causing her to skin her knee. Wincing, she pressed against the scrape to hold in the blood.

"Oh, for goodness' sake!" she said.

Cordelia yanked at the bottom of her nightdress, pulling off a long strip. Without having to look, she tied it tightly around her wound.

She then pulled herself up and looked around, the glint of her anger visible in her sharp gaze. This was Walter's fault. It had to be, and he would pay for it.

As she made a list in her head of all the punishments she could possibly give him, she scoured the landscape.

Realizing there was no one else for miles, she was worried that, perhaps, she had been stranded there. Suddenly fear cracked through her angry shell. Had Walter abandoned her? Had she really been that unpleasant to be around?

Cordelia shook her head, tossing away the thoughts. No, he wouldn't have done that. Maybe someone else, but never Walter.

She spun, taking the sad, empty landscape in with renewed energy. The fear was pushed back by anger once more, something she felt comfortable with. She wouldn't allow herself to be scared. She would just have to find Walter.

But where could he be?

After a brief investigation Cordelia decided that there was only one place to go: into the mine.

This normally would have frightened Cordelia quite a bit, but nothing frightened Cordelia when she had murder on her mind.

By the time Dreg had plodded down the final few stairs, his captive flopping at his side, Walter had noted that the walls here were made up more of the mysterious stone than regular rock. The pair no longer needed the headlamp; the whole cave was bathed in a soothing glow.

With a final hop, Dreg tossed Walter to the ground. The boy fell in a heap, the marble rolling from his hand. . . . At least, it should have rolled. But the marble was no longer a marble. Somehow, having been squeezed in his fist, it had taken on that shape—a sort of squashed star thing, with peaks where his fingers had pushed in and a rounded bottom where his palm had been. If he were to look closely, he would have even seen the spiderweb lines of his hand imprinted into the stone.

Walter was flummoxed. He had been quite sure this thing was solid and not squeezable. But there it was, and for a second, he thought, he could even see it beating to the rhythm of his unusually fast pulse.

Then someone grabbed him by the arm. Walter had to snatch the thing up again quickly as he was snatched up by someone else.

He heard her raspy voice before he saw her.

"Now, whatten we have here?"

Dreg piped up, "A thief, Ms. Galena, ma'am!"

Her body was thick and round, like a globe. Around the globe had been wrapped a swath of dirtied denim. She wore coveralls that were rolled up at the arms and legs—and, boy, what arms and legs they were, as thick as tree trunks and covered in hairs the size of toothpicks. By the time Walter saw the woman's face, it had already become violently red in anger.

"A thief?!"

Walter quickly and correctly noted that Galena did not like thieves, like a number of other people he knew.

She brought him inches from her huffing mouth, surrounded by black, twisted beard hairs, tinged with gray.

"We don't take kindly to thieves in the Borough, young 'un."

Her breath smelled vaguely of dirt, and for a moment Walter saw her lips curl up enough to reveal a single . . . green tooth?

"Factwise, we don't take kindly to intruders of any nature, even little 'uns."

Walter found his breath caught in his throat, the same feeling he had when he sat across from his mother as she read one of his disciplinary notes from school. Suddenly, and for the first time in his entire life, Walter thought he'd rather like to be there instead of here. Galena squinted at him before spitting on the ground. "Prove you ain't one."

A whisper rushed through the cavern, causing Walter to look around. He was at the bottom, it seemed, of the cave—but from this place dozens of other paths had been drilled. In front of many were welcome mats. Walter saw big bearded miner faces peering out of the holes, watching from the mouths of their cave homes as the impending action unfolded.

Walter then noticed that many more miners were standing in the wide, open gut of the mine, spanning surprisingly far around. The miners were armed with colorful spinning top drills and equally colorful hard hats.

That, however, was not the most notable thing in the mine.

The most notable thing in the mine was that there was a vast river of the glowing green rock bleeding through it. They had even constructed a bucket system that carefully scooped up the warm liquefied rock and hauled it into the many off-shoot tunnels. This was what they mined for, the mysterious stone, just like the nugget Walter held gripped in his palm, beating in time with his own heart, which had begun to speed faster and faster. The giant woman held him between two sausage fingers, right in front of her furious face.

Walter croaked, "I'm sorry." He then reached up a hand to hers, trying to dislodge himself; but along the way he dropped his marble. A gasp echoed around them. Walter gulped, and Galena became far, far redder than before.

An angry roar then filled the chamber as the miners all halted their work. Galena spat as she shouted, "Bring me my Round About."

Galena swung Walter easily to the side as she was handed a particularly large and pointy-looking red spinning top drill. "Let's see if the innards of a thief are as sweaty as the outside!"

The group roared again. Walter's mouth was now hanging open. This had gone from unfortunate to disastrous in a matter of moments. Mother had always said that such things were like that, but Walter had rarely listened to her.

Two long-armed miners grabbed him and held him up by an arm and a leg each.

"Put him up there, I 'magine. That's the target." She squinted one eye, pointing a thumb toward the back wall of the Pit. The miners carried Walter over and suspended him against the wall.

Walter's throat was becoming tighter and tighter as the miners gathered around. Still, he managed to squeeze out a few words, "There's been a misunderstanding. . . ." But that was all he was able to say before one of the long-armed miners stretched a finger across Walter's mouth, clamping it shut.

Meanwhile, Dreg, for his part, was standing to the side looking quite pale. For the first time he genuinely wondered if a plaid pickax was really worth someone else's life.

If Walter had thought his descent into the miner's cave was unpleasant, he would be glad to not go with Cordelia.

For one thing, she would have made him suffer. For another, he had at least had a guide (who, okay, perhaps *had been* making him suffer—but the world isn't always a perfect place).

Cordelia was forced to make the decline by herself without any light. It meant quite a bit of stumbling, toe-stubbing, and knee-scraping.

She was particularly relieved when the walls began lighting themselves. Though, unlike Walter, she didn't question it. She was just happy to see again.

The scramble down was still long, but far more tolerable, allowing her anger to mount again. She discovered that she wasn't the only one ready to scream, however, as angry shouts began to drift their way up the tunnel. Once she heard Walter's voice, she felt compelled to walk a bit faster.

It wasn't, of course, because she wanted to help him, she insisted. No, it must have been that she was intent on being the one to finally kill him.

Actually, I suppose Walter would have rather descended into the mine with Cordelia, for the simple reason that then he probably wouldn't have been there now, suspended against the mine wall, green stone hot on his back, as two miners stretched him to the breaking point, the tip of a massive top drill held a mere foot from his belly. Galena, from the other side, spit another threat, "For the last time, thief. Who sent you to steal our Blood?"

Walter's voice came out hoarse as the miner removed his finger, allowing the boy to speak, "N-n-nobody. I s-s-swear. . . ."

Galena nodded to the miner, who covered Walter's mouth again. Then she said, "All right. If that's how you're wantin' it." She began ripping the rope out of the top, one notch at a time, causing the top to slowly spin to life, but was interrupted by a tiny voice behind her.

"Walter Mortinson!"

A gasp rippled through the room.

Galena let go of the cord, looking down at the tiny inter-rupter. Cordelia—out of breath, hair knotted, and knees bandaged—continued, shocking even herself.

"You . . . you let go of him!"

Her heart was beating faster than she felt comfortable with (though she didn't notice the tiny misshapen marble, discarded by her feet, speeding up to meet her own pulse).

Galena just stared at the child whose head was as wide as the miner's knees, then let the drill drop. Walter puffed out a breath of relief, but sucked it back in only moments later, when Galena's growl returned.

"Walter . . . Mortinson?"

Perhaps out of reflex of his own politeness, Walter nod-ded. "Yes?"

Tears welled in Galena's eyes, her own voice bobbing. "Like . . . Maxwell Mortinson?"

Now Walter couldn't respond, afraid of what would come next. Cordelia saw the fear on his face and stepped forward, placing a hand on Galena's arm.

"That's his dad."

Galena nodded, sucking the tears back into her eyes as she gestured for the long-limbed miners to drop Walter. To his surprise, they did so not only promptly but with an oddly gentle touch. As soon as Walter's feet met the ground, Cor-delia rushed to him and hugged him tightly.

Walter's face became scarlet—his worst moment blossoming into his best. Before he could hug her back, however, Cordelia had pushed herself away. She held a finger to his face, her own face as flushed as a plum. "Don't you . . ." But the threat died on her tongue when she remembered who surrounded them.

Cordelia scooted closer to Walter, his clammy hand clasping hers. She was too scared to notice how sweaty he was. She was busy watching Galena, who was taking the scene in with visible chagrin.

"Our, uh—our most humblest apologies, Mr. Mortinson."

Both Walter's and Cordelia's heads quirked up in surprise.

Galena then looked around at her fellow miners, who stopped whispering. She nodded, awkwardly dipping into a half bow as she continued, "We owe your father quite a debt."

As the rest of the miners fell into their own bows, Walter stepped back, stopped from stumbling only by Cordelia's tight hand around his.

"M-m-mine?"

"He was the bestest man I knew, gave us our livelihood, our freedom."

Galena bent down, dipping a finger into the glowing green goop flowing through the cave, as she gripped the now-quieted drill to her side. Almost instantly the rock solidified into a cap on her fingertip.

"We ain't never woulda gotten deep enough to discover the heart of the stone without him." She flicked the rock back into the stream below. It melted almost instantly. Galena sighed, pushing herself back to her feet.

"I guess it's been time enough for the Mortinsons to collect their debt."

The miners behind her began to whisper worriedly to one another. Galena then glared at Dreg, who was shrinking into the corner.

"Our young 'uns will do better next time to ensure it's a real thief scratchin' at the door." Her attention shifted back to Walter. "So what'll you be after? We don't have no money, if that's what you want. When we found the treasure, why, we realized we couldn't bear sellin' too much of it to the rest of the world. They wouldn't understand it like we do."

She flashed her green tooth at Walter again. He then looked into the crowd and saw a miner with long earlobes wave. The miner was missing two fingers, which had been replaced with green stone, and, even more miraculous, they bent and twisted like real fingers. As Walter looked around further, he saw all sorts of cracks—in both the people and the walls—filled with the green stuff.

"N-n-no . . ."

"Well, you'll be wanting the stone, then! Don't know much 'bout it still; as mysterious as the caves. Been calling it the Blood; seems like the blood of stone, it does. It's alive, though, sure of that. And it'll only go with you if it wants to. . . . Can't force it to do nothing it don't want, but we can try. How much you after?"

Her eyes squinted at him; he shook his head.

"Nothing like that. . . ."

"Then what is it?! You want the tops back? We won't be able to go no deeper! You want our cave, our homes?"

Walter managed to cut in. "Just a ride, please."

Galena's eyes widened as she stepped back. She took the two shivering kids in fully.

"A . . . a what?"

"We have places to be, ma'am, and we've lost our car. Perhaps you could help."

Dreg gulped as Galena sat with the kids, waiting for them to explain. This was not good for Dreg, very not good. Maybe it would have been better if he'd just squelched that pipsqueak after all.

Hadorah was thinking similar thoughts only a few towns away, her face a mix of frustration, fear, and day-old makeup.

Hauling hindquarters in the old carriage, she watched the metal horses gallop, the gears of which could be seen through their silvery musculature, spinning so fast, she was surprised smoke wasn't rising. The horses ran faster than real ones, powered by pumps composing their thighs.

Hadorah was fueled by the adrenaline that the climbing speed gave her.

Just wait until she found him.

"Walter?" Cordelia asked, the two holding each other oddly close, both of their faces indicating that they were regretting this position.

"Yes, Cordelia?"

"Are you sure this is a good idea?"

"I can't say that I am."

The duo stood on the very uppermost part of the top drill, the drill bit sinking into the earth below them. Galena, meanwhile, was directing a group of miners in from the slope leading down from the world outside. They were carrying the hearse, or what was left of it. Walter had insisted they retrieve it. After all, he had to find some way to get it back to his mother. Dreg trailed in behind the other miners, as white as a sheet of paper and outfitted in a harness. He hoped never again to be made to bungee down to pick up a busted car. He had found a few loose Worm Crunchies along the way, however.

"We got the automobile back for you right here, Mr. Mortinson. As soon as Flint has pinpointed your directions, you'll be on your way," Galena said, and nodded to the kids. Below them a miner was scratching his head as he used a compass (glowing peculiarly green), shifting this way and that. Suddenly he found the spot and stopped, pointing ahead . . . straight into the mountain.

"That's it!"

A group of miners picked up the kids and the drill, sending Walter and Cordelia sideways as the miners shoved the tip into the side of the cave wall. The two closed their eyes and held their breaths.

"Hold on, kiddins. It's going to be quite a ride."

Cordelia's sense suddenly returned, and she held up a hand and said, "Wait—" But it was too late.

"Pull!"

One of the miners yanked the cord out. Walter and Cordelia held on desperately, not trusting the straps that bound them to the machine. They screamed as the top spun madly, rapidly firing into the earth.

Their cries were lost as they disappeared into the dark.

No one noticed the marble that rolled down the hole after them.

CHAPTER 17 ½

. . .

WAX POETIC

Honeyoaks buzzes—literally. The entire town reverberates with the dull trill of the many round bees who bob dumbly through the air. People from Honeyoaks are so used to the buzz that when someone eventually leaves (though most never do), they are shocked by how quiet the rest of the world is.

The residents, along with the town itself, are generally accepted as being the closest thing to perfect that anyone else has ever seen.

When Hadorah first rolled into town, just barely engaged and even barelier pregnant, she quickly found herself as mesmerized as the rest of the tourists. It was as though a spell had been cast over the city, something hypnotic. Even the colors were brilliant in an otherworldly way. The blue of the sky shone more brightly than a cornflower, the grass seemed to gleam like a string of emerald lights, and the houses were per-fect identical boxes with painted shutters and well-tended-to flowerboxes.

Hadorah had never seen such flowerboxes. She had always just assumed they were meant to be dirty, seeing as they were filled with dirt and all. Not here, however. Not in Honeyoaks. There was something different in the dirt here, and, boy, was it sparkly.

It wasn't all luck or magic, though. The town had done well for itself, thanks to its plump, brainless bees. Honeyoaks was a sweet suburb covered in candles and beeswax statues, and even the five-tiered fountain in the middle of the park bubbled over with a cascade of gleaming honey.

The fuzzy flying workforce floated with the breeze, and to Hadorah's surprise, no one seemed to mind them. Happy families sat in the grassy park, all smiles. When a bee would fly by, no one thought to cringe or bat the plum-size thing away. Instead it would float over their heads, unless, of course, the person's head was just an inch too high—in which case the bee would bounce harmlessly off, then buzz away.

It wasn't just the town that was striking. Everyone who lived there suffered from the same perfect condition. Their clothing and hair were flawlessly polished; even their skin shone. It was as if they too were made of wax.

Max and Hadorah sat on the grass on a little blanket she

had knitted. (It was only a first attempt, Max reminded her when she would lament about the size of the holes in the weave.) Night had fallen, but in Honeyoaks it was never cold.

Still, Max wrapped his arms around his fiancée to fend the darkness off. Usually Hadorah would mind that others could see them like this—but today, for some reason, she didn't. They were watching the beginning of the Solstice Parade, and it was spellbinding.

"Could you do that, Max?"

"Do what?"

"Could you make one of those?" She pointed to one of the towering floats, a bright sun, lit inside by fireflies. Max appraised it, nodding, then held her close, perhaps still afraid the cold would roll in.

"Haddy, I'd do anything for you."

Usually skeptical, she snuggled into him, just appreciating the moment of watching the parade go by.

Hadorah loved parades.

"Have you ever seen something so perfect?" she asked as the butterfly float beating its yellow wings rolled on. But Max wasn't looking at the butterfly, nor at any of the rest of the dazzling floats. He was looking at her.

"Sure have."

. . .

CHAPTER 18

BUMBALLOON JUBILEE

It had already been fourteen years, Hadorah thought with a shake of her head. Recalling the past was among her least favorite pastimes.

She grumbled to herself, "No such thing as perfect."

Her eyes drooped, adrenaline wearing thin. She was hungry and tired, but when she saw that the next stop was Shrew's Borough, she decidedly zoomed past with an involuntary shudder.

Hadorah didn't much trust miners.

Walter's and Cordelia's screams were audible before anyone in Honeyoaks caught sight of them. Their chariot, the spinning top, thrust itself straight out of the ground in the middle of a big green park, tearing the grass up from below.

The top then righted itself, spinning lazily on its point,

and Walter and Cordelia were finally thrown off—both horribly woozy and even dirtier than before. Next to be spat out of the hole was the marble, which rolled innocently to Walter's feet.

Meanwhile, the perfect people of Honeyoaks stopped to stare. Walter, Cordelia, and their spinning travel companion were a bit out of place. Imagine the town's surprise when, moments later, a second giant, muddy top popped out of the ground.

The waxy onlookers' smiles melted off as two massive miners, with a creaking *thump*, dropped the hearse they were holding. The car had seen better days. To be fair, however, so had everyone else in Honeyoaks, days that included far fewer monstrous tops and grubby children. The two giants each boarded one of the devices. The stronger of the two waved to Walter and Cordelia as he hopped the colossal thing over to the hole. "Good rummaging, Mortinson."

The other chipped in, "And friend!"

"You too!"

Bemused, Walter and Cordelia waved as the two giants ripped the cords out of the tops and spun away, back into the dirt and out of sight.

Walter turned to Cordelia, seemingly unaware that they were the center of attention. "Well, that was interesting."

Cordelia, having only ever heard talk of this legendary

place, was disappointed that this was her introduction to it. She felt the hot stares of the locals burning into them. Usually she'd care quite a bit more about that fact than she did at this moment, for at this moment her knees were still bleeding, her hair would never be rid of its knots, and she had just experienced something that very few people ever would.

"It certainly was."

Cordelia and Walter left the hearse where it lay and trudged across the park, hoping to gain their land legs once again. They headed toward a table at the far end of the park, which was lined with yellow rosebushes. A woman with a pile of blond hair and a big, swooping hoopskirt sat with her back to them.

Walter wasn't worried about being turned away for being so dirty, or a child, or even late. He had to get to Flaster Isle, and there simply wasn't a moment more to waste. Galena had sent them here, promising they would find passage to the island. "It's perfect timing! So long as you have a bit of Max in ya, you'll be able to snap your aircraft together yourselves."

She had told Walter about the competition, the Quinquagintannual Hot-Air Balloon Competition, to be exact. Cordelia had explained that this meant there were fifty competitions a year. Seemed a bit excessive to Walter. How many hot-air balloons did anyone need? Cordelia wasn't concerned about the logic of the Quinquagintannual Hot-Air Balloon Competition. She was just proud to have known what "quinquagintannual" meant.

Galena had told the kids that Max had won this very competition many years before. Walter, of course, had already known this fact, but he chose not to tell Galena, because she seemed particularly excited to tell him about it.

Walter knew everything about Maxwell Mortinson that had ever been printed in a book or a newspaper, and he knew that on the sixteenth page of the album in his backpack was a newspaper clipping with the headline: MAXWELL MORTINSON RISES ABOVE THE COMPETITION! The headline was accompanied by a half-page image of Max smiling from his place in a big, bright hot-air balloon, Hadorah hiding behind him.

Now it seemed it was Walter's turn. He needed to get to Flaster Isle, and if he had to build a balloon to do it, well, he'd done far more difficult things.

The kids had to trek across the length of the park to reach the sign-in booth. Walter unintentionally bumped foreheads with three big bees along the way, but they bounced off like Ping-Pong balls and floated elsewhere, unperturbed. Walter felt similarly to the bees. He was too busy scribbling on a makeshift schematic, whispering to himself as they went.

As Walter and Cordelia tromped across the field, they passed their inquisitive competition. A dozen or so balloons lazed, uninflated, in various stages of completion. The competitors had designed their aircrafts with bright colors and cheery patterns. That's what most people think balloons ought to be. The teams working on them looked equally bright and cheery; no one was even breaking a sweat.

Cordelia smoothed herself down before approaching the blond woman with the beehive hairdo sitting at the booth. Cordelia got close enough to read the sign in front of the smiling woman: HONEYOAKS QUINQUAGINTANNUAL BUMBALLOON JUBILEE!

Cordelia tried to act like a local, but with her day-old nightgown, off-kilter eye patch, and general air of unusualness, she wasn't doing a fantastic job.

Cordelia sighed, adopting her fanciest, most adult voice, "Room for another?"

She was fairly certain that was the kind of thing a fancy adult would probably say.

The woman, however, wasn't impressed. Based on her expression alone, it seemed she could smell the blood and fish on Cordelia's dress and maybe even on the eye patch. The woman gestured to a sheet decorated with doodles of cutesy balloons and cutesier bees. Cordelia hurriedly signed Walter's name, sensing the woman's stare.

After eight years, Cordelia could always tell when someone was looking at her eye patch. It was the unfortunate consolation prize of losing the eye, she supposed. It was a rather lackluster superpower, up there with talking to snails and producing enough electricity to give someone an almost imperceptible static shock.

Cordelia criticized herself for getting lost in such foolish thoughts, then shuffled back to Walter.

He was already racing to the car. Cordelia desperately hoped it was just to get his backpack. When she met up with him, however, she found him rifling through the trunk.

This was not good, as there was only one thing in the trunk—or, rather, hundreds of things.

Cordelia's eye shot wide when she realized.

"Walter, you can't."

But she already knew that he not only could; he couldn't be stopped.

About fifteen minutes later Walter had successfully dragged the many butterflies to their allotted spot on the lawn. After hitting them with his car, he'd picked up every single one with reverent gentleness and placed them, stacked, in a black body bag. His mother kept a roll of them in the dashboard. Terribly convenient.

Onlookers kept their eyes on the pair as they unzipped the bag. Cordelia, meanwhile, was trying her best *not* to look.

Walter started pulling butterflies out of the bag by the

handful as Cordelia retrieved the rest of their supplies from the beehive woman—one burner, weights, a fan, and a rope—along with Walter's backpack and the entire roll of body bags (so convenient).

The rest of the contestants noticeably reared back when the butterflies emerged. The insects were, at this point, excessively dead and crispy, as were the flies that had gotten stuck in the bag with them. Most of the people in Honeyoaks had never seen something dead. The town made certain of it. The only person who liked death less than the townspeople did was Cordelia.

"Walter, this is too much. I can't . . ."

With no time to lose and a firm idea stuck in his mind, Walter grabbed her by the shoulders. The stare he shot through her was like nothing she'd ever seen.

"Cordelia Primpet. You are one of the bravest people I've ever known. You can do this."

She stared into his resolute gaze and found herself only able to nod in response.

"Excellent. Now hand me the needle and thread."

Cordelia felt queasy as she sorted through the tools and handed him a little box with sewing needles.

"No, the curved one."

She swallowed down her horror as she pulled out a needle as long as her finger, in the shape of a scythe. Cordelia had never liked needles, especially ones that dipped into people's skin.

The next day the front page of the *Daily Buzz* would read BLOOD FLEW, but that's because the author of that particular article didn't get to see Walter's work up close. Nor did they know that butterflies don't contain blood; their bodies run on something called hemolymph. The article should have read HEMOLYMPH FLEW, but that wouldn't sell as many papers, would it? Oh, well. It was still a spectacular show.

The rest of the teams watched Walter rapidly sew together wings. The Honeyoaks residents were more than appalled, only slightly less so than Cordelia herself. It was bad enough to be using . . . dead things, but to do so without any hesitation?

Even the marble, which had been doing its utmost to follow the two through the grass and over streets, seemed to shrink back a bit.

Everyone's thoughts, however, were about the same: What on earth did Walter Mortinson think he was doing?

As the rosy curtain of afternoon fell, Hadorah found herself no longer even checking her speed. She galloped past Honeyoaks, faltering for only a moment before shaking the memories away and continuing. She just barely looked up in time to see a practice balloon peeking out from above the trees.

• • •

The rest of the Bumballoon teams didn't seem to care for Walter and Cordelia much, as evidenced by the fact that they had bunched together on the grass in an attempt to get as far away as they could from the boy, the girl, and their lifeless creation. Whomever remained close to them risked getting a stray butterfly shot up their nostril or down their throat, thanks to the usually pleasant afternoon breeze.

Cordelia didn't feel much differently. She sat with her back to Walter, unable to bear watching him anymore. She was paler and sweatier than usual, looking more unwell by the minute.

She glanced down at her knees and saw that they were still bleeding from her time in the mines. She sighed, hastily ripping off a second strip from the bottom of her nightgown, and tied it tightly around the first, which had become soppy with blood.

"Hammer, please," said Walter.

Cordelia unseeingly handed Walter the hammer, refusing to face him. Her throat felt sticky.

"How can you take it?" she asked.

"Take what?"

"All this . . . death."

Walter shrugged. He'd never thought of it that way. "Well, they're already dead. Might as well give them a nice good-bye."

"Doesn't that bother you, though? Dying?"

He thought about that. In the silence—no words, no cutting, no sewing—Cordelia realized how loud the bees really were.

Finally Walter spoke. "Things shouldn't have to die, but they do anyway."

"What's the point of it all if we're just going to have to die, then?"

"I guess . . . that I get to be here with you."

Cordelia didn't mind the stray wings stuck to his face as much this time when she looked at him. She hardly noticed them, in fact.

Walter then thrust his arm out over the field. "And I get to be here. I get to make things." His shoulders bobbed. "I like to make things."

He nodded before ripping another antenna from its hold on the butterfly's head.

Cordelia was quite dizzy by now and was having a hard time keeping focus, but she did really try to listen to him. She spoke just to keep herself awake.

"I like the bluffs."

Walter didn't even turn. "What bluffs?"

"Ramsey Bluffs. My biggest dream would be to string a line through them and walk right across."

Cordelia had had that dream many times before. She

would sit alone in her room and close her eyes, imagining the tense rope pushing up against the bottoms of her bare feet, picturing the angle of the world below her. It always made her feel better to be up there.

She was torn from her reverie as a plump bee plopped down in front of her.

"I've never heard of them," Walter replied.

The bee crawled toward her, but it was limping. Cordelia had never seen a bee limp. She offered her hand, which it dutifully clambered onto. She brought the fat creature to eye level as she spoke.

"Really? They're south of Flaster Isle. No one knows who made them, but they're supposed to be one of the most beautiful sights in the world. For three hours every day, when the sun shines through them, it's like they're magic." The bee curled in her palm, spinning itself like a dog. She continued, her eyes trained on its warm, rolling body, "They cast shadows on the ground of amazing illusions. Beautiful things."

"We'll have to go see it!"

"You have to have both eyes for the illusions to work."

She refused to meet Walter's gaze. She already knew what it looked like. People's faces always grew heavy when they carried pity, causing their cheeks to sink down, their foreheads to crease, and their heads to tilt to one side. Cordelia didn't want to see Walter's face get heavy. Instead she flopped back the other way, legs akimbo. They sat in silence for a moment, accompanied by the humming bees.

"Is that why you want to go to Flaster Isle?"

Even though the bees were loud, Walter did notice when Cordelia stopped breathing. He turned back to look at her just as she spoke.

"No. I—"

She didn't want to say the truth. She was so used to lying by now that it was far more comfortable, but for some reason lying to Walter in this moment felt different. Before she could think about what she was doing, the truth tumbled from her dry lips. "I have to see a doctor there."

"Why? Are you all right?"

Walter stood and rushed around to face her. He kneeled and without thinking did what his mother always did when she thought he might be sick—he pressed the back of his hand to Cordelia's forehead and found it slick with sweat. In spite of herself, Cordelia laughed. "Of course I'm not, but I haven't been for a long time."

Cordelia's smile dropped when Walter showed even more concern. Her thoughts jumbled; she tried to come up with anything to make that look on his face go away.

"But I don't want to talk about that. I just want to . . ." She breathed in deeply. "Thank you, I guess, for bringing me here. My parents certainly never would have taken me.

They rarely let me leave the house except to go to school."

Walter shook his head as he walked back to his circle in the grass, surrounded by butterflies. "That's too bad, especially because school is the worst place to go. I bet if Wartlebug had her way, she'd be like your parents and never let us out."

He continued working, humming to himself. Cordelia, meanwhile, could hardly catch her own breath. She curled her fingers, only to feel the round bee still there. She hadn't known it, but he'd crawled toward her to feel something warm in his last moments. With the remains of her voice, Cordelia croaked, "I'm going to the bathroom."

She shakily stood, then looked down. The bee had died.

It took far longer than it should have to find a bathroom. It seems that Honeyoaks was so dedicated to its own image of perfection that it had tucked the only public lavatories away from view, behind a garden shed, a wax figure of Mayor Gloria Mae Honeybumble, and a very large circular mailbox.

Cordelia faced herself in the mirror, lit all around by soft, spherical bulbs. They were there to make you look better, but not even the flattering lights could hide how unwell Cordelia looked. The sheet of sweat covering her face reflected easily, she could make out every crack in her lips, and her hair was either very greasy or very sweaty (more probably both).

She set the bee down on the counter, then groped in her

pocket for her medicine bottle. She pulled it out and spun off the well-worn cap.

She peered inside to see only a single white pill staring back at her from the bottom. Hastily she dumped the pill into her hand, but her palm was so slick with sweat, the pill slipped from her fingers.

"No!" She grabbed for it, but the tiny pill spun in circles all the way into the drain. It was too late.

Panicking, Cordelia looked again at herself, skin paper white, dark rings around her eyes. She looked down at her leg where the blood was already soaking through her second makeshift bandage.

She hastily ripped another strip off her nightgown and tied it around, tightly, whispering to herself, "Please stop. Please just stop."

She tried to calm her breathing as she stood back up, grasping for the bee. They were almost there.

Cordelia had to remind herself how to walk as she returned to their hot-air balloon. She found it just before the sky went dark.

Moments later (or at least that was how it felt to Cordelia) she was quivering, facing Walter. In front of him were tree branches, latticed together into a basket.

He worked quickly, frantically even.

The almost-finished balloon was deflated nearby. It was made of a combination of butterflies, sewn together into sheets, and the thick black body bags. The two "fabrics" alternated like a circus big top. Cordelia liked that about it— that was all she liked.

Walter looked up from his work, ecstatic.

"Ah! There you are!"

Without thinking, he dragged her away. He didn't seem to notice her sweat anymore, nor the emptiness of her eye as he pulled her to a fresh grave. The dirt had already been replaced, and there were two branches, whittled into gargantuan antennae, poking out the sides. They looked like grave markers because that's precisely what they were.

Walter cleared his throat, giving Cordelia a meaningful look, then continued his speech where he had left off.

"As I was saying, I really didn't mean to hit you all with my car. I want to thank you for being such good butterflies and for providing us with this valuable opportunity. We are forever grateful."

There was a pause as both kids looked down. Walter was being respectful; Cordelia was trying to figure out what in the name of Flasterborn was going on. Then Walter nudged her.

"What?" Cordelia was a bit snappish when she felt close to death.

"Well, don't you want to say something?"

"They were bugs. Dead bugs. I don't like dead things, and I don't like bugs, and I'm not that sorry that they're gone."

Walter turned to her and raised his eyebrows. Cordelia groaned and ground out a final: "Thanks anyway."

But she wasn't happy about it. Walter, for his part, was very happy.

"Thanks. I really wanted to do it right," he said, before spinning back to his work, humming his incessant tune.

Cordelia watched him, her vision becoming fuzzy with fatigue. She didn't understand how someone could care so much about the life of some insects. She instantly felt worse about all the times when she hadn't cared about stomping on a spider or slapping a fly. She petted the bee, hidden in her hand. He had been a nice bee, after all.

Squatting on the grass, Walter rapidly sewed the tiny wings of the butterflies tighter, and with such speed that Cordelia could hardly keep up just watching him. His precision was perfect, like a machine. He cut the thread with his gold knife.

The woman with the beehive hair circled the park with a clipboard, cheerfully shouting, "Prepare for liftoff, Bumballooners!"

Cordelia turned to Walter. She was anxious because the world wouldn't stop spinning, "Will it be ready?"

Water nodded, not looking up.

"Will it work?" she pressed.

"My inventions always work."

It was late, and the sky was growing the color of an eggplant cooked to blister. That meant it was time for the crowd to begin forming. Cordelia could hear the whispers start, winding together with the buzz of the bees into something thoroughly incomprehensible. But she hardly had the energy to care. Her legs were wobbly and were already giving out under the anxiety and strain. She plonked beside him on the grass. "Good."

Cordelia sprawled out, holding the dead bee so close to her clammy face that her wheezing breaths caused the little thing's fur to drift back and forth, back and forth.

Someone in Honeyoaks, a long time before, had thought it fit to make tiny candles and put them on tiny saddles, which were then affixed to the backs of the unaware bees—but only the biggest bees (otherwise it'd be silly). Bees carrying candles now circled the grass, the inky trails of the flames following their haphazard paths.

All the balloons but Walter's were inflated and ready to fly. He was still setting up the burner. Cordelia's face showed no emotion. There wasn't energy for that.

"One minute, contestants!" The beehive woman's voice was high-pitched and seemed to vibrate.

Cordelia stroked the bee with her thumb. During one

pass she accidentally slipped over the stinger. It was rounded but still grating enough to break her thin, pruned skin. She watched the blood ooze out in thick droplets.

Her voice was quiet. Walter almost couldn't hear her. "You said it would be ready . . ."

He attempted to light the wick, the matches burning down to nubs between his fingers. "It'll fly."

Cordelia began coughing and wheezing and was unable to stop. Walter turned, panicking. She was staring at her thumb.

"Cordelia! Are you all right?"

She shook her head. Her eye had rolled back and her chest was heaving. She raised a squeezed fist, and Walter forced it open. Inside he found the bee, curled in the nook of her palm.

"Cordelia? Cordelia!"

He laid Cordelia on her side, then jumped up, abandoning the balloon. He rushed toward the high-pitched beehive woman.

"Miss, my friend needs help!"

The crowd, to his surprise, offered nothing, their faces painted on wax, watching the show. Beehive was just the same; her teeth were spectacularly white.

"How can I assist you?"

"Call an ambulance. She needs a hospital!"

She laughed, batting him away. "Oh, Honeyoaks doesn't have a hospital. We hardly ever get sick here."

"Where's the closest one?"

"On Flaster Isle, of course, just over the bay." She smiled warmly, checking her watch. "You have thirty seconds."

"You have to help me."

"Good luck! May the best Bumballoon win!"

The woman teetered away on her swirly-heeled shoes. Walter ran back to Cordelia and felt her pulse. She opened her eye and managed to wheeze, "I wanted to thank you . . ."

Walter's eyes whipped across the crowd.

"Please, is anyone a doctor? Anyone?"

"What you did for Grandpa . . . No one liked Grandpa, except for me."

He looked down at her, panic exploding across his face.

"He would have loved that more than anything."

"Cordelia, I don't know—"

"Ten seconds, contestants!"

"We have to get there." That was the last thing Cordelia said before drifting off.

"Five seconds!"

Walter shot up and desperately tried to light the burner, and to his shock, it flickered on—but still the wretched balloon refused to inflate. No matter. He hurriedly picked Cordelia up and placed her inside as gingerly as he could.

"And, liftoff!"

All the balloons but one rose upward, their flickering fires adding to the light of the stars.

Walter rushed, tripping on his own feet as he cut the lines for his weights.

He flicked his flame as high as it would go, and the onlookers were astonished to see the balloon finally inflate. Walter threw himself into the basket just as it began hovering.

Then, in a most miraculous feat, it hobbled into the air.

As soon as it was up, however, there was no stopping it. Walter's balloon soared, careening through the clouds, speeding above the rest.

Those below were in awe of the sight—the butterflies glowed, like a gorgeous kaleidoscope, spinning with warm colors, contrasting with the stark strips of black. In a moment of ingenuity, Walter had even affixed dead flies to the top with long, rigid wires, making it appear as if they were the ones carrying the craft toward the moon.

Walter's creation stood out among a blanket of pastels. For all their bright happiness and festivity, the other balloons paled in comparison to the black one.

Walter wasn't thinking of the other balloons, however. He was too busy looking down at the girl curled into the corner of the wooden basket.

He kneeled to her, hesitantly brushing the wet strands of

hair out of her eye. "It'll be all right, Cordelia. Dr. Automaton will save you. He can do anything."

Walter then pretended he was rocking her to sleep, humming his tune as they finally disappeared into the night.

Fourteen years before, a brilliant black-and-gold balloon had floated down as the rest had floated up.

The basket had sparkled as if made of real gold.

When it hit the ground, Maxwell and Hadorah could be seen kissing inside.

He held a box. She wore a ring.

They hadn't a care in the world.

And that was just the way it was.

CHAPTER 19

· · ·

WELCOME TO THE FUTURE

Flaster Isle was renowned for its spectacular sights (and equally outstanding smells).

It was a city built on an ordinary rock sticking out of the sea. At least, it used to be an ordinary rock, before Flasterborn went to work on it. Then it became a very shiny rock.

Its namesake had designed the metropolis in his image—and, as stated on the flashing sign entering town: FLASTER ISLE IS THE *FUTURE*! Below that was another flashing sign that said 50% OFF ALL TOAST BOXES, but that had very little to do with the point.

And what was that point? That this bubble of a city—literally, surrounded in some marriage of glass and plastic that Flasterborn had trademarked "glasstic"—represented everything Flasterborn thought the future should be.

The first thing you might notice upon entering the golden gates was that Flasterborn apparently had decided that there were no cars in the future—too primitive. Instead people traveled in enormous situlas—massive iron buckets, with the achievements of Flasterborn carved into the sides. The situlas slid on invisible wires that crisscrossed the city (horribly dangerous for parachuters—which is why, Flasterborn decreed, there were no parachuters in the future). The wires were so traceless that the only way one could tell precisely where they were was by the lines of crows perched on top of them—oh, but not regular crows, mind you. In Flaster Isle future-history classes, it was discussed how all the crows would die as a result of a combination of a very hot summer and an uprising of aggressive slugs. Because of this, Flasterborn had preemptively created robotic crows for any and all of your crow needs.

In any case, the streets had to be extra wide, not only because they were already jam-packed with tourists, but also because the buckets zoomed every which way, pouring people out at their destinations as an afterthought along the journey. No one had any idea how the buckets knew where to drop them, but the buckets were *always* right. . . . Well, *usually* right. If they weren't, it was probably the passenger's fault for not wanting to be in the right place.

Buildings, made entirely of glass and gold, shot so high

into the air that there were constant fears that Flaster Isle would one day fall over from the weight of them. Flasterborn, however, had reassured his citizens that he would find a way to permanently get rid of falling. No one likes falling anyway—well, except maybe parachuters, but fortunately, in the future, they won't exist.

Vendors sat on every corner of every street, wearing flashing ties and glasses, peddling Flasterborn's inventions from their carts. Even the carts themselves were impressive. They spun, both upward and outward, in gyroscopic patterns. There were endless products piled into them that could only be revealed by spinning the spherical cart this way and that. The vendors would do this as they put on shows to entice visitors into their webs. There the guests would be hypnotized into buying many more gadgets than they had planned. Luckily, every product was one that the buyer definitely needed, whether they had known it before or not.

And the smells—*oh, the smells*. Flasterborn had invented a system by which the grates in the ground puffed out delicious scents. First Street smelled like fresh, steaming bread. Second Street smelled like a warm cup of cocoa. Third Street— well, Third Street was Flasterborn's personal favorite smell. Third Street smelled like sugar that had been burned in just the right way.

Flaster Isle was a wonderful place, or at least that was what just about everyone thought. Those who didn't were probably just upset that they couldn't live there, in the high-rise houses, sleeping in the clouds. (Literally on clouds, actually. Flasterborn had invented a bed of clouds to replace beds, for obvious reasons.)

The fact was that everyone wanted to live on Flaster Isle, with its flashy lights and glasstic halo. As a result, the city was packed, sprawling with people and the results of those people.

The streets were so often clogged, in fact, that only those who paid a fee were allowed to walk on them. Everyone else was relegated to the underground passage system that coursed beneath called the Elevator Highway (or "EH" for short). Tourists were advised to steer clear of storm drains, as you never knew when someone would be shot straight out of one—to hobble on to their next destination. Flasterborn didn't imagine there would be any other kind of elevator in the future, because elevators were widely known to be very scary and very dangerous.

The only trouble with Flasterborn's EH occurred after the holidays. If you ate one too many Figgy Flasterpies or a bit too much Hamborn, that extra weight would get you into a sticky jam in the middle of a lift. Such an accident was occasionally fatal and, even worse, quite embarrassing. But that was unavoidable, Flasterborn proclaimed, because his elevators were simply much better than any other variety.

Walter had dreamed of seeing Flaster Isle his whole life. Not only was it the subject of innumerable glorious tales, but he knew that his father had worked there many years before.

Even at night—which, for Walter, floating into the city, it was—Flaster Isle looked constantly in the middle of a celebration, filled with lights, sounds, and people.

As Walter passed over it, however, he didn't see much. He was too focused on Cordelia's slowing pulse. He needed to find the hospital immediately—or, preferably, before then.

Fortunately, that wasn't very hard.

The Flasterbornian Immortality Center and Laboratory was an unbearably large building. It was the kind of absurd structure that if you tried to see the top of it, there was a very good chance that your neck would stay that way forever.

If one *could* see the very top of it, past layer upon layer of reflective gold glass, one would find a lone tower. Rumor had it that this tower, of bronze and white, was solely for Flasterborn's own efforts against dying.

That was the ultimate prospect. Flasterborn insisted that there was no point in a future if you had to die before you got there. Therefore, there was no death on Flaster Isle. . . . At least, they pretended there wasn't. It wouldn't be long, Flasterborn insisted, before he'd finally rid the world of its ultimate calamity.

Below the tower was the finest hospital in the entire world. It was so successful because Flasterborn's main goal was to keep the inhabitants alive at all costs—or, rather, at whatever cost they were able to pay.

Walter found the hospital easily. All he had to do was navigate toward one of the gated entrances lining the glasstic bubble and pay a small fee to enter.

Once he did, he saw the flashing red building. Plastered on every side were advertisements for casts that wrote on themselves and bandages shaped like lips that delivered kisses straight to booboos every five minutes.

There was no parking lot because there were no cars, so Walter let the balloon down as easily as he could onto a wide street near the entrance. He bumped only one situla wire on the way down. It sprang up, scattering birds above and causing the passengers stacked inside the situla to bounce madly as they listened to their newspapers. (Flasterborn had decreed that people wouldn't read in the future—it wasted time—so these newspapers read to you.)

Walter staggered a bit as he carried Cordelia in.

To keep himself awake, he repeated the same mantra that had been running through his mind for their entire journey: "Everything will be all right." Then he added to himself with a relieved sigh, "We made it."

• • •

It was so late when Hadorah's ferry arrived at the gates of the small island that the sun had reawakened.

The woman, her head a torch of red, stumbled over the lip of the boat as she stepped out.

She trudged up the familiar rocky path to the wrought iron spikes—decorated with vines made from precious gems in green and amber. In between were solid gold letters: WELCOME TO FLASTER ISLE.

Hadorah approached, and the spikes opened for her, glasstic gleaming from between the bars, offering a glimpse of the dazzling lights in the city beyond.

CHAPTER 20

. . .

TIPPY THE SNOOP

Tippy was early to work on Friday, because Tippy was always early to work. She hadn't, however, expected to see Hadorah Mortinson waiting for her at the door.

Tippy was not excited to make her acquaintance.

The moment Tippy had unlocked her office and stepped in, Hadorah followed, stalking her uncomfortably closely. Tippy finally turned to face her, forcing them nose to nose.

Tippy counted things when she was nervous. There were precisely twelve and a half wrinkles around Hadorah's mouth when it moved.

"Where is he?"

Tippy set off the Code Red strategies in her mind. These strategies had been put in place for the most dangerous intruders. She was prepared to take Hadorah out if necessary.

"Good morning, madam. Can I offer you a beverage on your way out?"

Hadorah released a squawk that Tippy thought sounded uncannily like a robotic crow. Then Hadorah said, "You cannot. You can offer me Horace Flasterborn or else . . ."

Hadorah tried to push passed Tippy, but the taller woman held firm, pushing right back. Hadorah fought her the whole way, muttering terrible things about Flasterborn, which only made Tippy push harder.

Alas, just as Tippy had a hand on the hallway door, she heard a hollow *ding*. She closed her eyes tightly, knowing exactly what that sound meant.

She and Hadorah both looked to the opposite side of the room, where a large, ornate vase began glowing. Moments later Flasterborn's bowler-encased head burst out the top of it (followed, thankfully, by his suit-encased body). This was his personal elevator.

"Ah, Hadorah. Pleasure to see you again! Come in."

Then Flasterborn, in full tailcoat, removed his bowler and entered his office.

Tippy let herself be pushed aside as Hadorah barreled into the room after him. But this wasn't right. It couldn't be. This was a Code Red, and Tippy knew that in Code Reds she had a job to do—privacy be rot! So Tippy did what Tippy did best: she took care of Flasterborn.

Quickly, so as not to miss a word or murder attempt, she hurried back to her desk, kneeled onto the ground in a rather un-Tippy-like position, and removed the little gold button she had sewn into the carpet.

With a yank, it came loose, revealing a black tube. Tippy sat on the floor, eye to ground and nose squashed several times over, looking into the hole and straight into Flasterborn's office. This was an emergency periscope she'd installed on the duo's fifth anniversary. Of course, Flasterborn didn't know about Tippy's emergency periscope. She hadn't wanted to worry him. Tippy would be sure to protect Flasterborn at all costs.

Peeking around, she finally got a glimpse of the horrid woman sitting across from Flasterborn. Even the lady's appearance paled in comparison to his. She was hunched and gray, while he was straight-backed, smiling, and wonderful.

Tippy turned up the sound on her gold listening device and settled in.

Hadorah sat in front of Horace Flasterborn for the first time in fourteen years. She had expertly ducked when the train running through the maze had come shooting by, but had forgotten about the Puffumes (one of her favorite of Maxwell's devices) and was surprised when a cream-colored one plopped out. She watched with dreaded fascination as the little ball wobbled and burst; coils of cream mist spiraled toward her.

Despite her best effort to stay above all this silliness, Hadorah breathed in when the cloud of Puffume particles hit. She was suddenly soothed by the lovely, familiar smell of magnolias.

Hadorah's father had loved magnolias, and for one instant she was transported back to her room when she was a little girl, the yellow-trimmed windows and the stuffed pug plopped onto the pink carpeted floor. (Hadorah's mother had insisted that all the children have stuffed animals—but it wasn't until much later that Hadorah had learned that for most people, "stuffed animals" rarely referred to deceased pets.)

Hadorah recalled waking up to the smell of the top-heavy white flower sloping toward her sleeping nose. Her dad had liked to swipe magnolias from the neighbor's yard and leave them by Hadorah's bedside for her to find the next morning.

She had almost forgotten about that.

Hadorah pulled herself out of her reverie and was startled to find that her face had slipped into a little smile. She looked up to see the man across from her smiling back. It was a grin she had learned to despise.

"Hello, my dear."

Even his voice sounded the same—somehow booming and crackling all at once. Hadorah's, on the other hand, just cracked.

"What have you done with him?"

"Why, it has been a while."

"And the girl, was that your idea too?"

"I was sorry to hear about Maxwell. I hope you received our card." He leaned back in his immense chair. Hadorah could see the arms of it creeping around him in a big, cushy hug. "Although, I can't imagine what he expected. I did warn him. Love makes people do very silly things, sometimes."

Flasterborn shook his head and, for a moment, thought he might have heard a whimper from the other side of the door, but he ignored it.

"That was what it was, right, Hadorah? Love?"

Hadorah, growing redder and sweatier by the second, slapped a hand on his desk.

"You're trying to recreate us!"

Flasterborn shifted his eyes back to her without a twitch of surprise. His smile curled.

"Now, now, Hadorah. Don't be foolish. After all I've seen—why on earth would I want to recreate you?"

Fifteen years before, a vibrant young woman with ivy-vine curls winding down her back had worn a million-watt grin and her prized black-and-gold lab coat. The possibilities of the entire world had shone in her eyes, and she'd already been well on her way to discovering them.

Or so she had hoped.

"Wrench!"

Hadorah had adjusted her goggles and rushed to the tool rack to retrieve a wrench, then had brought it back to Flasterborn, who'd been sitting over a solid gold device armed with a claw and many wheels. She had eagerly stood over his shoulder, watching the master at work.

This is how you achieve your dreams, she had reminded herself as she'd dabbed the sweat rag across her boss's damp forehead. *You have to help others achieve theirs first.*

"You were nothing more than a tool belt, and if that was all you had remained, perhaps none of this would have happened." Flasterborn's grin was vile in how disarming it was—how disarming it *still was.* "But that was you—then there was Max. He was one in a million. . . . No, not even that. He was his own kind, wasn't he?"

Hadorah was slammed back by memories. They rushed over her with a lucidity they didn't have at home. She couldn't escape now and could only gasp as she was plunged into another memory.

Genius, young Hadorah realized, must take a very long time to grow, because Flasterborn had been screwing and unscrewing little wheels all over this darn device for far too long. And, of all things, this invention he'd been slaving over had only one func-

tion: to extract the hair from cats so that they'd stop getting hair balls.

Hadorah had already figured out what Flasterborn was doing wrong. Now she tried to warn him that if he just moved those wheels over a smidgen, the contraption would stop lighting things on fire. But the second she got out an "Excuse me, Mr. Flaster—" he admonished her for missing the sweat that was precariously balanced over one of his fuzzy gray eyebrows. She apologized and wiped it away.

It was then that she remembered that Flasterborn didn't need her thoughts. He was probably figuring out how to do it better on his own. How could he not be? He was famous. And what was she? Only his assistant.

Just then, she heard the soft tutting behind her. She breathed in deeply as she turned. She knew who it was.

He had been here only a month or so. Hadorah had been here for at least six times that. But he was special. He'd been brought here to become Flasterborn's apprentice, but it was clear that he was to be more than that. The promise of his future was written in the way he held himself, in how everyone spoke of him.

Maxwell was thoroughly unlike Hadorah. It hardly seemed fair. See, rumors rarely held water, but for Max they unveiled an ocean. Max wasn't just special. He was impossible.

Just then he was surrounded by his creations. There were so many of them. He tinkered with the ease of breathing. Little *invention equivalents of doodles sprang to life around him as he worked. A tiny metal girl spun in a circle; a copper carrot seemed to grow out of the table; and amorphous bubbles and blobs melted themselves, turned to vapor, and then morphed back into bubbles . . . but how? The cogs in Hadorah's brain ground together so hard, she was worried sparks might fly out of her ears. Still, she could come up with only one answer: Maxwell could accomplish anything simply because he thought it'd be neat.*

Maxwell, Hadorah begrudged, was extraordinary.

That just wouldn't do.

Hadorah snapped out of the memories, sweating. She shook her head. "You know why I'm here. Where is my son?"

Flasterborn stared at her a moment, sucking the air between his gapped front teeth. "I'm sorry to say, Maxwell's boy has yet to arrive."

She hadn't considered this. It . . . it couldn't be right. Where could he be?

"When he does come, I want you to do the right thing. He's still a child. He needs to be at home."

"I seem to remember another 'child' who felt differently." He leaned forward, face hardening. "The daughter of morticians dreamed of greater things."

• • •

All those many years ago, Hadorah had worked on her own invention as Flasterborn had busied himself. She had been going to prove her worth. Finally he would take her on as an apprentice—he had to if she succeeded.

It was only a flower—an undying one. It was meant to be simple, just a toy for children; perfect for the vendors, with pretty cobalt petals. At least, it was supposed to be, but Hadorah was having a hard time finishing it.

"Assistant!"

Shocked out of her concentration, Hadorah let go, and the flower fell to pieces. Again.

Drat.

"Yes, Mr. Flasterborn! Sorry, Mr. Flasterborn."

She turned to him, his station right next to hers. He just waved her away, never looking up from his Cat Dehairer. "Stop fiddling and pay attention."

"Yes, Mr. Flasterborn."

Hadorah stood behind him, staring uselessly as he screwed a screw, then unscrewed a screw, then screwed a screw, then unscrewed a screw. . . . Her fingers itched to finish her own project, but she didn't dare even turn to look at it. Then she felt a tap on her shoulder.

Maxwell stood beside her, leaning against her station, hands behind his back. He smiled and revealed her flower— not only fixed, but made to spin like a pinwheel. Hadorah blushed, taking it from him without meeting his eyes.

"Let her fail on her own, Maxwell. She has to learn. Help is for the weak."

Max hummed, passing Flasterborn and then tapping a box of factory-made mechanisms on the old man's table. "That's funny. I thought premade parts were for the weak."

Flasterborn harrumphed, nudging the box out of sight. Max winked at Hadorah, making the blush creep to her ears as her head shot down and she began fiddling again.

Max went back to his own device, tinkering on an impressive display of what would later become his Mechanical Puppet Theater (which Walter had enjoyed very much before he could speak but would certainly no longer remember).

She then looked down at her own measly flower. Suddenly filled with a new disappointment she hadn't before known, she took it apart, hoping to start again, and maybe . . . just maybe she could prove herself.

She had managed to remove every screw before Flasterborn had placed even one of his own. Never looking away from his Dehairer, she dropped the broken pieces of her flower onto her table.

A dark little thought nipped at the back of her mind. *There's nothing to prove when you are a nothing.* And though Hadorah swatted the mean gnat back, it was too late.

The wound had been planted, and it was ripe to fester.

• • •

"You never gave me a real chance." She scowled, trying to look brave, but Flasterborn knew; he always knew.

"There was no chance to give. You were only an assistant, Hadorah."

Hadorah tried to push the lump out of her throat so that she could retort, but no words would come.

Flasterborn continued, "The biggest mistake I made was assigning you to my most promising apprentice. Where did that leave him?" Hadorah's eyes prickled. She couldn't meet his gaze as he placed a hand over hers. He had worn the same black leather gloves every day since he'd met her. They felt cold and sterile. "In the ground. Buried by that daughter of morticians."

Hadorah yanked her hand back. "He left because he was too good for this horrid place—"

"He left because of *you.*" Flasterborn's voice broke only for a second; he lost his composure just enough to send a loose hair twanging out of order. He sucked in deeply, smoothing the hair down again, along with his honeyed voice. "I suppose you did prove your worth after all. Speaking of Walter, maybe Maxwell wasn't the only one who ran away because of you."

"Leave my son alone. If you don't—"

"If I don't what? Tell him to leave after inviting him? He's old enough to decide for himself."

Hadorah kept up the veil of anger, but she knew it was slipping in favor of fear.

Flasterborn spoke with dangerous calm. "I hear he's smart?"

"Very."

"Then neither of us can tell him what to do. He's isn't Maxwell, Hadorah, so you don't have the same hold over him."

With that single truth, Hadorah became deflated and suddenly very, very tired. Those three words, "He isn't Maxwell," reminded her of one very sad thing: she couldn't win. Max had listened to her. Walter did not.

Hadorah struggled to stand and then slowly headed for the door. Flasterborn's voice floated after her. "Just tell me . . . is he as good as I think he is?"

She paused in the doorway, fingers around the handle.

"Better."

The door slammed behind her.

In more than a decade Tippy had learned very few things about Flasterborn's past.

She was so struck by what she'd heard in this peculiar meeting, she didn't even bother standing as the crazed woman, red hair sticking out at every angle, stormed out of the office.

This was a very strange position for Tippy, and not just because her face was still pressed against the floor. Flasterborn had sounded almost . . . cruel when he'd talked to Hadorah. But that couldn't be right; Flasterborn wasn't cruel. And what did Hadorah mean that Walter's place was at home? He couldn't want to stay in Moormouth.

Who should Tippy agree with? Her boss, the most amazing person she had ever met, or the wild woman who couldn't even keep track of her own son? The answer seemed obvious, and yet she was infested with niggling discomfort. Something about the way the woman's face had been clenched and flushed as she'd burst out. Something about Flasterborn's smile . . .

"TIPPY!"

She yelped as the device screamed in her ear, still turned up high. She scrambled to her feet, twisting the dial back down.

"Yes, Mr. Flasterborn?"

"A cup of molasses when you get a chance."

"Of course, Mr. Flasterborn."

• • •

CHAPTER 21

DR. AUTOMATON AND THE IMPROBABLE

Walter awoke after precisely three hours of sleep, squashed inside a wood-and-wool chair, his knees by his ears. As his eyes groggily found focus, he struggled to remember where he was. This didn't look like his room. It was far too . . . clean.

The searing lights were painful. They built a wall in his mind—a blank haze. He peered down, seeing his pocketknife in one hand and the little white sphere he had been working on in the other.

What the . . . Oh yeah, his invention.

Last night, just as soon as he'd handed Cordelia off, he'd plonked himself into a chair across from the doors she'd been wheeled through.

The hour had been late, and he'd known he should be sleeping, but he couldn't possibly have managed that, with his best and only friend potentially dying right in front of him. Walter had known many dead people, but none of them had been Cordelia.

As he'd sat, waiting to hear news, a little green marble had hit his shoe. He'd gasped, "How did you get here?"

That's it? the marble had thought.

After all, it hadn't been easy following around the red-haired boy for the previous day. The boy had been walking over grass, rocks, and mud even. Do you know how hard it is to roll in mud? Then the boy had somehow found himself in the middle of the sky! The marble hadn't been happy about that but had managed to hop itself right up there with the boy's stinky black shoes. Then upstairs, across tiles, over many, many sick people's feet. (Why, the marble hadn't been sneezed on so much in its entire existence—humans were terribly wet things.) Finally, it had found its way back to the shoes it had been following.

And those shoes, attached to the boy, had been able to ask one only question: "How did you get here?"

Maybe the marble shouldn't have even bothered.

But then the boy had picked the marble up and gotten an idea.

In the wee hours of the night, when nearly everyone on Flaster Isle had slept, the boy had pulled something out of his sock, an old frog, made of gleaming white petrified wood. He'd begun, then, to invent.

That, thought the marble, *is more like it.*

But this had all happened the night before, and it was now morning. Walter's head was so overstuffed with the fluff of sleep that he could hardly remember the color of his underpants (which was uniquely impressive, as all of Walter's underpants were the same color).

He was staring down at the white wooden sphere, filled with green, and was trying desperately to push the fuzz from his mind, when an operator-less gurney rolled over his foot, causing him to jump—"Ouch!"—and instantly remember where he was.

Foot all but forgotten, he leapt to the door across from him, which (he checked for the eleventh time) was still locked. He peeked through the square window, crisscrossed with blue laser lines that zapped anyone who tried to reach beyond it. As he got closer, he could see between the laser lines, into to the empty hallway beyond. He desperately wished to see inside because his skin had started itching in anticipation; he couldn't wait any longer. He had planned to ask the next person who walked by—but he never got a good chance.

In the city of inventions, it was no wonder that humans were scarce. The hospital's janitor was a two-legged broom that sucked debris up through its bristles, and the nurse that patrolled the waiting room was a set of two robotic hands that would pop out of the wall with either a lollipop or a bandage. Very few people had come to wait, and those who had, stayed only a very short time. This worried Walter, though he didn't want to admit it.

He jiggled the knob, waiting for the door to open.

Meanwhile, the marble in his pocket, now surrounded by a strange new shell, was feeling much, much better.

Cordelia sat on a table—at least, that's what it felt like. It was cold, hard, and metal. Whoever had designed it knew very little about comfort. Neither did the man standing across from her—that is, if you could even call him that.

Dr. Automaton was very, very famous for being both a very good doctor and very not human. He was, in fact, the world's first and most successful nonhuman doctor. He had made a name for himself by curing all manner of diseases. The critics said he managed his incredible feats by extracting data in ways most human doctors would find . . . icky.

This is because human doctors know what pain is like. When you know what pain is like, and you see someone else in the midst of it, you begin to feel rather bad yourself. If you *don't* know what pain is like, and you see someone else experiencing it, it seems you might want to discover what it's all about. Sometimes that means creating pain where there isn't any, simply so you can see it up close.

That's what the critics said, anyway, but that's critics for you, always saying mean and nasty things. Who wants to hear about mean and nasty things? That's why most people ignore critics, even when they're right.

Cordelia had been much like everyone else. She had heard Dr. Automaton's critics but had just assumed they were jealous that *they* weren't robot doctors. It didn't matter anyway. She hadn't had a choice; no human doctor had been able to help. And, fortunately for Cordelia, this doctor had taken a liking to her case as soon as it had been wired through him.

"Curious."

His voice was synthesized to sound like a fifty-four-year-old man—which Flasterborn thought was the most trustworthy sort of person. He sounded like a mix of all the world's accents— which, at the time when he was invented, had felt like a good idea, to make him approachable. In reality it served more to make him sound like he was chewing on an irate parrot.

They had tried at first to give him skin, but the results had been . . . uncanny. Instead Flasterborn and his team had opted for a more traditional approach to a robot doctor. He had bungee tube arms, a speaker mouth, and camera lens eyes. His extendable limbs could make him as small as a toddler and so tall that the upper limits had never been tested. His hair was made from springs and screws because his creators had thought it would be a soft touch . . . so long as you didn't actually touch them.

"What's curious?" Cordelia's voice was sticky and more ragged than she remembered. Near-death apparently wasn't great for the vocal cords.

Dr. Automaton looked up at her, his eyes dimming. Cordelia's pupil shrank when met by the light, and she was forced to look away. There was something unsettling about him.

"Why, you should be dead already."

"H-how dare you! I should not!"

She scuttled backward on the metal table when Dr. Automaton's head shot several feet toward her, his neck extendable like his limbs. He stared at her a moment, taking her in.

"You will be."

Cordelia's breathing had become unnaturally fast. "Well, can you fix me?"

His eyes brightened for a moment, forcing her to squint, but this time she didn't look away.

"No." His neck retreated into his body.

"But you're the best doctor in the world . . ."

"And I am telling you, there is nothing more to be done."

Cordelia looked away. She had gained some hope during this trip and had thought that if she could just see the doctor, she might be okay. She refused to look at him as he continued, "But I am not the first to tell you that."

She shook her head.

"I have reviewed your files. You are a rare specimen,

Primpet child. Very rare. Have you ever been able to stop bleeding?"

Cordelia shrank with her voice. "Only sort of. The pills help."

One of his hands reached out for her, a blue laser shooting from his palm.

"Very interesting. Do you have family, Primpet?"

She suddenly tried to remember what those blasted critics had said after all. Something about how Dr. Automaton's patients would return, sometimes, more machine than human. They behaved strangely, almost like they were robots themselves, although no one had been able to prove anything. Cordelia found herself speaking rapidly as his hand approached.

"Yes! A lot of family! And they love me very much!"

Dr. Automaton's hand suddenly retracted with a thin *whoosh*.

"How unfortunate."

"So there's nothing you can do?"

He stared at her a moment. "There is nothing anyone can do."

And that was that. Cordelia suspected she had known the answer before she'd come.

"Be cautious, Primpet. If you lose much more blood, you will not need it anymore."

She nodded, the tears prickling at her eyes.

"I shall leave you with more of your required pills. I do not know how long they will help you. Hold out your hands."

Cordelia, confused, put her palms together in front of her. Dr. Automaton's head then shot out, causing her to flinch. A stream of pills spat from his mouth. She struggled to catch them all. The doctor then hacked a few times, and a bottle squeezed from between his metal teeth and fell on top of the pile.

With a bit of difficulty, she managed to drop the pills into the bottle, losing only one that fell and rolled beneath a cabinet.

"You have an allotted ten minutes remaining. Thank you."

The door shut behind him.

It had been a long time since Cordelia had been alone.

She curled up on the bench, remembering the bee. She buried her head in her knees and was surprised to feel them become wet as the tears escaped her best efforts.

Walter nearly left the waiting room, desperate to find a human nurse somewhere in the lifeless hospital, but was both ecstatic and terrified as Dr. Automaton loped out the door. He nearly passed right by Walter, before the boy tried to push into the hallway. A sensor blared, and the doctor stopped him, keeping the door closed with an iron grip as his eyelids unfurled like camera shutters.

"Who are you here to see?"

"Cordelia Primpet."

"Who are you?"

"Walter Mortinson."

In a fraction of a moment, Dr. Automaton was able to scan his archives and come up with that very important name. Then, as was proper protocol, he released the door.

"Room 505. Please have a nice visit . . . for the allotted eight minutes remaining."

"Thank you!"

Walter didn't need to hear it twice, and he bowled past the tall robot and down the hallway, nearly as gangly and unnatural as the doctor himself.

Dr. Automaton watched until Walter disappeared. Then the doctor pressed his ear, which was really an ear-shaped button, and spoke in a long code of clicks that roughly translated to: "Walter Mortinson has arrived."

Cordelia was still curled into a ball, even more tightly now. Her head was thoroughly stuffed. It was stuffed with worries and with sadness, but mostly with the Nothing.

The Nothing was something Cordelia had felt many times before. The Nothing was a lukewarm wave that would rise when she was very sad, or very angry, or very afraid. When Cordelia would worry, or anger, or sadden herself so much that she could no longer stand it, she would then become filled with the Nothing.

It was wonderful at first because the Nothing would wash everything else away. With all that Nothing, there simply wasn't space for anything foul, like being mad at her mother for taking away her book about aerial acrobatics ("because it's too dangerous for a girl like you"), or anything horrid, like worrying about what her mother would do if she found out that Cordelia had stolen the book of aerial acrobatics out of the garbage and hidden it under her mattress. There wasn't room for draining dread or excruciating gloom when you were stuffed with Nothing.

But after a while the Nothing would become pretty nasty too. See, at first you don't have to be sad or scared . . . but then, with all that Nothing, you don't get the nice things either. There is no happiness, no pride, no satisfaction, nor surprise, not even that lovely little flutter when you eat a delicious slice of your favorite sliced thing. Instead there's just . . . nothing.

And it keeps pouring and pouring, filling you up bigger and bigger with more and more—with every ounce of Nothing added, you feel even less of anything.

Then, suddenly, it all becomes gray. The world around you no longer has a smell, nor a taste, nor even a shape. Everything becomes dull and blobby. That dazzling sunrise out the window? A big ash-colored blob through the see-through square blob. That adorably fluffy puppy dog? A slobbery blob of hair. That delectable ice cream sundae? Cold blob.

That is the Nothing. Cordelia hated the Nothing. But there was little she could do to stop it.

And right then, curled on that metal slab, Cordelia felt the Nothing. She didn't notice how cold the table was underneath her. She couldn't feel the throbbing of her knee, which still refused to scab. She heard only the patter of her own heart.

She was so stuffed up with the Nothing that it was making her head feel very full—so full, in fact, that the Nothing was dribbling out her eye and her nose.

She sniffed back a wave of snot as she heard a rap on the door. She stayed silent, deciding that Dr. Automaton couldn't possibly be back. She wasn't dead yet—and even if it was him, she wasn't leaving.

"Cordelia?"

But she knew that voice, and, in spite of herself, she found it horribly comforting. Cordelia scooted up and disfigured her face into an impassive one, just barely remembering to wipe the tears away from her eye with her patch before she smoothed out what was left of her nightdress.

"Come in, Walter."

He peeked his head in, the words tumbling out. "How are

you? You look good! Or you look fine. I mean, it's good, though, and you don't look bad, but—"

She had to stop herself from smiling as she held up a hand. "I'm fine."

"What did the doctor say—was it Dr. Automaton?"

"He said nothing I haven't heard before."

"They couldn't . . . fix it?"

Cordelia shrugged, hoping it looked as normal as she didn't feel.

"Well, that's all right, then. You'll be all right, though, won't you?"

Now she had to force a smile. "As all right as ever."

"Great!"

The two stared at each other in a way that made the other person even more uncomfortable. Cordelia became suspicious when Walter started sweating.

"Hey, would you mind maybe going somewhere with me . . ." He faltered, trying to wipe the sweat from his forehead with the back of his sleeve. "I mean, if you're feeling up to it. You don't have to, though."

She stared at him, deciding something. After far longer than Walter felt comfortable with, she spoke. "I'd love to."

Walter beamed, taking her hand and helping her off the table. He knew she didn't need it, and she knew that he knew. . . . But he did it anyway, and neither felt like arguing.

CHAPTER 21 ½

. . .

WHERE THE END BEGAN

Eleven years ago Hadorah was no longer pregnant but somehow still glowed. The envious gaggle of Moormouth ladies supposed her famous inventor husband must have had something to do with it—a cream he'd conjured or a machine she'd slip into at night that would zap her wrinkles away. Hadorah would rather not have been the center of discussion but was amused in this case, as the local squawkers were right for once. Max was to blame.

But it wasn't anything to do with inventions. She was finally happy.

Still, he continued to tinker anyway—not that he could have stopped if he'd wanted to. For as long as he could remember, Max had had a horrible case of the tinkers. The tinkers resided in his fingers, he supposed, or maybe the part of his brain that dealt with his fingers, and they would compel him to do wonderful things. Now that he had a workroom in the house's garret all to himself, he wasn't going to stop anytime soon.

Hadorah clambered up the attic stairs. She didn't love to. It was strange up there, full of bizarre things that could sputter or spark or ignite at any second. But he'd asked her to come, and there was no saying no to Max, because he never said no to anything.

Today was particularly difficult, as her eyes were covered. The red bandana was tied extraordinarily tightly.

"I'm going to break something, Max."

"Well, then I'll have to fix it, won't I?"

She didn't need to be looking to know he was smiling. He didn't need to see her to know she wasn't.

Finally, after what felt like far too many stairs, they reached his table, and he gently unfurled the knot behind her head. The handkerchief fell, but her eyes were still closed.

"All right, you can open them."

She did and immediately gasped. Hadorah had thought that Max wouldn't be able to surprise her anymore—she'd already witnessed the impossible—but this was something else entirely.

"You made this for . . ."

She couldn't finish; she couldn't believe it.

A massive parade float stood in front of her. The base was

a garden, littered with blossoms, toys, and photographs of her and Max. Twisting above it all, with a thick, braided stem, was a great dahlia bud, shimmering in opalescent purples and reds.

Hadorah felt the skin on the back of her neck flutter as Max came up behind her and put his hands on her waist. His whisper in her ear sent shivers down her spine. "It's always for you."

He kissed the back of her head. Hadorah blinked away her fears, giving in to her own awe. She knew she would never be able to make something like this, but for once she didn't mind. She was in a never-ending dream.

A little voice, quiet but hopeful, rose from the floor below. "Fo' me?"

Hadorah turned as Max grinned more widely and kneeled to pick up Walter, only a toddler, with eyes taking up half of his round face. Max swung him around, to Hadorah's ire.

"Careful! Not in the workroom!"

But father and son laughed, in on the joke of being utterly infuriating together.

"Yes, always for you, too."

• • •

CHAPTER 22

THEY ALWAYS WORK

Nearly a dozen years later Hadorah sat, blankly watching the thin beginnings of the parade stretch across the plain in front of her.

She was unreadable as she took the familiar shapes in, waiting for them to finally disappear into the blinding sun beyond.

Hadorah hated parades.

Cordelia's sweating palm hooked on to the bar above her as she steered the balloon through the clouds.

She had begged Walter to take the reins, but he'd uttered four of the very worst words and had somehow convinced her otherwise. He'd annoyingly insisted, "You can do it," and she was certainly doing her best to prove him wrong.

Thunk!

Cordelia swung off course, away from the black projectile that had bounced off the balloon. The angry "Squawk!" of a robotic crow followed.

"It's fine! It's fine . . . just another bird."

Cordelia did her best to ignore Walter as he desperately tried to turn the balloon, but it wouldn't listen. Walter placed a hand on hers. Cordelia, relieved to no longer be in charge, relaxed at his touch, trying to let him guide the balloon—still he refused. He spoke right into her ear, so close that she could hear what he'd had for lunch.

"It's not working because you won't relax."

She huffed, her face puffing as her blood grew warmer. "Don't tell me to—"

"Relax." He squeezed her hand before releasing.

In spite of herself, Cordelia remained loose as she guided the craft once more. To her utter annoyance, she was flying more smoothly than ever. "Where are we going exactly?"

"You'll see. Take a right."

Cordelia did as he said, pulling down to coax the balloon over the tips of the mountain range below.

"We'll never find our way back. This is so far—" Cordelia's whine elongated into a gasp.

"Welcome to Ramsey Bluffs."

On the inside of a half-moon mountain range were clear stalagmites that had been built into the hills themselves.

These strange additions jutted hundreds of miles into the air, straight from the ground, all the way up to the peaks of the mountains. Walter looked on, enthralled. It was just as she'd promised.

Like movie projectors, the rocks cast shadows of the most amazing visions onto the mountains around them. Among the silhouettes were dragons, dancers, and lions—flickering together like a galactic snapshot.

Cordelia knew the answer but couldn't help asking—

"Is that them?"

Walter, seized with anticipation and fear, managed a nod. She responded with a sad smile.

"Is it as wonderful as they say?"

"You'll see."

"How?"

Walter turned, pulling something from his jacket. It was the white orb he had been tinkering on. In the middle it was green. The device was palm-size, round, and perfectly distinct.

He'd made an eye.

It spun in his palm, the mechanical pupil rolling up to meet Cordelia's matching one.

"Is that for—"

He nodded, and she stared, dumbstruck.

Walter regained his confidence and reached for her eye

patch. Cordelia jerked away, out of instinct and panic, before grabbing for the shiny black fabric herself.

"Let me."

She pinched the material between two fingers and slowly inched it aside—revealing a shadowed cavern where her second eye had once been.

Walter took her in for a long moment, and for those few seconds Cordelia lived out every nightmare she'd had for the past nine years. But unlike any of her bad dreams, Walter didn't run away. In fact, he even smiled.

He then handed her the orb. It was warm somehow. She hesitantly fit it in, then clenched both eyes tightly.

She jerked when Walter placed his hands on her shoulders, guiding her to the edge of the basket. "Don't worry."

She sighed, taking his advice once more. To her frustration, she couldn't stop doing that.

"Now open."

Slowly her eyes flickered. The mighty mountains stood before her in all their magnificence. The silhouette he'd guided them to was the largest, most intricate of all: two people embracing. Cordelia's face fell. Walter stood behind her, fearing her silence but emboldened still.

"Does it work?"

She forced a smile, pivoting to look at him.

"Of course," she lied. She glanced over the lip of the

basket at the mountains beyond. All she saw, however, were hulking gray stones. "It's exactly what I imagined."

Walter closed his eyes, breathing in sharply. He had to do it now. So, he leaned in and kissed her. It was slight and unsure, almost nothing, really. Cordelia reeled back with the electric shock of it.

Walter blinked wide. "I've wanted to do that . . ."

He met her eyes, both of them, and was humiliated to see that they looked very sad. Her voice was airy and forced, like a stranger's, when she said, "We should be getting back."

"I'm so sorry. I didn't—"

"You didn't do anything. It's just time to go."

He nodded, his heart melting and dripping down to his shoes. He reached up for the handle and guided them back as quickly as he could. He offered her a smile, trying to bring back the thin hairs of normalcy.

"Take a last look," he said. "It may be the last time in a long time that we get to see it."

She turned, looking out at one of the most wonderful sights in the world . . . but all she saw were the mountains. She took the eye out and looked again at the view. It was the very same.

The eye didn't work, but she couldn't bear to tell him that.

"Why did you make this for me?"

Walter looked down, surprised to see his invention back in her hand.

"Isn't it obvious? I've always . . ."

He glanced at her, staring a moment too long. She looked away, replacing the eye so that she would look ordinary again. Looking ordinary was the best defense against just about anything, she'd found.

"Never mind."

He nodded in response. They floated back without another word.

Walter let the balloon down, the hospital in front of them and the glasstic dome gleaming above. After the basket weave of branches rocked to a rest, Walter held a hand out for Cordelia, who ignored him. Instead she gracelessly hopped over the side, catching a leg on the basket as she went. Cordelia righted herself, airsick, and brushed her stained nightdress off, trying to rid herself of the embarrassment.

She refused to look at Walter as he spoke. "I have to go see Flasterborn now, but you wait here and I'll come right back."

She turned, placing a hand on his arm, looking only at the space between her fingers on his hound's-tooth coat. "I have to go home, Walter."

"You could stay with me."

"No, I—"

He ducked down to her, his voice hitching, higher and faster, saying things he'd only before thought. "Really! I'm sure Flasterborn would let you. You don't have to go—"

She blinked up at him, one blue eye, one green, both resolute. "You may not belong in Moormouth, but I do."

Walter's shoulders folded in as his spirit caved. Cordelia shook her head, avoiding the eyes of the mother at the door of the hospital, who'd stopped to stare curiously at the two. When she wouldn't leave, Cordelia quickly popped out her eye and shot her a look. The woman hurried her son inside.

Cordelia replaced the eye and ducked down with Walter, whispering into the cavern he'd made between his chin and chest, "Do what you were meant to."

"What about you?"

"What about me?"

He stared at her, desperate, searching. "I—"

"Need to leave."

His head swam as he stared back, the truth that she wouldn't stay with him pooling on his surface, refusing to sink in. Then he had a thought. "How do you plan on getting back, if I stay here?"

Cordelia shrugged, gesturing to the balloon behind him. "*When* you stay, I'll just take the balloon. I know how to steer now, after all."

He nodded, unable to think of anything more to convince her. "That's fine; take it." He stuffed his hands deep into his pockets, then walked toward the tallest building in the most desirable city in the whole world. Cordelia watched him and tried to stop herself—she really did—but her voice escaped anyhow.

"Oh. And, Walter!"

He turned quickly. She smiled, as sincerely as she knew how. ". . . Happy Birthday."

He smiled back, nodding, then turned, hoping she didn't know how crestfallen he really was.

But of course she did.

CHAPTER 23

. . .

THE TEST

Tippy was preparing for the horribly frightening task of cleaning the vaselator, which involved a very long bungee cord and several pairs of underpants, when she heard a timid knock at the door. This was particularly curious, as the door knocker installer wasn't due until next week.

"Come in?"

Tippy nearly had a heart attack on the spot when Walter Mortinson poked his big curly head in. "Oh! Sorry. I can come back—"

"No!"

She rushed over and dragged him into her office. Tippy had waited far too long for Walter to arrive. They finally got to meet, and all she could do was stare. Walter also couldn't look away, finding her oddly familiar.

"Hello. My name is Walter—"

"Mortinson. I know. We've been expecting you."

Walter's cheeks burned as he rubbed the hairs on the back of his neck.

"Sorry about that. We got caught up."

Tippy didn't bother asking who the "we" was. She had been watching Walter for the last eight years, and he hadn't had a single friend for the entirety of that time. Perhaps it was an imaginary friend, or maybe he was talking about the voices in his own head. Geniuses often have voices in their head, she decided.

Tippy then tapped expertly on the mechanism in her ear, informing Flasterborn of their visitor. Her lips turned up shyly as she realized that Walter was investigating the listening device.

"It's a communicator, runs on taps that it translates into—"

"Fabulous. Let him in!" Flasterborn's voice boomed through the communicator, causing both to reel back.

"Flasterborn will see you now."

"Th-thank you, Miss . . ."

Tippy knew everyone's name who entered the office, but people rarely asked what hers was. After a second of surprise, she stuttered, "T-Tippy Tedesco."

"Miss Tippy Tedesco."

Walter nodded his head at her as he rubbed his palms on

his pants. Tippy hurried forward, smiling as he stood before the door, waiting as patiently as he could.

"Welcome, Mr. Mortinson, to the office of Horace Odwald Flasterborn."

Tippy pressed a button, hidden in the shape of a roaring lion in the doorframe's engraved molding. The ornate doors creaked open, revealing a positively gleeful Flasterborn sitting inside, beard like a pig's tail.

"Walter, my boy. Finally."

Walter smiled back, not looking at Tippy as he followed the closing doors in. It was no matter. Tippy couldn't have stopped staring at Flasterborn's glowing face if she had wanted to.

The doors shut with an audible suction, locking the magic in—and Tippy out. She shook herself from her reverie and hurried back to business: lying face-first on the ground, eye to the hole under the little gold button.

This was going to be good.

Walter entered Flasterborn's office and suddenly felt something he hadn't before: a sense of purpose. Maybe this *was* where he was supposed to be.

Walter ducked out of the way just as a toy train zoomed over his head, racing through the maze winding around the room. Lips parted, he took in the rest of the room with a slow glance across.

It was, well, *wonderful*.

There were inventions that were as tall as the ceiling and thrummed and whirled in tizzies, spitting out miniature firework shows. There were inventions as wide as Walter could stretch his arms—those that bore strings thinner than strands of dust, which danced in the windless air, making soft but tremendously pleasant sounds. There were inventions that looked just like pocket watches, but which fluttered around, struggling against their chains affixed to the ceiling. Then, of course, there was the machine that puffed out smelly bubbles—one of which, a deep mahogany, circled Walter's head before bursting and filling him with the scent of home.

"Welcome, Walter."

Walter's eyes shot open. He had all but forgotten that perhaps the most famous man he had ever heard of was sitting but a few steps away.

"Hello."

Walter debated bowing, as he bounced from foot to foot. Then he dove into the seat across from his hero. Flasterborn looked on, eyes alight with flickering curiosity.

Despite his nerves (or perhaps because of them), Walter could not pull his attention from the pretty perfume bottle that the bubbles arose from.

"One of your father's, I admit. He did most of the fiddle-faddle in here." Flasterborn swept a hand coolly over the room. Walter was unexpectedly filled with awe and pride.

When Flasterborn leaned in to whisper, Walter couldn't stop himself from mirroring the action.

"He was always the dreamer. I'm more . . . practical, you see."

Walter's head quirked. What could be more practical? Flasterborn's smile slipped for only a second before growing wider than before.

"But there's no need for us to talk about me. I want to learn about you."

Here we go, thought Walter. His mouth went dry as he tried to open it. He urgently dug through his thoughts, trying to strike upon something, anything, that would explain why he was worthy of being here. His creations were nothing like the ones in the room, or others his father had made. His inventions weren't pretty, happy things, and he suddenly felt a bit ashamed of them.

Walter's fear only grew as Flasterborn leaned in closer, whispering with such intensity that Walter almost didn't hear the words.

"What is . . ."

This was it.

". . . your favorite sandwich?"

Walter blinked, confused. That was not quite what he'd expected, but Flasterborn's eyebrows dipped in with a sincerity that made Walter answer without thinking.

"Uh, I don't know. Maybe pudding—"

He was horrified when Flasterborn's smile fell and his mustache drooped back down. Walter had disappointed him? As Flasterborn opened his mouth, Walter continued, desperate to bring the smile back.

"Or maybe pickles and cheese?"

Flasterborn's fist smacked the table with audible delight.

"Ah! Pickles and cheese!"

Walter released a sigh of relief as Flasterborn snuggled back into his overstuffed chair.

"Your father liked pickles and cheese too. I'm more of a cheese and onion man myself, but we're all in the same family. Now on to the serious business . . ."

Walter was reassured by the idea that his dad had liked pickles and cheese; maybe he and his father did have some things in common after all.

Flasterborn picked up a little pair of gold glasses that pinched his upturned nose. He then squinted at Walter.

"Turn this way."

Without thinking, Walter followed the older man's finger to the left.

"And that way."

Walter then looked to the right. Flasterborn squinted at him for a moment more before nodding thoughtfully to himself.

Walter put a hand to his cheek, trying to feel what Flasterborn had seen.

"What is it?"

"Everything, my dear boy. It's everything."

Flasterborn flipped up a secret panel on his desk, revealing a set of glowing, spinning, humming gears beneath. Flasterborn selected a circular toggle, twisting it slightly to the right. As he did—"Whoa!"—Walter found that the chair he was sitting in swiveled the same way.

Flasterborn looked up at Walter, nodded, and clipped the panel back into place, out of sight. He then folded his hands.

"You look quite a bit like your father, but mostly from the left side."

Walter's head bobbed again, dazed, and he switched his hand to feel his left cheek.

"Good enough. You pass," declared Flasterborn.

"I do?"

"So now I would very much like to tell you something."

Shoving his concerns down to the bottom of his belly, Walter sat up in his seat. He definitely wanted to hear a secret. He didn't even particularly like secrets, but he had never heard one from a legend before.

"But first I have something I think you'd like to see."

Walter's eyes opened as wide as saucers as Flasterborn heaved himself from his cushy chair—the arms of it releasing from their hug and settling back into their usual shape. Walter allowed himself to stare for only moment at the bizarre fixture before stumbling up and following the shorter man to the corner of the room.

Flasterborn stopped before a black vase, just like the one outside the office, that was as tall as Flasterborn himself, inked in brilliant gold swirls.

"Alleyoop!"

The old man winked before vaulting himself into the broad mouth with one hand. Walter ran after him but arrived too late, and glanced down into the abyss below. But there was no water nor dead things (which were found in the bottom of the vases in his own home) down there. It was an elevator shaft of sorts.

Echoing out from the bottom he heard, "Come along!"

Walter looked about cautiously before easing himself down the tube as well. This felt like a test, and it also felt very frightening. Before his fear could get the better of him—

Shoop!

He was sucked out of sight.

Neither was around to notice when a very curious (but not at all snoopy) Tippy counted to ten and then hopped into the second vaselator outside, following after them.

. . .

Walter was surprised that when the tube ended, he was softly pulled to the top, or was it the bottom? Somewhere along the way, he supposed, he must have been upsided down. Nonetheless, now that he was upsided up at the top (or bottom), he could easily lift himself out.

He jumped off the lip of the vase to the ground below. Walter could hardly take in his surroundings before being pulled away by a whistle ahead. Flasterborn trotted alone down a long hall. Walter had to jog to catch up.

They were in a bizarre sort of hallway—all black and gold. There were huge darkened glass panels on both sides. It was extraordinarily shiny for a room without any windows. Walter couldn't help but think that someone had spent a lot of money to make this room look like it had cost a lot of money.

He finally caught up to Flasterborn, who stood before one of the great glass sheets lining the walls. The man casually walked to the left side of Walter as he spoke.

"Do you know where we are, my boy?"

Walter shook his head. He felt this interview was going poorly. Flasterborn just beamed, however, clapping his hands.

Lights glittered on above them, illuminating rooms behind the glass, on both sides of the hall. Walter gasped, spinning to take it all in. Each one of Flasterborn's fantastical inventions was housed inside an exhibit, like in a museum.

"Where are we?"

Walter regained his senses, rushing to the window on the other side of the hall. Beyond the window was a cubicle filled with water. An old man, with a beard and hair so long that they floated to the top of the tank, swam behind the glass. In his mouth was a device that puffed up with each breath into rainbow-colored chipmunk cheeks.

"The Swim Bladder!" Walter shouted as he held a finger out, pointing at the bright *F* logo on the side of the device. Out of the corner of his eye, Walter then saw the adjacent window, and his face lit up again. He rushed there next and pressed his nose up as he watched.

Beyond this window was a room, a young girl's room. A twentysomething woman, wearing bright pink princess pajamas that were a tad tight, was asleep, drool pooled on her pillow. She wore a metal helmet that had a pipe that shot out the top of it and turned into a paintbrush in her hand. The brush moved feverishly, despite the girl's lack of consciousness. It painted a mural of the woman's dream on the wall, one of a little girl riding a unicorn.

Walter pointed again, hollering, "Paint by Slumber!"

Flasterborn sniffed, his smile faltering. "Yes, but—"

Walter turned to look at him, but was distracted by the display across the hall. He grabbed his chest, already certain of what it was, but hurried over to see it up close.

A man rode a winged tricycle, flying in circles around the room, which had been made to look like the sky outside.

"The Flycycle—"

Flasterborn grabbed Walter's shoulder, cutting him off, and then spun him around so that they were face-to-face.

"Ah, yes, but those are all inventions Maxwell—er, that your father *helped* me design . . . antiques."

He snuffled again, sucking through his front teeth.

"You must know some of my more recent products; they're household staples."

Flasterborn steered the boy down the hall to an even fancier section of demonstrations. The exhibits here were quite a bit larger and more ornate. Flasterborn planted Walter in front of one—inside which was a little boy, sitting at a lone table with a single cup of water. He held an oddly intricate straw in one hand that seemed to be trying to wriggle out of his fingers. He slowly lowered it into the drink. Flasterborn pointed to it, his voice confident.

"The Self-Stirring Straw."

Just as the boy let go, the straw dropped into the liquid and sent up an impressive bolt of electricity that caused him to squeal as it singed the hair hanging over his eyes.

Flasterborn yanked a confused Walter to the adjacent window. Beyond it was a very large woman at a desk, working on a delicate model airplane, tongue sticking out as she positioned the rudder on with tweezers. She reached for a roll of tape on the edge of the desk.

"Double-Sided Super Glape."

The woman peeled a piece off and gently stuck it to the plane. After pressing for a second, she pulled her hand away. The rudder stuck to the tape well, but, unfortunately, so did her rubber glove and a number of her arm hairs. She winced as she ripped the tape off.

Flasterborn spun Walter around hastily, allowing him a view of the grandest-looking exhibit. Walter peered in, unsure.

"What is it?"

On a crystal pillar was a square plastic box, encased in glass, floodlights illuminating it from every angle.

"The toast box."

Walter looked back at the display blankly. Flasterborn rolled his eyes, pointing at the inscription on one side of the box: "The best thing since sliced bread!" Flasterborn then read the other side out loud: "Every family has one."

Walter shrugged, craning his neck to see other interesting contraptions. "Mine didn't."

Flasterborn grabbed his shoulder again, tapping on the glass.

"That invention alone made enough money to add four floors to the building you are currently standing at the top of."

The boy finally nodded, impressed. "That's good. Otherwise we'd be suspended in air."

There was a pause as Flasterborn considered the oddling in front of him. *Perhaps a bit too much like Max,* he thought. Flasterborn then shook the idea from his head and directed the boy into one of the empty rooms behind the glass, inside which were long worktables composed of thick marble slabs. On either side of the room were ceiling-high displays of the finest tools Walter had ever seen.

Flasterborn waved Walter to one side of a table as he took a seat on the other side. The lights lowered, as did Flasterborn's voice. Walter supposed it might not be a coincidence.

"Enough about me. I've been . . . looking after you since the tragic passing of your father."

Walter was surprised when Flasterborn reached a hand out and gave him a sympathetic squeeze. The expression on the old man's face made him look even older. Flasterborn seemed to catch himself and smiled again.

"I know about some of your inventions. A revived rabbit?"

Walter pulled his hand away in surprise. How could Flasterborn know about that?

"Ralph. I just made him for fun."

"But don't you see? It's more than fun! It's marketable!"

Walter wiggled in his seat, not quite able to get comfortable. "I don't know . . ."

"I do. You were given a gift."

Walter took in the cheery face across from him for a second and was warmed by the hope that the man might be telling the truth. Flasterborn persisted, "Why else would you invent, if not to make money from it?"

Walter shrugged and looked down; the warm feeling had extinguished. Flasterborn ducked, catching his eye.

"Why did you come here, Walter?"

"You invited me."

Flasterborn shook his head, wiping his gloved hands off on a handkerchief, then stuffing it back into his pocket.

"But there must have been a reason why you traveled all this way. You want something. Money? Power? Fame . . . like your father?"

Walter's ears perked. He had heard more about his father in the last twenty minutes than in the previous nine years.

"Is that why he came here?"

Flasterborn shifted his belly, leaning back and closing one eye as he continued, "Your father was much like you. He had grand ideas and was looking for someone to guide him." Flasterborn's voice became quiet. "He could have done great things, if only . . ."

Walter looked around the lavish hall, at the many tools on the walls around him—all he would ever need. "Why did he leave?"

Flasterborn shook his head, petting his mustache with his pinky. "That's difficult to explain to someone your age. First I'd like to tell you why he came here."

Walter nodded vigorously, but Flasterborn looked more severe than ever.

"I don't tell you this lightly, Walter. You and I will be the only ones to know now, and we must keep it that way. It will be our bond. Can you do that?"

Walter simply couldn't believe this was happening. No one had ever trusted him with so much as a secret that everyone else already knew.

"Of course."

Flasterborn then breathed in deeply as he looked way up at the ceiling in the way people do when they try to retrieve something from the spine of their memories. "It was a very hot year, I remember. The kind of hot that melts your bones. Summer came, and I'd nearly sweated out every good idea I had. I had just built this place, and I do believe it stole something important from my gears, something I didn't get back until your father was given to me."

He stared at Walter in a sharp way that made the boy want to say something.

"I see."

Although, he didn't really.

But this seemed to satisfy Flasterborn, who went on,

straightening his beard as he concentrated on something invisible in the walls.

"I had been feeling horribly lost. I couldn't devise a single contraption that was worth even a penny. The darkness loomed, and I worried I would never have inspiration again. Then I heard about something rather fantastic that could change it all." Walter found himself leaning over the worktable as Flasterborn continued. "News traveled to me from very, very far away, from an island long forgotten, about a boy who was making impossible things."

"Who was he?"

Flasterborn chuckled. "Your father."

Walter sucked in, his eyes wide.

Flasterborn laughed loudly now, remembering. "Why, he hadn't even a proper tool set. He was a poor, dirty thing with no money and no family. He scrounged up whatever he could find and, somehow, transformed it. He could make anything fly or blink or sing. Ask him to turn a plastic bag into dancing shoes? No problem. Nothing could stop him."

Walter blanched. Maxwell had been that amazing? He was really nothing like his father after all. Flasterborn only laughed more loudly, however.

"Any other year, any other season, and I would have thought him a threat and squashed the poor boy. But, no. Max was given to me so that my magic would return."

Flasterborn held his hands out wide. "I invited him here and took him on as my apprentice."

Walter's mind spun, filled with fuzz. "My father . . ."

He couldn't finish the thought, too overcome by what he'd learned.

"Was special," Flasterborn supplied, reaching out two fingers and tilting Walter's chin up to the right, into the shining bulb above.

Walter could hardly breathe as Flasterborn pulled away, a glint in his eye. "Your father had amazing promise, but he gave it all up. He left me with only his old inventions, a bucket full of memories, and this." From out of his coat Flasterborn brought a little silver cube, encased in a clear plastic box. Flasterborn reverently unlocked the plastic box and retrieved the cube. He held it out to the boy. It looked so innocent and ordinary.

Walter's hand shook as he reached for it. As soon as his bare fingers rested on the gleaming surface, however, Flasterborn tutted, pulling a handkerchief from his pocket and handing it to him. Walter flushed, grabbing the box with the fabric.

"What is it?"

"That," Flasterborn began, "is very much what I wanted to ask you. Your father eventually made the decision to leave. I begged him to see some sense. Instead he gave me this blasted box and told me it was the only thing I would ever need. He never explained it, however, and I've been puzzling over it ever since. You must solve the riddle for me, Walter."

Walter delicately twisted the box one way and then the other. But there were no buttons, no levers, and nothing seemingly extraordinary.

After a very close look, he finally set it down. Flasterborn's eyes were wide. "Have you figured it out?" he asked.

Walter thought very hard. This was a test, he knew, but unfortunately, he worried that he wouldn't be able to solve the mystery. If Flasterborn hadn't in fourteen years, then how would Walter?

"I think . . . ," Walter began, "that some things aren't meant to be known. Perhaps . . . the point of it is that we do not know, and that's the loveliness of it."

Flasterborn's face grew dark again. "Yes, well, you can continue working on it. There's time."

Walter sighed. That wasn't the answer? Why, he was horrible at tests. Then Flasterborn smiled again.

"Your father was wonderful, Walter. The only mistake I made was allowing him to slip away." He fell back into his chair, face twisted. "But now we've been given another chance, see?"

He smiled at the boy, a big bright smile that very few had ever seen.

"In life you make decisions—some that determine the rest of your days. Your father made one of those choices when he left for Moormouth—a wretched place where no one has any worth beyond making it all the more wretched. He was on the brink of everything and gave it away."

Walter could feel the skin on the back of his hands prickle as Flasterborn stared into him, his words now clipped and his gaze unblinking.

"Say yes, and you will stay here with me. You will have everything you could ever dream of. Say no, and I will have you dropped wherever you would like to go. It's up to you, really, but remember what your father did. You and I . . . we could finally figure out that blasted box, Walter—together. We could have everything."

Flasterborn squinted at the boy, whose forehead was scrunched in concentration.

"So, if I stay now, will I ever go back?"

"There would be no reason to."

Walter thought so hard, his head hurt.

"When must I decide by?"

Flasterborn snorted in a way that reminded Walter of when Ms. Wartlebug had explained to the children that she wasn't going to be teaching math because they wouldn't understand it.

"I can't say that I care to miss another moment of what

could be. So . . ." He leaned in, his gloved fingers sliding on the glossy table below. "Everything? Or nothing?"

Though his whisper was soft, it rustled out the open door and into the long hallway that Tippy was waiting at the end of, still peeking up from inside the vase.

She couldn't see their faces, which made her heart pound faster as she waited for a response.

CHAPTER 24

TIPPY TEDESCO

Oh, conflab it all—Tippy had done it again! It was her fault. She was certain of it. She had almost quite definitely snooped. What was worse, she had rushed away, hoping not to get caught. Why should one rush, unless they are horribly nosy?

Tippy brushed the snout in question, aggravated with herself as she paced, puffing out quick, soft breaths. When the door behind her finally cracked open, she shot straight up, speaking as she spun around.

"Mr. Mortin—"

But it was Flasterborn's glowing cheeks, not Walter's, that greeted her.

"Just me, Tippy. Molasses, please."

He winked, which would have normally caused her to melt, but she was feeling particularly solid today.

"Of course. . . . Should I make a cup for Mr. Mortinson as well—before he goes?"

Flasterborn's chuckles trailed him as he clipped toward his office.

"No need, my dear. I'm glad to say that my boy will be staying."

Tippy's head quirked. "For how long?"

Flasterborn looked back at her, hand on the knob. "Indefinitely."

"But he said . . ."

He bristled, stopping in the doorway. "He said?"

And Tippy instantly knew she had made a mistake.

"What did you hear him say, Ms. Tedesco?"

Tippy stumbled back, stuttering, "I-I don't—I just—I—"

He got nose to nose with her—a mere five inches from her face (three and half inches for her nose and one and a half for his)—and flicked her gold listening device, causing it to whine unpleasantly.

"What did you hear?"

She stared into his eyes. It was like many dreams she had had, and yet it was so different. For one thing, the vein in Horace's neck had never bulged this way in her fantasies. But she still hoped beyond hopes that this encounter could end the same way her dreams usually did. This was Flasterborn, for Flaster's sake! She had to trust him.

"Everything. I heard everything." The words spilled out, and though she felt relieved to no longer hold the secret, she found herself quivering.

He raised an eyebrow and then, to her delight, smiled, pushing himself away. "So then you know."

"That he wants to go home."

He met her eyes again. "You know that we cannot let him make that mistake."

"What choice do we have? He doesn't want to stay."

Flasterborn shook his head. "Oh, don't be silly. We have everything here for him."

"But what about his family?"

"That woman doesn't deserve him."

"But she's his mother."

"She's a murderer!" Flasterborn's head snapped to her, face distorted and maroon. His nostrils flared momentarily before he closed his eyes, calming himself. "Hadorah Mortinson does not deserve Max. She deserves Moormouth."

Tippy's head was pounding, trying to keep up. "And you deserve . . . Walter?"

She cringed, waiting for the explosion that was certain to come, but instead she heard a laugh. "Of course I do. Have you seen them, Tippy? My elevators and situlas, my ever-burning bulbs? Have you seen what I did? I was the most amazing inventor in the world."

Tippy nodded rapidly, remembering who this man—no, legend—really was.

"But the world hadn't seen Maxwell yet."

Tippy stopped nodding.

"I created this city from nothing, and the effort of it drained me. I had lost my spark, years of building for nothing. And then a boy appeared who could turn his very dreams into reality. Even if *my* ideas had become dusty, there were so many more. He gave those sparks to me. All they needed was my name on the side. Now everyone knows them. Everyone was able to have me again, thanks to Maxwell." Flasterborn shook his head. "Then as quickly as he'd arrived, he disappeared." His face, as creased as it was, lit up—a child's again. "But he's been returned, and now everything will be splendid. And before molasses hour, no less!"

Something had changed inside Tippy forever. Now when she looked upon Flasterborn, her tummy didn't flip; it wrenched. "But we can't make him—"

He placed a hand on her shoulder. "We must do what's right."

Tippy Tedesco had been working for Horace Flasterborn for precisely thirteen years, zero months, five days, and twelve hours—and right at that moment, she didn't care to spend a second more with him.

"I understand, sir."

"Oh, I'm so pleased, Tippy. I knew you'd stand behind me. You always do."

He shuffled into his office, a skip in his step. Not a second later her earpiece blared, "MOLASSES, PLEASE!"

Tippy jumped, shaking her ringing ear. Then, with a smile, she realized that she could finally do something wonderful. She plucked the earpiece off and tossed it onto the ground. She didn't need it anymore. Tippy had something far more important to attend to.

She then spun on her heel and hurried to the vaselator.

What she didn't see was Flasterborn sitting in his desk chair, thinking about an old silver box that he was doomed to never understand.

Walter Mortinson stared at the box. He was careful not to touch it with his bare fingers, for Flasterborn seemed terribly certain he mustn't.

It was difficult to maneuver, however, with the fabric in the way. He poked and prodded it, then shook it gently. Nothing. It was just an ordinary silver cube.

Walter finally set it down. It seemed he was condemned never to understand his father. Maxwell was too brilliant, too mysterious, too remarkable, and Walter was just . . . Walter. It never seemed good enough.

With a deep sigh from the bottom of his belly, he gazed

hopelessly into the metallic surface, only to see his own distorted reflection staring back. His face looked tired and unusually frowny. Instinctively he swiped his thumb across his reflection in the cube, and for a second he saw something— something rather colorful.

Had it been only a trick of the light?

Emboldened, Walter pressed his thumb into the cube's surface. When he pulled away, the colors lingered for slightly longer.

Now his heart beat quite fast. This . . . this might be the answer. He might just solve it after all. Walter bit his lip, thinking. Maybe it was a technology activated by finger-prints? He rubbed the back of his hand against one side of the cube, testing it. The colors emerged again and lingered long enough for him to see the faded silhouettes of what appeared to be people.

So it wasn't fingerprints, but perhaps warmth? Walter brought the cube up to his face, excited now, and breathed on it in a mighty puff, but nothing happened. Not heat, then.

With another sigh he thought hard, before making a deci-sion. Maybe it needed your skin and warmth at the same time?

Looking around the room cautiously, he untucked his shirt and lifted it up as best he could, and placed the cube underneath, close to his chest. In this final effort he wrapped his arms all the way around it, forcing it further into his body

CHAPTER 25

. . .

WONDERFULLY SHARP TEETH

Buddy Moberly had always dreamed of being a janitor. He had never, however, faced such a mess as the one in the middle of the Honeyoaks Park after the Bumballoon Jubilee. Why, there had been oil and tree bark and butterflies even. It had taken him all day to mop the grass, and now he was on his hands and knees with tweezers and a magnifying glass, picking out every stray antenna. He was so focused that he almost didn't notice the strange scuttling thing running in from the west. It had many legs and a stout, square body, but no head. This was no animal at all; it was a vehicle.

All at once, mere feet from Buddy, the machine halted and a door popped opened. Out from the vehicle stepped a lanky kid whose wild red hair in the darkness looked like a match on fire. The boy was wide-eyed from the journey, and he held on to the door as if he were worried the world around him

in a tight embrace. He squeezed his eyes shut, willing this to work.

Walter focused on his heartbeat, warming the cube, until its coldness no longer bit at his skin. Finally satisfied, he opened his eyes and saw something most peculiar. From between the gaps in the buttons of his shirt came a bright, shining light.

Wide-eyed, Walter pulled the box back out. It had been activated. Lit from within, there were flickering pictures of people—happy people.

He recognized them and gasped. Facing him was a shot of Hadorah and Maxwell kissing. They were young and so very cheerful that he couldn't quite believe it. He'd never seen Hadorah so happy.

His eyes tickling, he turned the cube around, taking in the different pictures on each side. They shifted after a few moments to new pictures. All were of Max and Hadorah, working together, going on adventures, testing inventions. Walter flipped to the bottom of the cube, where the photo featured not just Max and Hadorah but Flasterborn as well.

He looked younger too and much, much happier than he seemed now. His arms were thrown around his employees, gripping their shoulders tightly.

That's all it is, thought Walter. A box of pictures.

With a smile, he looked at them again and again, noticing

Flasterborn in more than a few—in each one looking more cheerful than before. When the colors began to fade, Walter hugged it to his body once more, filling it with all the warmth that he could.

That was all the box did, and it was truly quite lovely.

Tippy pulled herself out of the vaselator and stepped into the hallway, the rooms glowing around her. People were testing all sorts of inventions, prisoners of this place. She would free them, yes, but there was someone she had to see first.

Tippy peered into each cubicle before finally coming to Walter's. He sat alone at the worktable, peering at a small silver box, head down and eyes dazed, as though in a trance. Tippy tentatively opened the door, hoping greatly that he was unharmed.

As soon as the door opened, a rush of wind pushed past her that smelled a bit sweet and intoxicating. When the air cleared, Walter shook his head, face returning to normal.

"Oops! I just started fiddling and lost sense of myself. Sorry." He perked up. "Did Flasterborn send you to take me home?"

Tippy breathed in, debating how to explain what Flasterborn had actually said, but then she dashed those thoughts. Walter looked so nice, sitting at the table. Instead she replied, "Yes, Mr. Mortinson."

"Oh good. I was worried for a se
here forever."

He smiled to himself, standing to me
the cube, now a plain, polished silver.

Curious, she brought it up to her
exactly?"

"It's for Flasterborn, I think. My fat
have it."

Frowning, Tippy flipped it around. The
be anything particularly special about this l
see . . ." And for a moment she did. As she sh
she thought she saw something colorful in the
a second later it was gone. How strange. She s
slipping the box into her pocket.

"Right this way, Mr. Mortinson. Let me sh
fastest vehicle. It will take you wherever you
We'll go the back way, I think."

wouldn't stay put long enough for him to find his footing.

Once he finally let go of the door, it instantly clipped shut. The scuttler then shot into motion, racing the way it had come—sending terrified bees scattering.

Walter ambled across the field toward Buddy. "What are you doing?"

"What does it look like I'm doing?"

Walter pondered the question seriously as he watched the man tweeze the grass. "Mowing the lawn very, very slowly?"

Buddy snorted. "I'm cleaning the mess that butcher made."

Walter screwed up his brow in confusion. "What butcher?"

"From the contest, with that awful butterfly balloon. Sad to hear about the crash, but serves him right for making such a mess."

"The crash?!"

"Oh sure, just off Elverpool a few hours ago. Real explosive, I hear."

The boy took off running, shouting a polite "Thank you!" as he went.

Buddy shook his head, plucking a butterfly leg off a daisy. He truly hated messes.

Walter ran faster and faster to where he hoped his car would be. He felt a lump rise in his throat, however, when he remembered the state it had been in the last time he had seen it. Even if it was there, it wouldn't be drivable. He'd need to fix it or find something else. But there wasn't time; what was he going to . . . and then he caught sight of it.

The hearse sat right in its spot on the grass where he'd left it, and yet it was nothing like he'd ever seen.

It had been completely renewed, beyond what it had been before the journey, even. All the dings, dongs, and dents had been pounded out. The scuffs and the scratches had been unscuffed and unscratched. Why, even the chunk of tire that had been knocked out by the side of the cliff had been somehow glued back.

Why on earth had the car been cleaned this well?

The answer, of course, was because nothing in Honeyoaks could ever look dinged, scuffed, or scratched. It simply wasn't allowed. So the bees, as they'd been trained, had lifted the car at night and had brought it to the town's Fixers. The Fixers made sure nothing in Honeyoaks was amiss . . . no matter what.

The next morning the hearse had been returned to its spot, looking newer than new, just as shiny as the town around it—waxed so nicely that Walter could see his own terrified reflection.

He was also surprised to see that the windows had been rolled down. The interior was littered with half-nibbled cabbage leaves.

Cautiously Walter opened the door—still unlocked.

He glimpsed inside for the nibbler and came face-to-face with a fluffy white rabbit, midway through a chomp. The rabbit squawked, sprang to the floor, and scuttled between the pedals.

"Who are you?" Walter asked. He had rarely dealt with bitey things, but he thought it best to grab it from the other end. He slid his hand behind the rump and edged the rabbit back toward him. From there Walter lifted the entirety of the sharp fluff out. Around its neck was a ribbon with a note. He opened it. The scrap read, in scrawled writing: "Happy Birthday. I think you'll find that you'll like a living one even better. —C"

Walter flipped the note over. On the back were scribbles that looked suspiciously like those Cordelia was fond of making.

Walter carefully folded the note up and placed it in his pocket. He set the rabbit down on the seat next to him and buckled him up as the bunny stretched his neck to grab another leaf.

Walter then shot out of the park, anxiety making everything move faster.

CHAPTER 26

· · ·

THE PRIMPETS

Hadorah trudged toward her house, her tired feet slopping through the mud. She looked up to her stoop—two figures huddled together beside the porch light. They stood still, forlorn silhouettes, the smaller of the two leaning on the other.

"Who are you?" Hadorah called out, fearful of the answer.

The couple stepped forward, into the light, revealing the Primpets.

Hadorah sighed. "Why are you here?"

Mr. Primpet twiddled his finger as he responded, voice high, "Oh, we were just in the neighborhood and popped by to say hello, you know how it is, and—"

Mrs. Primpet stepped in front of him, unblinking. "We've been waiting for hours."

Hadorah pushed past them. She unlocked the front door

and stepped in. "I see. Well, if you don't mind, I need to—"

"We received a call from the hospital on Flaster Isle," Mr. Primpet began. "It seems Cordelia went there to try to convince them to 'fix' her. I can't imagine what she was thinking. The doctor sent her home, and we don't know when she'll return, but . . . we're worried." Mr. Primpet stared pleadingly as Hadorah looked back. Befuddled and drained, all she could think about was her own bed.

"I'm sorry to hear that." Hadorah stepped inside, nearly shutting the door on Mr. Primpet's hand as it shot out to catch the doorframe.

She stepped back in surprise as he inserted his face between the jamb and door. His words unfurled rapidly. "Well, um, we wanted to talk to you about the, uh, the—"

Mrs. Primpet's eyes were as vacant as a ventriloquist's doll as she whispered, "She's dying."

Hadorah couldn't think how to respond, unable to process those two words.

Mr. Primpet broke the silence. "We're scared, Hadorah, and you're the only person we could think to talk to."

Hadorah nodded slowly, opening the door wider. "Come in."

Mr. Primpet's lips turned up just slightly in relief. "Thank you."

Mrs. Primpet didn't smile at all.

CHAPTER 26 ½

. . .

WHY HADORAH HATES PARADES

When Walter was four years old, Max thought he would be ready to stand on a parade float with his mother. "He'll love it!"

Hadorah wasn't worried about Walter, however. Walter liked just about everything (and, as a consequence, everything liked him). No, Hadorah was worried about herself.

Hadorah didn't mind watching parades, but being in one was another story altogether.

Max had somehow convinced her to clamber up onto the float with her son, and now here she was, waving wearily at the crowds of people. They blurred together into a wall of smiles and shouts, caging her in on every side. "They're staring at me."

Max laughed at his wife as he operated the float from a wheel in front. His feet danced across a myriad of pedals below. "I think that's the point!"

The Solstice Parade continued its festive romp down the gray streets of Moormouth. Maxwell's float stood out in the middle of the colorful amorphous blobs. It was bigger and more wondrous than the rest.

The crimson dahlia closed and bloomed lazily, raining petals onto the onlookers below. Everyone in Moormouth had come out to watch. Everyone in Moormouth loved Maxwell.

Hadorah was in the back, near the ladder, hoping people wouldn't notice her there. But she could tell they did, which caused her to heat up and sweat uncontrollably.

Her blood rushed in her ears so loudly that it began to overpower even the screaming around them. She couldn't take it. "Stop. We're getting off."

Max turned, hesitant, but then he saw that his wife was terrified. He nodded, slowing the float for them. She readjusted Walter, who dropped his metal toy car, a gift from his father, in the process. The toy fell into the float's gears, without anyone seeing it do so. Then Hadorah climbed off, Walter balanced on her hip.

Max grinned his famous grin and shouted after the two, "Don't take your eyes off me!"

He laughed and powered the dahlia forward, to the crowd's delight. No one paid Hadorah any mind as she carried on, following the float on foot.

She walked more quickly, trying to keep up with the dahlia.

Finally Max looked up from his controls to find her—when he did, he smiled widely, winking. Hadorah smiled back.

This was one of the few moments that had been burned into her memory.

There was a click, just one click, then a wail. Everyone turned to look as the great dahlia stopped. In that second, no one knew what had happened. And then the mechanical float burst, in a great fiery explosion that seared the air and rocked the earth.

Hadorah and Walter were thrown back, along with the entire front row, and splayed onto the ground. Everything smelled burned and wrong. The parade dissolved into chaos as the little creatures abandoned their own floats, fleeing the fireball encompassing Maxwell's. Hadorah could only stare in shock, holding her son clutched to her chest.

The first thing she saw was nothing. There was nothing but black where the float had exploded. Nothing was left.

The second thing she saw was Walter sobbing into his empty hands.

The third thing she saw was a little girl lying on the ground, long black hair covering her face while her father shouted, trying to pull something smoking from her eye.

And the fourth thing she saw was the townspeople, turning from the mess to stare.

Hadorah heard no sound in those moments, but those four sights she would never forget.

CHAPTER 27

. . .

THE VERY BAD KISS

Walter tore down the empty road while the rabbit nibbled.

The rabbit was a lot less concerned than the human was, see, because the rabbit had cabbage. Cabbage is the nicest thing for a rabbit to have.

Walter wasn't in the mood for cabbage. His eyes squinted in the darkness for any sign of life, but he couldn't see anything. There was no one.

He passed miles and miles of desert, the same desert that had lulled him to sleep those few nights before.

I shouldn't have told her to take the balloon, he chided himself. *It's my fault.*

He slowed as he came upon a blackened tree, a flame licking the desert sand around it. The car rocked to a halt, and Walter stumbled out of it toward the wreck. He held the rabbit in his arms. The rabbit was displeased by the lack of cabbage in Walter's arms.

Everything around the fire had burned to a crisp—the balloon was just a heap of ash.

Sifting through the mess, Walter found the fuel line. It looked as though it had been chewed through by a rodent. Sighing, he let the squirming bunny down onto the ground as he continued searching through debris.

He picked up the burner, which was still spitting out a little flame, and saw the rabbit hopping along a shiny trail on the ground. Walter lit up the trail with the burner—drops of blood.

He followed it a few paces, before pulling the light up higher and revealing that the trail went on for yards, far out of sight. Walter ran after the rabbit, scooped him up, and hurried to the car.

Cordelia limped forward, her clothes torn and dirty. Her calf was mangled from the wreck, where it had been crushed in the branch-weave basket as the balloon had smashed into the tree. But she didn't care about that, because she was alive.

The tree had met a power line above the ground, and instead of falling, she had caught it. She held on tightly to the line and pulled herself up. After great effort, she managed to steady her feet on top of it.

Every few seconds Cordelia's leg dripped blood. She winced, continuing on slowly toward the bend. In her hands she held a long, thin branch from the tree. She had been able to tear it off before starting her trek.

As Cordelia made it past the bend, she became fully illuminated by bright lights behind her. She couldn't turn, but she knew who it was.

Walter stumbled out of the hearse and was running as soon as he hit the ground. Once he reached her, he stopped and stared up in shock, amazement, and frustration with the absurdity of it all.

"Cordelia! What are you doing up there?"

Cordelia couldn't turn around. She simply wasn't a skilled enough tightrope walker. The best she could do was keep her toes pointed and feet steady, one behind the other. It was just like the books said, but even better.

"Going for a walk."

He could hear the smile in her voice, and that only made him more concerned.

She looked strong up there, balanced on the high wire, simply a cutout in the headlights. She was not only taller than he'd ever seen her, but her back was straight and she looked magnificent. Then he saw something; from her silhouetted form fell a bright red trickle of blood. That was no good.

"I suppose it's time to come down now." Her voice was powerful but still soft somehow, tired.

As she walked to the nearest pole, Walter's chest seized.

"Wait! Stop! Let me help!"

But he was too late. He could only bite his fingernails as he watched the girl grab hold of metal brackets stapled into the pole and climb down horribly slowly. At the last bracket, she had to hop a good distance to reach the ground. She hit the dirt in a heap.

Walter ran over, then held her tightly as he hoisted her up. Cordelia allowed him to hug her. It was comfortable and warm.

Walter examined her face, dirtied with ash. He grabbed a strand of her once-long hair, now fried short.

"What were you thinking? Are you all right? I thought you were dead and—"

Cordelia smiled. "Hello, Walter."

He looked her over, and his eyes came to rest on her still-bleeding leg. "Oh no."

He unbuttoned his shirt, pulled it off, and ripped it into strips with his teeth. He crudely wound it around her leg but, if he was being honest, wasn't entirely sure what he was doing. The blood seeped through the thin fabric nearly instantly. Cordelia appraised his work.

"You know, you're not very good at that."

Walter nodded, mostly to himself. "I'll take you home."

He tried to usher her to the car, but she stopped him, planting her feet. "I am home."

He continued to try to coax her in, pulling her hand. "Come on, Cordelia."

"It doesn't matter anymore."

"What are you talking about? We have to get back." He tried to pull her again, stretching his other arm out to open her door, but she remained anchored outside. "*Come on, Cordelia. I—*"

She crossed the space between them and pulled his face to hers. (It's fortunate that there was no preparation that went into this act, because it would have only made matters worse.)

Neither knew what to do with their faces. Walter's was soft and unmoving, while Cordelia's mouth was stiff and pressed so hard against his that he could feel imprints of his teeth being made against his lips.

She finally released him, and he reeled back and stared at her, fish-eyed.

It was truly a tremendously awful kiss, and both immediately wanted to do it again.

The road ahead was dark, and the beams of the hearse lights peeked through with little hope. Cordelia smiled, petting the rabbit's ears with the back of her tired hand.

Walter glanced back and forth between the road and the girl. His eyes lingered on the soaked bandages. She looked paler, and her breath was coming out in wheezes. Cordelia felt his stare.

"What do you think of Periwinkle?" she asked. Walter glanced around the car, confused. She held up the equally confused rabbit. "He's like my rabbit."

Walter allowed a one part surprised, one part sneaky glance at her. "I don't know what you mean."

"Of course you do. That rabbit you made for class. He was for me."

"What are you—"

"A long time ago I told you that I wanted a rabbit but my parents wouldn't let me, because"—her tired face screwed up into a scrunchy-nosed impression of her mother—"'rabbits have teeth, claws, and the desire to maim you.'"

Walter stared straight ahead, his face bearing every sign of a bad lie. "I had no idea."

"Which is why you reanimated that rabbit for me."

"How are you so sure?"

"Because I know you, Walter."

"Since when?"

"Since we were four." She dug in her knapsack by her feet until she found what she had been looking for, the sweat from her hands darkening the torn scrap of fabric around it. Cordelia unwrapped the little thing. Inside was a windup rabbit, just small enough to fit in her hand. It had used to be a nice bright orange, but had become chipped, revealing the silver metal underneath.

Walter looked, his back instantly rigid in surprise.

"You still . . ."

"I had to hide it for years. You have no idea how much trouble you gave me."

Walter didn't mean to swerve, and yet he did swerve. She didn't even look up, smiling her waning-moon grin, slipping the rabbit lovingly into its place in her bag.

Walter spoke slowly to avoid stuttering. "I thought you didn't remember."

"It'd be easier if I didn't." She looked up. "You were the best friend I ever had."

They stared at each other for a moment too long, before Cordelia began petting the real rabbit again.

Walter looked to Periwinkle and back to her. "Why would you do that for me?"

"They have wonderfully sharp teeth, don't they?" she replied.

He opened his mouth to say something, but no words came.

She edged her fingers on top of his. "I'm going to leave this here, if you don't mind."

This felt like a dream, but Walter was soon shaken from his bliss when he looked at her again and saw things that the adrenaline hadn't allowed him to see before: her head was lolled to the side, her forehead slick with sweat, her eyes drooping.

"Are you sure you're all right?"

She spoke with such earnestness that he nearly believed her. "Never better."

CHAPTER 28

• • •

THE END

Walter drove as Cordelia fought looming unconsciousness.

The car beeped. He looked down at the dash; the tank was almost empty. "That's it. We have to stop."

Her voice wheezed out, as demanding as she always was. "No. Keep going."

"But I have to stop for—"

"You can make it."

Cordelia's body was curled into a little ball, Walter's hand resting on her back. He slowed, fighting with himself, as he approached the WELCOME TO ELVERPOOL sign.

The sigh forced itself out of his tight chest. Then he looked back down at the girl.

He pressed all his weight into the pedal, passing the off-ramp, faster than before.

. . .

Cordelia was deathly pale, her clothes drenched in sweat. The bandage on her leg was covered in both fresh blood and some dried, caked around the edges.

Walter drove in a fury, the bunny peeking through the steering wheel, the hearse kicking up dust.

Walter saw colorful, amorphous shapes up ahead; he accelerated to beat them.

"Not this time." He burst between two ambling floats, and the ever-marching parade disappeared behind him. The smog of Moormouth could be seen in the distance. Walter didn't notice, his focus on the road before him and the girl to his side. "We're almost there, Cordelia. You're all right. Everything's all right."

She sounded distant, like in a dream. "Walter?"

"No!" The car sputtered, jolted hard once, and skidded to a halt. Dust shot up in a cloud around them. Walter tried to restart the car frantically, but it stubbornly refused. He tried again and again. "No! No, no, no, no!" He slammed his fists onto the steering wheel.

"Walter?"

"What?" He looked at her, breathing hard.

She just smiled, grabbing his hand. "Everything's all right."

"You're not all right!" He pulled his hand away, looking across the endless desert on either side.

"Walter—"

"No. I'm going to get help."

He yanked his door open, but stopped when Cordelia tugged on his sleeve. "Stay with me," she said.

He felt the tears of frustration and fear rise as he tried to argue once more, voice cracking. "But I—"

"Please."

She eased her head onto his lap. He could only stare down at her, his stomach sinking as he noticed how drenched the floor below her was with blood. Her blood.

Cordelia nestled her head into him. "Do you know any lullabies?"

Walter nodded, numb, his eyes red. He opened his mouth and sang. *"Leubiet vost tuv . . ."*

Cordelia recognized the song at once, though she didn't know it. It was the tune Walter had hummed their entire trip. How she had hated it then, and how she loved it now. Walter, for his part, couldn't remember learning it, but he knew it still. His voice matched perfectly with the memories tucked away that he couldn't quite grasp. Though Walter didn't know it, it was his father's voice that he heard.

Max had hummed the song to a pregnant Hadorah as they'd sat in Sturgeon's Rowhouse Gill. He'd hummed leaving Shrew's Borough, and as he and his wife had basked in the dying light of the Honeyoaks parade. He'd even hummed to her as they'd gazed out from the black-and-gold balloon, high above it all.

Hadorah had looked at him, face scrunched up in questioning.

"You're always humming that song. What is it?"

Max had grinned at her as he'd gathered his courage and sung the very same words Walter would come to know. "*Leubiet vost tuv, leubiet vost tuv.* Back home that means 'I'm a fool.' That is what I say when there is no way to tell you how much I love you."

Hadorah had laughed, thinking it marvelously silly. "That's funny."

She'd stared out at the clouds as Max had stood behind her, pulling a ring box from his pocket. "Why?"

She'd turned, seeing Maxwell's bright face—

Hadorah, fourteen years later, tried to recall the proposal and how her husband had looked—but instead she saw what haunted her mind whenever she tried to remember him: the explosion.

She saw him humming just before she jumped off the dahlia float.

As she had walked to keep up with the float, she had looked down at her son in her arms, his hands now empty.

"Where did your toy car go, Walter?"

He'd pointed to Maxwell.

It was the last time she saw him.

Hadorah saw all these things, running endlessly, unstoppable as she lay alone in bed. His voice invaded her memory.

"Leubiet vost tuv . . ."

Cordelia lay in Walter's lap, barely holding on. The parade had caught up to them and was beginning to part around the car as the floats continued on their long journey.

Walter sang, keeping his voice strong for Cordelia, doing what she had asked.

". . . Back home that means 'I'm a fool.' That is what I say when there is no way to tell you how much I love you."

She smiled faintly up at him, eyes half-closed. Her lips parted as if to say something, but no words came.

Walter's heart pounded as he waited for her to speak.

"Cordelia?"

He brushed wet strands from her face, wanting to know she was warm but instead feeling for the first time what true coldness was.

"Everything's all right." He repeated it to himself as he held shaking fingers to her neck, searching for a pulse. There was nothing.

He broke down, and he hugged her tightly, repeating her name.

As if sensing the misery, floats on either of the hearse sank to the ground and shifted underneath the car.

Many years before, the creatures of the floats had seen their friend die in their parade. At long last they were able to make amends.

They lifted the hearse above them, and it drifted on the back of the parade toward Moormouth.

CHAPTER 29

THE CLOUD WALKER AND THE PUPPETEER

C ordelia Primpet" is no kind of name for a girl. It is the kind of name for an old, wrinkly woman who smells slightly of stale cookies—but the bad kind with raisins. In fact, she'd look quite a bit like a raisin, and she'd make it her daily mission to do absolutely nothing interesting. Instead she'd sit in her rocking chair, pulling melted butterscotches out of her big, droopy purse, while telling long stories that had no end.

Cordelia's parents had known this when they'd named their daughter. In fact, this had been the primary reason why they'd chosen the name. Cordelia's parents had hoped most hopefully that Cordelia Primpet would never do anything interesting and would never dream of doing anything interesting. That way, they would know that she would be safe.

Unfortunately, they hadn't been able to stop her from trying.

Oh, Cordelia had tried brilliantly. Ever since she'd been a young girl, she'd dreamed of walking in the sky on a wire. How free it would be, how sweet the air would smell, how impossible it looked. That was what she knew she had to do.

Her parents, however, had named her Cordelia and wouldn't settle for anything more. So, they had locked her up and given her sad, gray storybooks about children who were made to hit stones with hammers and eat cookies . . . but only the bad kind with raisins.

Alas, the more Cordelia's parents wanted to stop her from dreaming, the bigger her dreams became.

No, Cordelia's parents wouldn't let her walk on the clouds, but her grandfather was another story. Arlo Primpet had had dreams too, you see, and late at night, when the rest of the world was asleep, Cordelia and her pop would play circus. He was the puppeteer, and she was the cloud walker. That was their secret.

And then the circus was found out, and it was ripped apart at its seams. Cordelia's parents decided to smother her dreams once and for all. If the steel locks on the windows and doors wouldn't keep her inside, then perhaps the locks in her own mind might. They told her the truth, in all its most terrible details. Soon the world looked dark, and Cordelia didn't wish to escape into it any longer.

She then turned to her books, where anything was possible.

The worst thing about books, she decided, was that they ended. When the end came, that meant the adventure was over.

Cordelia was afraid of the end, most afraid. She lived her whole life clutching to her pages, trying to stop them from turning. After all, there are no pages beyond the end. Then *her* story would be over, and there was nothing more frightening or unimaginable than that.

It took her many years before she was able to fulfill her own dream, but then Cordelia saw something. In the darkest black, high above the ground, she looked back and realized: there were no pages before the beginning, either.

Perhaps that was it, she thought. It was exciting to begin, and the end was just the same.

Out there somewhere beyond the pages was a puppeteer searching for his circus, and now there would be a cloud walker to join him.

CHAPTER 30

PLANNING THE IMPOSSIBLE

Hadorah's eyes were rimmed with deep circles the next morning. She had slept, but not well. She worried that she'd never be able to sleep again unless Walter returned.

Hadorah idly stirred a cup of tea while staring out the front window.

She nearly thought she'd gone mad when she saw a long black car appear in the distance.

It certainly didn't help that the long black car was atop a group of sunshiny floats. Still, she couldn't help herself. Hallucination or not, she raced out the door, knocking over the tea in her haste.

The car-bearers set the hearse down carefully. Before Hadorah could reach them, the parade had already moved on, disappearing into the fog.

Walter held Cordelia in both arms. His eyes were wide, and his lips were clenched tight. He lightly petted the bunny sitting on Cordelia's chest.

Hadorah wrenched the driver's door open. Walter turned to her, his eyes red and voice hoarse.

"Call the police."

Walter watched from his window as Officer Culpepper spoke to Hadorah. He knew she'd show him Cordelia, and he couldn't bear to watch that.

He turned back to the diagrams scattered over his bed. They were complex, written in a way that only Walter would understand.

Periwinkle sat beside him, right on top of Cordelia's journal.

Hadorah trudged up the stairs and sidled up to Walter's door. She thought, perhaps, to peek in and listen but decided against it. She knocked, pushing the door open slightly. The locks lay lank in disuse.

"Walter? They left." He lay on his side, back to her. She continued, "I'm sorry, for what you had to go through, but there wasn't anything anyone could do."

He continued drawing, out of sight, but she knew he could hear her. Hadorah turned to go, before adding, "I'm glad you chose to come home."

She waited by the door a moment, hoping he'd tell her something he needed. Give her something to do.

He didn't.

She looked down and saw Periwinkle staring at her from the doorway.

"If you need anything, I'll be downstairs," she said to Walter, avoiding the rabbit as he twitched his nose and took a hesitant hop toward her.

She shut the door, and Periwinkle was just able to scurry back in. He bounded up next to Walter, who petted him as he added the final drawings to his diagram.

It looked oddly like a human schematic.

CHAPTER 31

. . .

THE PROJECTOR

That night, after hours of work that had turned his eyes blurry, Walter crept out of his room. The diagrams were rolled into his pocket, away from prying eyes.

He quietly shut his door, setting the rabbit down outside it, along with a pile of cabbage. The rabbit thought Walter was wonderful.

On his way down the stairs, Walter stopped when he heard footsteps. He inched to the bottom and peered past the wall to see his mother, who should have been asleep but instead was . . . sweeping?

She looked tired, dragging the broom across the kitchen. Walter pushed down a pang of guilt when he realized she looked older now than when he had left.

His eyes tracked her as she trudged into the living room, mindlessly cleaning.

She slipped the broom under the couch, and it returned with the newspaper article that she had unknowingly dropped all those nights before. Walter forgot to breathe as Hadorah picked it up, her hands shaking. He recognized it instantly.

An unassuming news clipping. On one side was an advertisement for bundles of bread clips (those square things that keep your bread bag closed); on the other side was Max's obituary. His smiling face met Hadorah's lined one. And though she tried to stop them, her eyes were drawn to the small picture in the corner, a grainy shot of the explosion.

But Walter didn't need to see the picture. He'd memorized the whole page.

It reminded him of that moment, of that day, of the week that had followed. It reminded him of watching his mother saw AND INVENTORIUM off the sign swinging out front. He remembered how she had thrown away every last invention she could scrounge up, including Walter's mechanical toys. She had tried and failed to explain to him that they were too dangerous. In the end she had decided just not to explain at all. He remembered walking into town, hand in hand with her, and the faces of the two women selling sweet potatoes on the side of the road. They had stared. He would never forget the way they'd whispered to each other, or how Hadorah had pulled him along before he could hear what they were saying.

He remembered everything, thousands of things. He

remembered watching in the basement doorway as his mother had worked on his father's funeral. How as soon as she'd finished his urn, she'd dropped her own wedding ring inside.

Walter was snapped out of his memories when he saw Hadorah moving again. He flattened himself farther against the wall. She looked as if she were in a trance, the article clutched tightly to her chest.

She stepped into the kitchen and went straight to the highest cabinet. Walter's skin tingled. He'd never been allowed to go into the highest cabinet.

He watched closely as she unlocked it. She then pushed it open and pulled out a dusty film reel from inside.

Walter's interest only grew as he watched her laboriously set up an old video projector that had sat rusting in the front closet.

Hadorah placed the reel inside the projector. She fiddled for a moment and then finally got the blurry image to project onto the white wall in front of her. As the wheel started turning, the fuzzy image adjusted into Maxwell holding an infant Walter. The older Walter, watching from his hiding spot, couldn't pull his eyes away.

In the video Max looked adoringly down at his son, whispering softly, so as not to wake him, "Hello, Walter. I'm your dad."

Walter hadn't seen this film in years. Neither had Hadorah. For her, however, it brought on a whole different mess of memories.

Six years before, Walter's room had been very different. There had been no inventions, only a few toys that had littered the floor, foreseeing the mess that would one day replace them.

Hadorah had approached from the hallway, carrying a pile of clean linens. She'd stopped by the door, hearing Walter's high voice echoing beneath it. She'd peeked inside, curious.

Walter faced the other way. There was a projected image running on the wall behind him. What was odd was that he sat with his back to the film. He had connected the projector to an old rotary phone with scraps of odd wires he'd fitted together.

Hadorah noted that the projector didn't show one video but a choppy film made up of clips. Every few seconds, every few words, the film cut to an image from an entirely different video. The only valuable part of this collage was the audio that was fed through a bulky wire straight into the telephone.

The volume on the receiver was too loud, and Hadorah could hear it from the hallway. Max's voice sounded tinny as it bounced out of the phone.

"Everything—is good—here."

Walter spoke into the receiver, clutched to his ear with both hands.

"Good!"

"Is—your mother—all right?"

Hadorah's mouth dropped, watching her son as he held the phone tighter.

"Yes."

"You are—taking care of—her?"

He nodded.

"That's my—boy."

There was an odd pause, and then Max's voice returned.

"Walter?"

"Yes, Dad?"

"I miss you."

"Me too."

Hadorah sank to the ground outside, clasping the clothes to her chest.

Hadorah, in the present, pale and limp, sat on the ground, watching the reel project onto the living room wall. The film was almost over.

In the video, Maxwell stood over the crib, placing his son inside. Walter, an infant with big brown eyes, woke and looked up at his father. Max put his finger through the bars, and Walter reached a chubby fist out to grab it.

Hadorah remembered the final words Walter had whispered into the phone, so many years before. His sweet voice echoed in her head.

"I love you, Dad."

In the film, baby Walter's grip was firm, refusing to let Max's finger go. Max responded with a soft smile, leaning in.

"I love you too, Walter."

Mascara tears tracked Hadorah's sallow face. The video flickered off, and she sat alone. Little did she know that Walter was only a few feet behind her, feeling just the same.

. . .

CHAPTER 32

AFTERMATH REANIMATED

Walter returned upstairs, overcome by emptiness. It wasn't a normal kind of empty, though—not like you're hungry or tired or even bored.

It was a kind of emptiness that cannot be filled. It felt like he'd had an arm cut off . . . and yet there were two by his sides. It felt like his brain had been swirled out his nose and replaced with cotton. It felt like an aching pain deep in his chest, and yet he knew he couldn't be healthier.

The feeling reminded him of his inventions. It made him feel like a machine. So that's what he'd be. He'd try to forget all the pain and instead just do what he was supposed to.

Walter silently stepped onto the landing and walked to the very back corner, where no one ever went.

He needed a large space to work, but he couldn't sneak past his mom to get into the basement. Plus, he didn't want to be left alone in there with . . . *her*. Not yet.

Instead he decided to investigate a place that he thought might fit his needs.

Walter took the ladder from his room and leaned it against the back wall. He then climbed, his whole body numb. In one hand he held a crowbar that made a soft *clang* as he grabbed each rung.

When he reached the top, he was inches from the boarded-up room. He balanced with his legs and slipped the edge of the crowbar under the slats. With a hollow *crack* the old planks gave way, and a cloud of dust and decaying wood followed.

Walter swallowed back his coughs and slid the broken pieces back into the hole, so that Hadorah wouldn't discover them while he was investigating. He then continued, cracking away one slat at a time until the gap was large enough that he could hoist himself up into it.

Once inside, Walter brushed himself off and pulled the ladder in behind him. After setting it to the side, he looked up from the floor. Instantly the breath became caught in his throat.

It was his father's workroom, as if preserved for a museum. Warm red wood tables sat up against walls, covered in hanging tools. The tools didn't seem to be in any particular order—some were catawampus, and others upside down.

Walter even discovered a dirty fork balanced between two pegs.

He smiled. He hadn't known that his father was messy. None of the newspaper articles had thought to mention it.

His knees now shaking, he walked farther inside, taking it all in.

The room should have been dark, but there was a large, round attic window that took up half a wall. It was patterned like the top of a jewel, with facets that glinted endlessly. The beauty of it couldn't be spotted from the outside. Walter had only seen it as blackened, dirty glass. From the inside, however, it cast a brighter light than he had ever before witnessed in Moormouth.

Someone had made it—Maxwell, perhaps—so that the meager natural light of the town would be amplified. Moonshine flooded in, through the center of the jewel, and filled up the room with a gentle, cheery glow.

Walter walked to a table in the back. On top of it were sheets of scrap metal, the edges shorn and tinged with age.

He ran a thumb over the warped and uneven surface of one, removing layers of dust and revealing a brilliant copper color underneath.

This would do. This would do just fine.

He removed the pile of schematics from his pocket and

unrolled them, pressing them flat against the wood. As he did, his hand hit a hammer on the edge of the table. It had been laid there and forgotten. Walter picked it up in awe. It had been the last one his father had used before he . . .

Walter couldn't finish the thought as he gripped the cold handle.

Maxwell had used it, and now Walter would too.

Walter glanced over his schematic, then checked his watch. With a renewed sense of vigor, he tapped the metal flat, as quietly and quickly as he could.

Hadorah, bleary-eyed, walked downstairs. She'd just had a horrible nightmare.

She pushed the basement door open and breathed a sigh of relief to see that her son wasn't up to anything. Her expression then clouded when she saw the girl lying on the cold gray slab. Cordelia's face was soft and peaceful, as if she were only asleep.

Hadorah couldn't bear to look any longer. Instead she went straight to her workbench, where a plain coffin waited.

The funeral was in two days, and she couldn't think of anything more important to do.

As the sun rose over the Mortinson home, it met Hadorah, asleep over the coffin, a whittling knife in her hand, and

Walter, creeping down the basement stairs. Slung over his arms were various sizes of copper bands.

He eyed his mother only for a moment before moving quickly to Cordelia.

He gazed at her face, feeling the sting of sweat rolling from his hair into his eyes. Brushing the sweat away, he looked down to see that she was no longer wearing a nightgown, nor her usual school uniform. Instead she had been dressed in a light blue gown of silk, a matching ribbon in her hair.

Walter shook his head, unable to look any longer. Instead he slipped a ring off his arm—the smallest of them—and snapped it around Cordelia's wrist. The click of the band closing was quiet, but loud enough that it echoed in the wide basement.

Walter looked up to see if Hadorah had awoken. She hadn't.

Perfect.

He moved more quickly, snapping bands around her joints, connecting them with a spine of gears that he'd had tucked under his arm.

After only minutes, he was fastening the final ring around her neck, on the side of which was a curious key slot.

Walter's hands quivered as he fit a key inside. He turned once.

The gears of the spine ground together unpleasantly, hissing at the tension. Hadorah's eyes fluttered as she was drawn from sleep. Walter twisted the key again, and the hissing became louder. Another twist, and louder still. He continued, round and round, until the turning became effortful as the tension grew tight.

The fuzz of Hadorah's dreams finally dispersed, and she looked up to see Walter fighting to turn the key again.

A humming began to emanate from the mechanisms surrounding Cordelia's body.

Hadorah's voice was groggy but desperate as she stood, knocking the stool back behind her. "Walter—no."

He refused to turn around. "Leave me alone."

Her voice softened as she held out a hand. "You don't know what you're doing."

"I have to."

"I thought you were finished with all of this! It's too dangerous! Think of your father!"

Walter stopped cranking. "Inventing didn't kill Dad, and you know it."

Hadorah stepped toward him, but it was too late. Walter let the key go. It spun to life; now no one could stop it. Finally it slowed to a constant, turning rhythm. Cordelia's eyes eased open—one blue, one green.

Walter's heart raced as a smile broke across his face. It had worked.

Behind him, Hadorah suffered through nauseating déjà vu as she wrapped her arms around herself.

Cordelia's voice sounded like a mechanical version of what it had been, something Walter had devised from his memories. "Walter."

He laughed giddily, leaning over her, picking up the paper script to read from as he went. "Yes! Cordelia!"

She sat up slowly, aided by the bands that moved her limbs as a skeleton might, but her movements weren't quite human-like. They were disjointed and stilted.

"How are you?" she asked.

His eyes gleamed as he replied—she hadn't left after all. "Good, and you?"

"Just dandy. You look tired."

Walter smiled more widely. Hadorah looked on, increasingly uneasy as she waited for what she knew would come.

"You too," he said.

"I missed you."

Walter dropped the script, wrapping her in a hug and muttering into her hair, "Cordelia, I—"

But Cordelia couldn't listen. She kept on book, as she was programmed to do, unaware that Walter wasn't reciting with her anymore. "Of course you did. I would too."

Walter looked into her eyes, expecting to see the spark of life return. "Cordelia—"

But it didn't. She spoke nonsensically, unwavering. "Well, how would you explain it, then?" Walter looked on, his smile remaining but becoming increasingly as dead as his eyes. Cordelia continued with her one-sided conversation. "You would say that.

"If you did, I would go too.

"But do you know why?

"Of course you do."

Walter's smile dropped as he spoke her line with her, in unison—

"Because I love you."

Walter collapsed at the middle, bent over, the pain too much. Cordelia was oblivious as she tittered her mechanical laugh. "Now, don't get sappy on me—"

A screw turned loose. Her facial expression stayed the same, her eyes pinned wide in malfunction. "Walter? Walter? Walter? Walter?"

Through tears, he closed her eyelids with his fingers. She suddenly fell silent and motionless, sinking onto her back once more.

Walter sobbed silently over her body, tears and sniffles pouring out of him. Hadorah stepped out of the shadows. She walked over, slowly at first, and then smoothed a hand over his back.

Walter's ragged voice cracked through his sobs, "I just wanted to say good-bye."

Hadorah shook her head, looking over to Cordelia. "We will, at the funeral."

"I wanted to say good-bye to Dad, too. It was m-my fault—"

She stopped rubbing as the memories washed over her.

They had watched the explosion together, but Hadorah had hoped that Walter was too young to see the tire of his windup car land at her feet in flames. She hadn't wanted him to know that it had caused the explosion. She had been hoping that maybe she'd kept it from him this entire time. The pain clutched in her chest when she realized he knew— he'd always known.

Hadorah shook the memories from her mind and began rubbing his back again, leaning close to his ear as she spoke quietly. "It was an accident."

He cried, turning and latching on to her. "I didn't mean to. I'm sorry—"

"Shh . . ." Hadorah patted Walter's back as he sobbed into her. It was something neither had done before, but the experience came naturally. They were mother and son, after all.

As he wept, neither he nor his mother saw the green stone in Cordelia's eye begin to glow. They didn't notice when the stone pooled onto her cheek and rolled down, a marble again, nor when it rolled off the table and onto the ground, not even when it hopped into the safety of his shoe.

No, neither of them noticed, but for some reason Walter's tears began to dry up, and the emptiness inside felt filled by something.

He may have never known it, but the marble had melted. And now it was gone.

CHAPTER 33

• • •

WALTER IN THE WAKE

Walter returned, carrying a composition book that was immaculately clean despite the binding cracking off from overuse.

"This is it."

He dropped the book onto one of the workroom's dusty tables. On the front was written, in curly print: "Owned by: Cordelia Primpet. If found: Burn immediately."

Hadorah felt her ribs tighten. She wanted to do as Cordelia had suggested and toss it into the fireplace. But then she saw Walter glancing back with hopeful eyes, and she sighed.

"We'll see what we can do."

Walter knew that his mother had always dreamed of this moment, of them standing side by side over a body, working together in the "family business." Of course, neither of them had ever imagined it would be over this body. Both would have given almost anything for it not to be her. To distract themselves, they worked on their own projects.

Walter was twisting a screw into some kind of projection box. He had tried to explain it to his mother, but to both of their long-felt disappointment, none of it had made any sense. He had eventually given up, and she was relieved for it.

Hadorah, for her part, was finishing the too-small-for-comfort coffin. Walter had always secretly admired his mother's ability to make coffins, but this happened to be his least favorite kind.

"The soldering iron."

Hadorah didn't even need to look as she handed him the pen-size tool from the wall. Walter glanced up at her as he reached for it. "Are you sure this is all right?"

Hadorah grunted in response.

He took that as a yes and hurriedly grabbed it from her and went back to work.

Walter knew she didn't like it. Her face definitely said that she didn't like it. He was amazed, however, that she was doing it anyway.

He side-eyed her as she suddenly picked up Cordelia's journal and leafed through it. Walter watched over her shoulder. He'd already looked over every page. There were stories, drawings, and photos crammed in from corner to corner. Hadorah stopped at a page that was bookmarked. On it was a detailed drawing of a circus with many performers—clowns, lions, the lot. Two figures in particular, standing at the front, caught Walter's attention. One was a happy puppeteer; the other was a girl floating on the cloud above him, holding a long sunflower between her hands.

It was his favorite drawing in the whole entire book.

As twilight peeked into the workroom from the one small window, it lit the covered shapes now littered around the floor. The pair worked long into the night.

Walter looked over at his mother. She seemed tired, her fingers stiff and crunchy, popping every few minutes. She was hunched over the coffin, carving the final petal into an elaborate sunflower on its face.

She then looked up at Walter, who quickly turned away, poring over a drawing of a shadowy unicorn in the book. Hadorah's quiet voice drifted over to him. "As a little girl . . ."

Walter looked up, surprised. He had never heard Hadorah talk about her childhood; he'd previously wondered if she'd even had one.

Hadorah continued, "There was nothing that I wanted more than to create something out of nothing. To finally give people what they wanted. To make someone happy." She paused, and he dared to look over. She was staring at her own thin fingers. "I so wanted to invent. But then I met your father and thought I'd never be as good as him. I thought I might as well stop trying."

Walter felt the breath catch in his throat.

"I didn't appreciate him enough—or you, or myself, for who we are." She pushed her chair back, standing. She then turned to her shaken son, brushing a rogue curl from his forehead. "I'm sorry, Walter. I grew up surrounded by death, and I forgot how to live. I'm so proud that you're different."

She nodded at him. Her eyes looked watery—but then, didn't they always? She trudged toward the stairs. "Don't stay up too late."

The door clicked quietly behind her—a typhoon disappearing at sea.

Walter sat, reeling. Periwinkle was sound asleep at his feet, none the wiser. Walter looked back at the closed door. He had thought he'd known her, his mother, but he realized all at once that he knew very little.

What an odd week.

CHAPTER 34

. . .

THE END AGAIN

S oon enough the day came. Walter had slept only a wink or two in preparation. The days between hadn't been as terrible as he'd feared, however.

Walter had found that the time after death is not quite like the time we are used to. It moves slowly.

Luckily, Walter had discovered that by doing what he loved, inventing, he could stay sane, albeit numb, as he completed his most important project to date.

Walter entered the church for the first time since being thrown out. His arms were full of lights and cords. He plopped the pile in the middle of the room, then turned and plodded right back out. Moments later he returned, pushing a massive covered shape, nearly as tall as the room, on a dolly. The sheet over it slipped off momentarily, revealing a large clear . . . rock underneath?

Walter replaced the sheet, then he rushed away again without a second glance.

The noontime sun shone down on the modest steeple of the gray, stone-walled church. Moormouthians had crowded around the large arched doorway, ready for the next funeral. They were all so terribly bored of waiting and just wanted to go in. Finally the crowd heard a click, and Walter's head popped out of the door. "We're ready."

The Primpets pushed to the front of the mumbling, grumbling crowd as they filtered in. Mrs. Primpet released a strangled gasp, corking the doorway. Those behind her stopped to peer inside. Everyone was silent.

Inside the church were visible the most astonishing sights anyone in Moormouth had ever seen. Giant quartz stalagmites shot up around the room. From them, ghostly figures poured over the crowd. There was a dragon emerging from the quartz column by the door.

A little Moormouthian girl, with an unnecessarily long dress that pooled on the ground, reached toward the dragon's wing. Her mom yanked her back, but that made her only try harder.

An ax-wielding giantess and a knight battled, silent blades clashing.

Ms. Wartlebug (armed with a ruler) nearly jumped out of

her hunch and screamed as a curious projection of a swarm of lemurs surged out from a cliff right behind her.

In the middle of it all were the shadowy projections of a puppeteer and, above him, a tall-backed girl on a tightrope.

The church benches had been replaced with the mossy molehills Cordelia had doodled in the bottom margins of her journal (complete with scattered dandelions).

At the edges of the room, lining the walls, was a big top tent composed of Cordelia's favorite book covers. They had been arranged in an alternating swirling pattern like in a hot-air balloon. Between the covers were pages of text, marked up with Cordelia's looping scrawl.

In the center of the hall was a vertical bright yellow hoop of sunflowers. Strung from marionette strings in the middle of the hoop was a simple pine coffin with a hand-carved sunflower design. Inside lay Cordelia, eye patch and all, just as she was. She held the journal clutched in both hands.

Everything looked the same as in the drawings, down to the last detail of the string of softly glowing candles circling the room.

The funeral goers slowly entered, taking in the sights as if they were children again, both frightened and excited, with no one to tell them what to think. A young, nervous mother was the first to sit on a molehill, nearly tripping over and ripping her long skirt as she positioned herself. Her baby boy ogled a giant shrew as it sniffed him. He offered the beast a dande-lion—and to his delight, the shrew seemed to sniff that, too.

Walter stood in the shadows, not wanting to attract atten-tion, as his anxious gaze shifted across the room. He stopped momentarily on the lumbering figure of Alexander Grooblan as he hunkered down on a hill. He sat among his classmates, crying into a too-small hanky. He sobbed loudly, sniffing between words, "Thee wath my betht friend!"

He howled, blowing snot into the little square, before handing it to his tiny bespectacled mother. She shook the thing out, then folded it and placed it in her pocket, patting her boy on the head.

Ms. Wartlebug smacked Elliot nearby as he pulled on a loose screw coming out of a projector box on the ground. Walter could have sworn she nearly smiled as Elliot squealed, tumbling off into the open jaws of an anglerfish projected nearby. The curious kindergartner, Nicolette, looked on, switching between amused and horrified every other second.

Finally Walter dared to look at the Primpets perched in front. To his uncomfortable relief, neither smiled, though Mrs. Primpet sobbed into her husband's drenched chest. She pointed a shaky finger toward the front, and Walter nearly had a heart attack waiting for her to speak. Eventually she was able to whisper, "She loved sunflowers."

She turned back to watering her husband once more. Mr.

Primpet allowed a small smile flecked with smaller tears of his own. "Yes, yes, she did."

Walter felt himself relax, blending into the shadows again, but he felt hot, too, like someone was watching him. From the opposite side of the room, also hidden in a corner, Hadorah met his gaze. She smiled in a way Walter hadn't see her do before. It was the smile of the mothers in the picture books that he used to look at time and time again after he had accomplished something. For the first time he saw the expression in person. She looked proud.

The old preacher found his place in front of the coffin and spoke, in his booming voice, to the waiting crowd. Walter was surprised to see that his normally all-black suit was a bit different today; a little yellow flower peeked out of his pocket.

"We are here to honor Cordelia Primpet."

After the last of the sleeping children had been hauled off, the crying grannies (who, admittedly, hadn't known Cordelia personally but felt like they had) drifted into the night, and Mrs. Primpet was coaxed away by Mr. Primpet as Cordelia's coffin was finally carried away. Walter and Hadorah began the final part of their job.

Though the cleanup required more effort than usual, today it felt far more worthwhile. Taking out the inventions and fixtures was easy enough. Replacing the benches and podium was a bit harder. Now the two Mortinsons were left sweeping. Hadorah rubbed down a counter, a bag of trash clutched in her hand. Walter leaned on his broom, staring at the empty church.

"Now what?"

Hadorah looked at him with a shrug. "Dinner?"

"Just like . . . normal?"

Hadorah snorted, dropping the last piece of trash, her own washcloth, into the bag. "We were never normal, Walter"— she tied off the top of the bag—"but we can keep on anyway."

Walter slumped down onto a hard bench, sleepiness finally catching up to him. "How?"

Hadorah tossed the bag out the open door, then sat beside him in the pew. "Breathing, I think, mostly."

"It hurts."

"Give it time."

"And if it never goes away?"

"Oh, it won't. The hurt stays," she continued. "But it doesn't have to be all there is: sadness means there were things—and are things—to be happy about." Hadorah glanced down at him. "You know, your father always told me something, but I hardly ever agreed with him long enough to believe it: An invention never fails. You simply haven't found the right use for it yet."

Now that Walter was really listening, she continued, "One

day there will be a use for this moment, Walter. When you find it, you'll be a better person, I imagine."

"I don't want to be a better person."

"No one does. Welcome to Moormouth."

There was a pause, and neither knew what to do. Then Walter struggled up, cracking his back. "All right, let's go."

"Where?"

"Dinner."

She followed him. They walked together toward the door. Walter held it open for Hadorah. She turned to him, building the courage to say something that would change everything. "So, do you think you could make a ferret that twitches his nose for Mr. Everett? His just died, and he always did talk about how its nose twitched."

Walter's lips quirked. "I can try."

"I'm sure you will."

Periwinkle hopped quickly toward the closing door—and slithered out as it swung shut behind him.

No one in Moormouth paid any attention to much at all that night. They were too busy walking down the streets, chattering about their peculiar day. Children scampered past the junkyard piles on the edge of town, searching for an adventure and, perhaps, a dragon or two. (After all, no one could convince them anymore that dragons didn't exist.)

Some of the bravest children even stopped to scrutinize the one unique fixture Moormouth had to offer. The slouching building squatted a good distance from town. The space between gave the impression that either the house was running toward Moormouth or Moormouth was running toward it. There was a long mismatched chimney chugging away, an old chestnut tree, and a car and a carriage parked out front.

The illuminated attic window gave a peek into the quiet interior and the outlines of Walter and Hadorah sitting together, hunched over something.

Hadorah pushed a photo of baby Walter and Maxwell toward her son, telling a story that wasn't for anyone but the boy in front of her.

The sign out front swung in the rolling fog, now reading:

THE MORTINSONS

And that was all.

ACKNOWLEDGMENTS

I wrote this story first in film school with the help of three outstanding professors: Scott Sturgeon, who taught me that your idea is only as good as how you write it; Robert Ramsey, who showed me that your first draft is *meant* to be terrible and that your second draft is meant to be slightly less terrible; and David Clawson, who had six months to teach us what "books" were.

When I left school, I researched agents and stumbled upon John M. Cusick at Folio Literary Management. (Hi, Folio team!) Something clicked, and I instantly felt that he would understand me, which is a big deal because *I* don't understand me. No exaggeration: of the hundreds of agents I looked up, I thought he was the *best*—and I was right. What I didn't appreciate is that, on top of being a brilliant agent and writer, he's genuinely kind in a way you rarely encounter outside the pages of a book.

I was also lucky to have found John because he led me to Liz Kossnar, who must be one of the bravest editors in America. Liz has an incomparable ability to dig out what makes a story work and amplify it in a beautiful way. She's a genius and a warrior, and I'm so grateful that she's fought for this book and made it worth reading. Without her it would not exist; or, at the very least, it wouldn't be half as good.

Plus, without Liz, I wouldn't be able to say that I was published by Simon & Schuster Books for Young Readers—something that I will never quite wrap my head around. Watching them transform this manuscript into a living, breathing novel was an incredible experience. Some of the key people who contributed to that are publisher Justin Chanda, who I'm so thankful took a risk on this strange little project; designers Krista Vossen and Hilary Zarycky, who transfigured plain old words into a stunning artifact; managing editor Jenica Nasworthy and copy editor Bara MacNeill, who helped make me sound 90 percent more capable than I am; production manager Martha Hanson, who ensured there would actually be a book in your hands; and Gediminas Pranckevicius, whose gorgeous artwork gave my story a face.

And while I'm beholden to the dozens of talented people who have worked together to make this book possible, there are some people who make *me* possible, and I like that about them. Thank you to my entire family, particularly Harper Lily and Ava Yoshiko, whose road trips are just beginning; my friends from Santa Barbara who insisted I could write even when I couldn't (Devin Scott, looking at you); Tyler

Patterson, who made my Latin slightly less made-up; my Writing for Screen and Television class, who learned with me; and Eric Borsuk, who brought me many, many, many snacks, the significance of which I cannot overemphasize.

Thank you to Lynette, who acted as one of my two readers, along with my dad, Todd, who has given me everything even when he didn't have it to give. Then there's my brother, Max, who is the only person who will ever fully understand this book—not only because he and I are the only two people to have lived this story through our mother, but because he's much, much smarter than me.

Lastly, you. Without you, I couldn't write professionally. You also just plain deserve to be acknowledged. You are remarkable because you are you, and that's enough.

Now, that was all to say that I didn't write this novel, many people did, and I love them for undertaking it with me. It's also to say that if there's something that you don't like about the book, it's almost certainly not my fault, and there are plenty of other people to blame (please see all the names above). I commend you wholeheartedly for doing so.